Jimmy Murphy
The Man Who Kept The Red Flag Flying

THE MAN WHO KEPT THE RED FLAG FLYING

BY WAYNE BARTON

Reach Sport
www.reachsport.com

*Dedicated to the memory
of Winnie Murphy*

As a family we are immensely proud of Jimmy's contribution to Manchester United and to Welsh football. He was a great coach, a great football man, and a wonderful father and grandfather.

We're proud that his work and his legacy are acknowledged and recognised in this book.

*The Murphy family,
January 2018*

Reach Sport
www.reachsport.com

Copyright © Wayne Barton

The right of Wayne Barton to be identified as the owner of this work has been asserted in accordance with the Copyright, Designs and Patents Act, 1988. All Rights Reserved. No part of this publication may be reproduced, stored in a retrieval system, or transmitted in any form, or by any means, electronic, mechanical, photocopying, recording or otherwise without the prior permission in writing of the copyright holders, nor be otherwise circulated in any form of binding or cover other than in which it is published and without a similar condition being imposed on the subsequent publisher.

With thanks to the Jimmy Murphy family.

First published in hardback in Great Britain and Ireland in 2018 by Trinity Mirror Sport Media, PO Box 48, Old Hall Street, Liverpool, L69 3EB.

www.reachsport.com
@Reach_Sport

Reach Sport is a part of Reach PLC.

1

Paperback ISBN: 9781916811317
Hardback ISBN: 9781910335857
eBook ISBN: 9781911613107

Photographic acknowledgements:
The Jimmy Murphy family collection,
Mirrorpix, PA Images.

Excerpt of 'Without Whom' used by kind permission
(c) Tony Walsh, cdc Longfella Ltd 2023.

Every effort has been made to trace copyright.
Any oversight will be rectified in future editions.

Printed and bound by CPI Group (UK) Ltd, Croydon, CR0 4YY.

CONTENTS

Introduction and Acknowledgements   8
Prelude: 'Old Trafford, Son'   11

Part One

1. The Rise   17
2. Meeting Matt   29
3. Recruiting The Babes   45
4. Star Maker   63
5. Golden Apples   77
6. Like Clockwork   91
7. The Greatest   107

Part Two

8. Munich   127
9. United Spirit   177
10. A Proud Man   199
11. World Class   221

Part Three

12. Nothing Will Tear Us Apart   239
13. Resurrection   251
14. The New Crop   271
15. Destiny   285
16. The Fall   295
17. Legacy   317

Postscript: A Man Ahead Of His Time   343

INTRODUCTION & ACKNOWLEDGEMENTS

JIMMY WAS UNITED

Jimmy Murphy is, without hyperbole, one of the most important men in the history of Manchester United Football Club. Most are familiar with his name and his work because of how he took charge of the club in the horrific aftermath of the Munich Air Disaster on February 6th, 1958. Those with a keener interest know Jimmy as the youth team supremo who coached the 'Busby Babes' in the days before they were introduced to the first team.

Yet these bare facts do not begin to reflect how deeply Jimmy's contribution was felt in almost all corners of the club, before and after his death. Jimmy Murphy *was* Manchester United. And, accordingly, Manchester United *was* Jimmy Murphy.

Take any positive attribute of the club – its approach to youth development, its never-say-die attitude – and it was likely implemented by the fiery Welshman, either by instruction or by example. Instruction, in the innovative belief of how intensive coaching of ostensibly simple repetition to a group of young players could be of such long-term benefit. And example, in the way he inspired a group of young boys to come together to

INTRODUCTION

compete so that the team was almost greater than the sum of its parts.

He used his grief as fuel to continue and overcome; a humbling life lesson, and a moment in time which forever shaped the culture of a football club. Jimmy's response in tragedy not only saved the immediate future of Manchester United in February 1958 – it was used as a motivational tool for future successes long after he had passed away.

It has been a privilege and a humbling experience to listen to personal recollections of Jimmy's colleagues and family. It is clear that Jimmy was not only one of football's great men, but one of life's, too.

If words can do justice to such a contribution to football, and British sport history, then I hope this book does. Jimmy's story is one of the most remarkable in the history of the sport and it has been an honour to write it.

There are a number of people who deserve a hearty thank you for help and assistance which has been invaluable. So, firstly, and in no particular order: John Aston Jnr, Ron Atkinson, Alex Dawson, Tommy Docherty, Mick Duxbury, Jimmy Elms, David Gaskell, Wilf McGuinness, Harry Gregg, Gordon Hill and Alan Wardle for giving their time and sharing their memories. A huge thank you to Sir Alex Ferguson who was gracious enough to spend time talking about Jimmy and the legacy he left; likewise, thanks to Paul McGuinness who shares my dedication to raising awareness of Jimmy's contributions to Manchester United. A big thanks to Ally Begg and Jason Ferguson.

A sincere thank you to Eifion Evans and Tony Park, whose own knowledge and research has been so appreciated. And, as always, I have to thank Dan Burdett and Dave Murphy, two wonderful friends who not only gave support to this book throughout the years it has been in development, they gave their eyes and time throughout the lengthy proof-reading process. I also wish to thank Mark Armstrong and Michael Garvey.

Thanks to my family for their patience and support; my beautiful wife for enduring the long days where I was committed to working, and my mum and Uncle Stuart who listened as I enthused, at length, about Jimmy's work. Thanks to Lisa, the best mother-in-law I could have ever asked for, who always provided a workspace whenever needed.

Thanks to all at Trinity Mirror Sport Media for their help and enthusiasm about the project, especially Nick Moreton and Adam Oldfield on the editing and production side and Mark Frances for designing the jacket.

Last but not least, my sincere thanks to Jimmy Murphy Jnr, Nick Murphy, Paul Murphy and the entire Murphy family.

Wayne Barton, January 2018

PRELUDE

'OLD TRAFFORD, SON...'

Monday, February 3rd, 1958

Assistant manager Jimmy Murphy is with the Manchester United players at the ground as they prepare to depart for their European Cup game.

Their opponents in the quarter-final, second leg tie are Red Star Belgrade, United leading 2-1 from the teams' first meeting at Old Trafford. They are travelling to Belgrade via Munich where the plane needs to refuel.

Jimmy is laughing and joking with the players as they wait for Mark Jones, who is running late. Just after 8am, the coach leaves for the airport. On board the coach is the team that will take to the field at the Partizan Stadion: Harry Gregg. Roger Byrne. Bill Foulkes. Mark Jones. Bobby Charlton. Eddie Colman. Duncan Edwards. Kenny Morgans. Albert Scanlon. Tommy Taylor. Dennis Viollet…among others.

"See you all on Thursday lads," says Jimmy, "see that you do a good job!"

Some time earlier, Murphy had suggested to Matt Busby that he would travel with the United team as usual but Busby insisted that in his other role as manager of Wales, Jimmy should be at Ninian Park in Cardiff for the second leg of their World Cup play-off against Israel. Success for Wales would mean a historic qualification for the tournament in Sweden. But the game was scheduled for Wednesday, February 5th, 1958 – the same day United were scheduled to play in Belgrade.

"I usually sat next to Matt on the plane and had the next room to his at the hotel whenever the team went away," explained Jimmy.

"I had suggested that I went to Belgrade, with it being such an important European Cup game. He had said, 'No, Jimmy, you have a job to do,' so Bert Whalley went to Belgrade in my place."

Tuesday, February 4th, 1958

Tom Lyons of the *Daily Mirror* reports from Cardiff University on Wales' preparation for their crucial play-off second leg.

'On a works sports ground over on the other side of Cardiff, the Welsh team did a strenuous training programme,' Lyons wrote. 'Manager Jimmy Murphy put the players through a fast seven-a-side game in the morning, and talked tactics with them in the afternoon. Everyone is fit and confident.' A short article beneath Lyons' piece was headlined 'Fans Mob The Babes'. It chronicled United's arrival at Belgrade Airport in Yugoslavia. 'A crowd of autograph hunters stormed the Customs Hall,' it read. 'Officials tried to keep the fans back but they swept past them and through the barriers.'

OLD TRAFFORD, SON

Wednesday, February 5th, 1958

Wales win 2-0 in a tense game, scoring twice late on to settle the tie. Israeli officials, gracious to their opponents for accepting the game where others had refused, present their Welsh counterparts with bags of oranges as gifts. Bag in hand, Murphy thanks them for their generosity, saying his wife and family will appreciate the gift very much.

In Belgrade, Manchester United draw 3-3 to advance to the semi-final.

Thursday, February 6th, 1958

After boarding an early train from Cardiff to Manchester, Jimmy Murphy looks forward to a double celebration after learning of United's navigation against Red Star.

He arrives at Manchester's London Road station in freezing temperatures and hurries to hail a taxi cab. Knowing nothing other than the football and with thoughts only on getting back to work and catching up with the team and his friend Matt Busby, he settles back in his seat.

"Old Trafford, son," he tells the driver cheerfully…

Part One

1. *The Rise*

2. *Meeting Matt*

3. *Recruiting The Babes*

4. *Star Maker*

5. *Golden Apples*

6. *Like Clockwork*

7. *The Greatest*

CHAPTER | ONE

THE RISE

"I was determined to make the grade as a professional footballer. I appeared to be getting nowhere when a stroke of luck fell upon me... all players need that luck at the start of their careers" – Jimmy Murphy

If you were not to be told otherwise, Treharne Street, in the village of Pentre in the Rhondda Valley in South Wales, presents a vivid impression of the most uncompromising of upbringings. Two opposing rows of terrace houses line up, tightly packed together on a hill that overlooks the former pit sites.

Imagine the scene over one hundred years ago, when those collieries were active, and circumstances become harsher still. It was a battle to survive; and whilst it might be a fairytale stretch to suggest it was a miracle to thrive, it is nonetheless a sobering thought to consider that the man who is arguably more responsible than any other for shaping the cultural identity of football's biggest club was reared on these very streets.

JIMMY MURPHY

And yet, in some ways, it is hardly a surprise, when everything discovered about Jimmy Murphy's childhood sows the seed of the man he became. Late in the first decade of the twentieth century, William 'Billy' Murphy, a manual labourer from Kilkenny, a city in the South East of Ireland, arrived in South Wales with the intention of working in the pits. Billy was a widower and travelled with the son from his marriage, Patrick. When it seemed like the rest of Ireland was heading West, maybe it was the fact that he had a son which made Billy make the shorter journey to Wales. Billy travelled straight to one of the biggest pits in the Rhondda Valley, the Maindy Colliery, and was taken on at a time when the industry was thriving.

In Pentre, Billy met Florence Louisa Eynon (nee Scourfield), herself a widow, with four sons and a daughter. The pair began a relationship and married.

James Patrick Murphy was born to Florence and Billy on Monday, August 8th, 1910. "My father was the only child of that marriage," Jimmy's son, Jimmy Jr, said in 2016. "Their children from their previous marriages were quite a bit older than Jimmy; all of his brothers were miners. He had an elder sister, Mary, who was a lovely woman. She was good company. It would naturally have been a loud household – and I gather that being with his brothers is where he learned to handle his drink."

It may well have been expected that James would follow the path taken by his father and his brothers but it was clear from an early age that Florence wanted better for her youngest child. She was determined that he would have a good education and hoped that he would become a school teacher. One of Florence's edicts to James was that in order to have a successful life, he must be a good listener, and likewise, he should only speak when he felt he had something sensible to say. He described her as

THE RISE

upright and very honest, and said that she ruled the household with 'devotion and a rod of iron.' Florence was Welsh Chapel, William was Irish Catholic; Jimmy grew up a Catholic, though all of his stepbrothers and sisters were Protestants.

A school report dated the Christmas term of 1923, when James was 13, indicates that he was 'capable of better work.' He had obtained a full twenty marks in English and was noted as having 'very good' performance in Arithmetic, Reading, Penmanship and Composition. Overall, he scored a total of 134 from a possible 170 marks over the term; his teacher remarked that his conduct was *'very talkative, otherwise satisfactory'*, elaborating at the bottom that he was capable of better work, but talked too much, though it was noted that there had been an improvement in mental arithmetic and composition.

James was a naturally talented pianist and church organist. Florence was so keen for James to develop this skill that he was sent for lessons on both instruments and, in his teenage years, he played organ in the Treorchy Parish Church. He loved music, but by the time he was a teenager, he had shown more than just a touch of natural ability as a footballer. He retained his fondness for music, later explaining that he found Beethoven, Lizst and Chopin a therapeutic release from the intensity of working for Manchester United.

Having an Irish surname in the Ton Pentre Village School made James stick out like a sore thumb and he would get into various playground fights where his heritage was often used by others as an insult. There is no suggestion that this was any more sinister than general schoolchildren teasing but, growing up in the environment he had, he could more than handle himself.

At the end of a hard week's working down the coal mines, the miners enjoyed their downtime with a few games of football and more than a few pints to quench their thirst. Having observed and occasionally participated in these sometimes aggressive games between strong fully grown men, the young Murphy was not only well-equipped to deal with the rigours of playground football, he had all the tools to flourish. His natural ability as a footballer was complemented by an aggressive tackle, the likes of which were rarely seen in those who played as inside-forwards, as James did. Those rough edges of his game were smoothed out by schoolteachers George Tewkesbury and Arthur Hanney.

James played for a number of local teams; first of all, the Pentre Linnets, then, Pentre Boys, followed by Treorchy Juniors and then Glamorgan Boys. Though he would carve out a professional career in a position further back, as is often the case with the best boys in their local areas, Murphy played in a more forward position and attracted plenty of attention; so much so, that at the age of just thirteen, he was called up to play in an under-16 schoolboy international for Wales against England at Cardiff Arms Park.

Wales won the game and Murphy – having described himself as a 'little whippet of a boy, who, despite his size, had been taught to tackle hard' – held his own against an England team who were rated as far superior. His performance was so impressive that he retained his place for the next game against Scotland at Hampden Park. That game ended 2-2 and the prodigious young player was attracting the attention of a number of top English league clubs.

Murphy's ambition was to play for Cardiff City and the reasons were obvious; the Welsh side had only gained entry into the English league relatively recently and had created waves with their ascent up the ladder. Their status in the mid 1920s was as strong as any club in the country but unfortunately for Murphy,

THE RISE

Cardiff didn't express an interest in signing the youngster. However, after the Scotland game, West Bromwich Albion – themselves a formidable First Division club – made their move, approaching Billy and Florence and requesting their permission to sign James and take him to the Midlands.

Having never travelled, in his own words, beyond the pitheads of the Rhondda, West Bromwich may well have been a thousand and twenty miles away from Jimmy Murphy's home as it was one hundred and twenty.

"These days you can drive from the Midlands to Wales in two hours, but in those days, the journey was far more difficult," says Jimmy Jr. "So it was a brave move to go there by himself."

Brave, perhaps, but inevitable, for Jimmy described the roar of a soccer crowd as the only thing that sounded sweeter than the classical musicians he so adored. And so, at fifteen, he was off to ply his trade in the English game, though he would never forget his roots. "I came from a little Welsh village in the Rhondda Valley," he later said. "I played for Wales as a schoolboy and they were unforgettable times for me. I was passionate and extremely proud to have been selected…those results fired my imagination and brought me to the attention of English league clubs."

Jimmy's reputation was quickly developed; it would be neatly summarised in the most perfect way by the most perfect person in later years when Matt Busby told Tommy Cooper, the Liverpool defender: "You always need two pairs of shin pads when you play against this chap." It was a reputation Jimmy loved. "That's the way I always tried to play… (like) true professionals, who went in hard for the ball and got it."

His apprenticeship was far from an easy ride. And, at first, Jimmy became terribly homesick, but he worked even harder to make things happen.

In the late 1920s, as West Brom became more successful, it seemed as if Jimmy's chance may never come. He was rewarded with a professional contract, though it was his tenacity and application rather than his prolific goal return which seemed to impress. West Brom had no problem scoring goals; they registered 105 goals despite finishing in sixth place in the Second Division in 1930, and, with promotion out of the question, Jimmy was handed his first team debut against eventual champions Blackpool on March 5th.

Going into the following season, Murphy found himself back in the reserves, and looked further away than ever from commanding a regular place. It was his wholehearted perseverance that would make the difference.

"I was determined to make the grade as a professional footballer," Jimmy explained. "I appeared to be getting nowhere when a stroke of luck fell upon me…all players need that luck at the start of their careers. I had run out of goals as an inside-forward, and one day in a reserve game we had a player injured. I dropped back to the wing-half position and happened to play exceptionally well."

That opportunity and position conversion came against Tottenham Hotspur on March 28th, 1931 – a significant breakthrough in Murphy's career, though, unfortunately, a little too late in this particular season for the twenty-year-old to stake a claim for a regular place in the Baggies' remarkable run to promotion, or their successful FA Cup run that year.

Murphy's thoughts remained with his family back in the Rhondda Valley and as soon as he was reasonably able, he saw it as a duty to assist them. "After he'd been at West Brom for a while and had been earning some decent money he arranged for his father to move from working at the bottom of the pit, to the top, so it would be less dangerous, and he made up the difference in his salary," says Jimmy Jr. Jimmy remained close to his family; but, because he was so much younger than his brothers, some of his own children never got to meet them. This was a case of history repeating itself; Jimmy's mother Florence was one of thirteen children.

Having toiled for five years, a prolonged opportunity in the first team for Murphy was well overdue and his superb form as a no-nonsense wing-half meant that the Baggies' first team manager Fred Everiss could no longer keep the player out. Their form in the autumn months was exceptional for a promoted side; while their post-Christmas inconsistency cost them the chance of a serious title push, it was nonetheless an impressive effort for Everiss, Murphy and co. to finish in sixth place.

The following season began even better; West Brom won their first four games to really make the other teams in the division wake up and pay due attention.

Eventually, they finished in fourth place, but their reputation as one of the best teams in the league was now well and truly established. This was no flash in the pan success. And so, Murphy's form was recognised by an international call-up; having played against 16-year-olds as a precocious 13-year-old, he became the youngest player to appear for Wales at the age of just 22 when he lined up against France in front of 25,000 at the Stade Olympique in Paris on May 25th, 1933.

His own reputation established, Murphy began the 1933/34 season as first choice for club and country.

On October 4th, he made his home debut for Wales in the first game of their defence of the Home Championships. The 3-2 win against Scotland in front of 40,000 at Ninian Park – back where he'd made his schoolboy debut – was memorable for another reason. It marked the one and only appearance of Matt Busby at international level. Busby was playing at right-half – so, incidentally, was Murphy's direct opponent, though the pair had squared off against each other in the First Division when West Brom played against Manchester City.

Murphy would later suggest the reason Busby didn't get another chance was 'folly', because the Scottish selectors didn't appreciate that he was a Roman Catholic. He certainly couldn't have spoken in any higher terms of his future boss, later describing him as a master player, whose most memorable quality was the way he could 'rip a defence apart by cutely shielding the ball, and then suddenly (make) an astute reverse pass across the field.' Murphy also said that the way Busby brought other players into the game was something to be found prominently within Manchester United's own game plan when the two were in charge.

Murphy missed Wales' next game – this was a time when club games were occasionally scheduled for the same time as international games, and West Brom wouldn't release him as they had an important fixture against Tottenham – but he was back in for their final Championships game, against England up at Newcastle. Just 15,000 turned out as Wales achieved a famous 2-1 win to secure the tournament for a second year in succession. Unfortunately, domestically, West Brom were not quite able to match their exploits of the previous season, finishing seventh.

If he had a difficult year in his playing career then the 1934/35 campaign certainly presented Jimmy's biggest professional disappointments to date, despite only missing one game all season. Wales' defence of the Home Championships was a catastrophe; a 4-0 home defeat to an England side inspired by Stanley Matthews was compounded by a 3-2 loss to Scotland at Pittodrie, to end hopes of retaining the title.

THE RISE

At the end of the season, West Brom had the chance for glory as they faced Sheffield Wednesday in the FA Cup final. Wednesday had finished third in the league and West Brom ninth; they had, however, faced off in the league five days prior, and drawn 1-1. Manager Fred Everiss made a couple of tactical gambles, including the selection of Joe Carter, who had been missing with a knee injury. Unfortunately it backfired and Carter suffered a recurrence; in these days before substitutes, the Baggies were effectively carrying a passenger for eighty minutes. By that time they were a goal down and though they valiantly battled back to equalise twice (the second goal, scored by Teddy Sandford, was notably followed by the sight of Jimmy running into the goal to retrieve the ball so that they might benefit from the momentum that seemed to be swinging their way), Wednesday's advantage eventually told and the Owls won 4-2.

The next two seasons were unremarkable at club level as West Brom finished in 18th and then 16th position but there was glory to be found at international level again as Murphy won the Home Championships with Wales in 1937.

He missed the second of Wales' three wins (later bemoaning that he felt he would have won at least eight or nine more caps had West Brom always released him to play for his country when it was requested) but did play in the home wins over England and Ireland, the latter being a 4-1 win at Wrexham on March 17th, 1937, which secured the title, incidentally the last one Wales were to win outright.

Eight months later, to the day, Murphy played his last international game, against England, in a 2-1 loss at Middlesbrough's Ayresome Park.

Welsh football historian Ceri Stennett described Murphy as a 'key member' of that successful Wales team. Alongside the 1958 side and the 2016 team, there has been much debate about the potential of the 1934 Wales team and how, given that they were the pick of the teams in the UK, they might have even been good enough to be World Cup winners.

The fact that Murphy was seen as a key component in an international side that could feasibly be argued to have been the best around in its day gives some sort of indication as to the quality he had, beyond the anecdotal evidence that exists to support his aggressive approach.

"In modern parlance he was one of those players people would say are a seven or eight out of ten every week," WBA Historian Dave Bowler said in a 2016 documentary for MUTV. "You knew what you were going to get from Jimmy Murphy, he was just a regular, rock-solid member of the team."

Without doubt, Jimmy could easily be described as a top level footballer. He was a committed and clever player who commanded respect from his peers. He played for teams who lost more games than they won, be it at domestic or international level. He was a chaser of lost causes; the last man to be beaten; the one yelling and swearing at team-mates to get stuck in and yet, perhaps paradoxically, also a man who had thought carefully about how the game should be played.

Away from Saturday afternoons, he was an approachable and friendly chap; a modest man of simple pleasures. Of an evening he would have a pint of ale in the tap-room of his local in Wednesbury, where he became very acquainted with the landlords. On Sundays he took the Sacraments of Confession and Holy Communion.

By the late 1930s, and having enjoyed a career spanning more than two hundred first team appearances for West Brom, Jimmy Murphy was approaching his thirtieth birthday as a player who was no longer automatic first choice for his club and that had in turn prematurely ended his international career. When a move to Swindon on the other side of the Cotswolds presented itself, it was the appeal of first team football and probably not the appeal of dropping two divisions which convinced him to make the move south.

It can't have been a decision made lightly, though the relative closeness must have helped when taking into account the fact that Jimmy had married a local girl, Winnie, and they had a three-year-old daughter Patricia.

"Mum's parents ran a pub in Wednesbury, and Dad used to go in there drinking, and that's how they met," Jimmy's youngest son, Nick, says.

The family didn't move, which was just as well, considering the briefness of the sojourn – just four games – before the onset of the Second World War changed everything. Little did he know it, but the war years would see him make the first steps on a journey which would eventually lead him to the job by which his life would become defined.

CHAPTER | TWO

MEETING MATT

"Almost at once we seemed to fit. On the face of it we may have seemed like opposites. Our ideas were similar and from this understanding would be born what would eventually be known as the Busby Babes" – Sir Matt Busby

By the time Jimmy left to fight Rommel at the Siege of Tobruk – a campaign which, alongside the Second Battle of Alamein, marked a turning point in the War – his wife Winnie had already given birth to two sons, John and Philip, and was pregnant with another. The third son was born in July 1942; Winnie was sufficiently concerned that her husband would not return that the son was named James Patrick, after his father.

Jimmy's escapades during the War with the Eighth Army saw him in the deserts of North Africa, then Tunis and Sousse in 1943 before they got to Rome in 1944, and eventually ended up in Bari. By then, in 1945, his main responsibility was to help keep morale up by keeping fitness levels high, a role he had taken over from future Wolves manager, Stan Cullis. He organised football and cricket matches and whilst up on Italy's Adriatic coast, a PTI by the name of Matt Busby arrived with a few professional players, including Joe Mercer.

"By the time he got to Italy, the War was over," Jimmy Jr. explains. "He wouldn't talk about what happened. He would always say that he 'killed a snake, rode a camel and he cooked an egg on the bonnet of a car!' I didn't know where he'd been. After he died, my mother went through a suitcase of photographs and keepsakes. There were a number of postcards with very few words on. *'Everything okay, God bless, Jimmy.'* That was it. *'Hope Winnie and the children are okay, Jimmy.'* When he came home from the War my first words were, apparently, 'I don't like him'. But I can't remember that!"

Jimmy's army report described him as *'an excellent MCO who has been in charge of the camp's sports section for thousands of men passing through. He has plenty of drive and personality and is popular with all ranks.'*

In Bari, Busby – who had already been offered the manager's position at Manchester United – participated in an exhibition game that was being coached by Murphy. Jimmy's team comprised of six Polish players, two professionals and two amateurs, and even though they lost 6-3, the fiery Welshman caught the eye. Here was a man enthusiastically stressing the importance of various elements of the game. In reality, Jimmy had nothing to gain, nothing to profit from it, but he was just so passionate about the game that those watching couldn't help but admire it.

"We could have heard the guns in Bari had it not been for the loud entreaties of a tough little character in the act of training," Busby said. "I had bumped into him before. Or perhaps I should say he had bumped into me before, when I played for

MEETING MATT

Manchester City and Liverpool and he West Bromwich Albion. Jimmy Murphy was not averse, notwithstanding his great skill, to sitting an opponent on his bottom if by that means – and of course always within the law! – he was the more certain to relieve him of the ball. He was a master of the timing of the tackle. But it was his attitude, his command, his enthusiasm, and his whole driving, determined action and wordpower that caused me to say to myself: 'He's the man for me.' I asked Jimmy to join me at Old Trafford as my assistant when he had been demobbed and returned to England."

Matt had told him that they would have their work cut out – they had no money, the club had been bombed, and they had to try and develop their own players. This would be Jimmy's job while Matt looked after the first team.

Jimmy Jr. was three years old when his father returned from the War; the reunion of the family was short-lived, as Jimmy went to Manchester that summer to begin work with Busby.

In early 1946, Busby's United rebuilding job was well underway. Yet only on physically arriving at the football ground did Jimmy realise how literal that rebuilding job was. He walked into Old Trafford whistling and was stopped dead in his tracks. The ground, after all, had been bombed in the War, and all that remained was a scene of devastation. The club was training at the back of the destroyed stand on a concrete surface which Jimmy compared to 'a school playground'. It is perhaps a compelling early insight into his mentality that he saw these testing conditions and relished the challenge; indeed, he credited the environment with helping when it came to the cultivation of team spirit.

Despite the difficult circumstances, Jimmy was very much a fan of the team his boss had been putting together. He described them as 'brilliantly entertaining' and was equally enthusiastic about the components. Johnny Carey was arguably his favourite, Jimmy describing him as the best defensive organiser he'd ever seen, a quality that was emphasised by the fact that he wasn't the quickest, so used his intelligence to more than compensate. Murphy was also a fan of Johnny Morris' aggressive style and felt that Johnny Aston Sr. possessed a loyalty and a selflessness which were 'the backbone of any club whose ambitions were great.'

Morris was part of a frontline given the nickname of the 'Fearsome Five' by the press; the attributes of Jack Rowley (a rocket shot on him, akin to Bobby Charlton), Jimmy Delaney (a quick showman in the style of Denis Law), Charlie Mitten (a direct goalscorer) and Stan Pearson (a worker) meant that United's attack could mix it in any given circumstance. Not only did Murphy enjoy watching such variety, but he was a firm believer that football should first and foremost be entertaining.

'I cannot look upon soccer as a dry and uninteresting chessboard exercise,' he said in his 1968 book, *Matt…United…and Me*. 'It would have been ridiculous to have pulled seven or eight men back in defence with such a fine forward line as Delaney, Morris, Rowley, Pearson and Mitten at your disposal. With such an attack the only reasonable policy in those days was to use their great skills in trying to score goals. There was no room then for the frightened man of football who places all hope of success in unimaginative defensive tactics.'

In addition to his responsibilities as a coach, Busby trusted his new number two enough to send him on scouting missions. In December 1947, Murphy was deployed to cast his eye over a potential new recruit. The December 15th edition of the *Daily Express* carried the sub-headline *But Jimmy said 'No'* in a story by Henry Rose. 'Matt Busby, Manchester United's manager, has found it hard to avoid having the name of Hughie Russell,

MEETING MATT

Gillingham's 22-year-old young centre-forward, recommended to him. Russell, in fact, has for some time been one of the most-wanted players in the country. "A certain international in the making," was one build-up given to Matt. So he sent his aide-de-camp, Jimmy Murphy, former Welsh international half-back, along to watch Russell in the Cup tie at Rochdale. But Jimmy was not impressed, and that is good enough for Matt.'

His instinct and intuition for such things, for players who would be good enough to play for Manchester United, was one reason Busby had such an unrelenting belief in him. He believed Jimmy's was a priceless gift; the ability to not only identify whether a player had potential (or not, as the case may have been with Russell) within a matter of minutes, but to develop them to fulfil that potential.

United would finish second in 1948, 40,000-plus supporters making the trek to Maine Road to see their team play every other week. They at least defeated Derby County in the FA Cup semi-final to set up a final against Blackpool.

Blackpool boasted the world-class pair of Stan Mortensen and Stanley Matthews but this was not the only headache United faced in their preparation. Twelve days before the final, the *Daily Mirror* reported: 'With only two weeks to Wembley, two of Manchester United's stars, skipper Jack Carey and centre-forward (Jack) Rowley, are on the injured list. Unable to play against Everton, they were down for special treatment at Old Trafford yesterday. Rowley's leg injury is first priority. He is due to play in the Inter-League game at Preston on Wednesday. "We are doing everything we can to get him fit for this match, but I cannot say yet what will be the result," said coach Jimmy Murphy.'

In the *Daily Express* of April 19th, 1948, journalist Frank Butler reported a story relating to speculation that Rowley would miss the FA Cup Final. '*BURKE TOLD: STAND BY*' ran the headline that Monday morning. Eventually, Burke wasn't required and United focussed their play down their right wing to restrict their opponents' supply to Matthews. It was a successful strategy as United won 4-2, Rowley scoring twice.

A year before that Cup triumph, one of the most famous and influential conversations in Manchester United history had taken place between manager and assistant. It ought to be mentioned, because it's a truth that is most often lost, that Murphy's own start to life at United had been successful.

In his first season in charge, United's reserve side won the Central League Championship, registering these impressive wins along the way – 9-3 against Newcastle on September 7th, 1946; 5-1 over Stoke City reserves on September 21st; 6-1 over Burnley reserves on October 12th; 4-2 against Derby County's second string on October 19th; 3-0 versus Sheffield Wednesday reserves on December 14th; 4-0 against Sheffield United reserves on February 8th, 1947 and another six goal haul against Everton reserves on March 29th. Murphy had certainly adopted a very successful attacking philosophy.

At the end of the season, a party was held to celebrate United's second place in Division One, and their reserve success, but at the party, Jimmy confessed to Matt that he did not feel a single player from the reserve side was capable of coming into the senior side and strengthening it.

In Roger Macdonald's 1968 book *Manchester United In Europe*, the author says: 'Busby's response was to step up his recruitment of youth, an idea which had been in his mind since he took over at Old Trafford, until four teams of varying ages could be fielded every Saturday – the 'B', for boys of 15 to 16 ½; the 'A', 16½-17½, the Colts, 16½-18½; and the official third or 'A' team, 18½-20.

MEETING MATT

The system was always the same. First United's team of eight scouts, led by Joe Armstrong and Louis Rocca, would look at young players, concentrating on those who had represented their city or county. If Busby, or Murphy or Bert Whalley, the club coach, thought them sufficiently promising, they were brought to Manchester for one or more trials.'

Busby had laid out the game plan and Murphy set about implementing it. "I think it was at this point when Murphy was given responsibility for the development of the reserve and youth teams as he saw fit," says United youth historian Tony Park. And what commenced was a radical overhaul of the club's approach to youth development. "All of a sudden there were youth and reserve friendly games being played for the first time. These things weren't done before; clubs didn't take the time to arrange friendlies for their junior teams. But Murphy was trying all of these things. The club started going on youth tours to Ireland in the early 1950s and it was at this point that the name and reputation of Manchester United's youth team began to gain some serious traction."

Taking the youth team on the road was the most effective way of finding the best players from different regions; and, once found, Jimmy Murphy could attempt to lure those players to Manchester.

"The likes of Johnny Scott, Billy Whelan, Jackie Mooney, these players were all attracted to United from Ireland from these games and tours," Park says. "There was this interest, and there was a subsequent groundswell of local Manchester boys who had taken an interest. Then Jimmy had Joe Armstrong scouting the county football games, Sheffield versus Durham, Manchester versus Liverpool and so on. In these days before schoolboy terms were even a thing, Murphy and Armstrong were convincing players to come along by offering them apprentice positions. They'd come and join the ground staff and learn to become a plumber or an electrician alongside training at the club. Jimmy then started running summer camps, and then had them at Easter and Christmas too."

As early as late April or early May, Murphy and Bert Whalley would send out official invitations to talented local players. After an introduction informing the player of the date and time, the letter would read: 'Every player will have personal tuition on the theory and the practical side of the game. P.E and games will also be introduced periodically. We hope you will take advantage of this course and have no doubt you will derive great benefit and knowledge from the tuition received.'

Kids came from far and wide. "We watched English trials, Scottish trials, Welsh trials...and chose, as we thought, the best of the youngsters," Jimmy said. "I think we were the first to start making our own players at Manchester United."

At this time, Busby's efforts lay solely with the first team; he had a job to do to try and win them the League title, and he was also trying to get the club established as a name abroad.

Jimmy's innovation was noted by the national press; there was a report on his forthcoming camps in the *Daily Mirror* on May 16th, 1950. 'While Matt Busby and his Manchester United stars combine soccer and holiday-making in America and Canada, twenty young stars who hope to be United stars of tomorrow will take part in a specialised individual coaching course,' wrote Gerry Lofton. 'Each lad, average age sixteen, will be half picked. In charge will be United's assistant manager, Jimmy Murphy, and coach Bert Whalley. "There will be personal link up, and complete instruction in the theory of the game," Jimmy Murphy tells me. "Each lad will get individual tuition." Last season United ran this course for the first time. Six of the lads graduated to the reserves and one, Whitefoot, to the first team. United believe that this individual coaching of young players, instead of mass instruction, will provide better results. The course, which will be held two days a week, will be on an enclosed ground away from Old Trafford so that the youngsters have complete privacy and the use of a large swimming pool after training.'

Jimmy felt more comfortable dedicating such a comprehensive amount of his time to the task at hand, because Winnie and the children made the move up to Manchester in 1948. By now, the couple had another son, Nick, though the intervening years had obviously put a strain on the family.

"It's not just me who missed out on childhood memories of Dad," says Jimmy Jr. "My brother Phil is two years older than me, and Dad went to North Africa due to the War within nine months of me being born. John is two years older than him, so he would still have only been around ten when Dad came back and then went to Manchester. I was born in July 1942, and Dad came home from the War in 1946."

Behind the scenes Murphy and Bert Whalley were in charge of what would become a conveyor belt of talent. There were different age groups, four or five junior teams, with one or two men looking after each of these teams, and each of those men reported to Murphy. 'He oversaw the entire production from junior sides, to the A team, to the reserves, and then when there was a player who was ready, he would tell Matt," Park says.

It was an intense workload. Murphy coached the reserves every day, and still found time to dedicate two evenings each week to coach the younger players who were either at school or in the apprenticeships. It was quickly apparent that his family would simply have to accept Manchester United as a large part of their own lives. "My mother would stay in bed in the morning and Dad would get up and do the fire, and the breakfast for the kids," Jimmy Jr. recalls. "Then Joe Armstrong or Bert Whalley would pick him up in their car – that was him, he'd be out and Mum would be in charge until he came home. And even then it wasn't that straightforward – Tuesdays and Thursdays, in the evening he'd coach the youngsters. Back in those days it had to be done that way because the young players would have other jobs until they became professional players."

Murphy's approach was perhaps a more refined and improved version of the MUJAC (Manchester United Junior Athletic Club) system which had been initially established.

Along with this new potential to attract players from far and wide came some human issues – not least young players becoming homesick. Having experienced this himself, Murphy was able to be empathetic and also pro-active. He sourced lodgings for the youngsters where the landladies would be motherly and welcoming.

"He left home when he was seventeen to go to West Bromwich," explains Jimmy Jr. "He was a year younger than Matt Busby when he did, who also came from a coal mining village (Bellshill, in Scotland). Their upbringings were the same and so they were determined when they were bringing young players through that those young players would have it better. I wouldn't say he was ignored but he was put in lodgings without a second thought. So they would carefully choose the lodgings and make sure that they knew the landlady." So sound was his judgment on this score that those landladies were used for decades to follow.

Busby had expressed a wish that the youth and reserve teams led by Murphy would play in a similar manner to the first team, so that when the time arose, players could move into their next

MEETING MATT

senior side with more ease. As Matt's vision of carefree attacking football was one Jimmy wholeheartedly agreed with, that became the plan. Jimmy described Great Britain as a potential gold mine for the finest all-round footballers in the world, reasoning that in a population of 50 million, within the thousands who played football must be some of the very best in the world.

The best players coming to a club where they were receiving proper training, at the same time as learning a trade, in an environment that was not only conducive to their development, but was indeed centred around their comfort, had an obvious effect. United's kids were winning games and winning them handsomely.

Alongside him were Bert Whalley and Joe Armstrong. Jimmy affectionately attached himself to the pair and spoke fondly of their collective reputation as the 'Three Musketeers'. Bert was Jimmy's assistant and Joe was his chief scout, having taken over from Louis Rocca; it is abundantly clear, in any record, the esteem in which Murphy held the pair. The three of them had many things in common; Jimmy would speak glowingly of their honesty, dedication and hard work, their loyalty and their intuition; qualities present in his own personality.

Jimmy recalled a time when Bert was on holiday and saw a boy playing football on the beach; he went and said he would arrange him a trial, only to be told that the boy had signed for Sheffield Wednesday. The boy was Albert Quixall, who later of course did sign for United. Jimmy would tell the story to illustrate what a good eye for talent Bert had but there is an underlying subtext to it; it is clear that Bert's dedication to the cause, going so far as to continue to look for players when he was meant to be on holiday, was most certainly something Jimmy found appealing.

Bert, like Jimmy, was indebted to Matt for having his job at the club. Bert had played for United and was a dependable centre-half – in fact, he was almost ever-present in Jimmy's reserve side in his first year in charge. However, Bert suffered an eye injury when he was coaching some schoolboys and despite initially thinking it was nothing, he went to hospital after suffering from some trouble with his vision and he was told it was so serious that he may lose the sight in his eye. At the age of 34, his career was winding down anyway, but Busby visited him in hospital on Christmas Eve 1947 to reassure him he would have a job at Old Trafford should he have to retire. He was good to his word; Bert described it as the best Christmas present he ever had. Later, Jimmy would describe Bert as a 'brilliant' coach. He said that Bert and Joe could spot future stars on a foggy day – using the literal example of Joe first watching Bobby Charlton on a misty February morning in 1953.

Such was the prolific and pronounced nature of United's growing reputation that it was thought that the club had eyes in every town. They did, in fact, employ only one full-time scout – Armstrong – and for a long time never numbered more than ten in part-time scouts. Names like Bob Bishop have become familiar in United folklore but it wasn't the case that United had eyes everywhere. Instead, it was the dedication of those few names who became revered which counted so significantly in the eyes of parents whose children had been identified as future stars. United's scouts had been deployed with this mandate from Murphy – "there is no substitute for skill or character" – with the idea that if a player was found who had both qualities, then Manchester United stood a good chance of making a gem from the rough diamond.

Of course, it wasn't long before other clubs cottoned on and started to imitate, but United had a few distinct advantages. They were the first, and had established a strong reputation when it came to how they conducted their business. They were not only transparent with their intentions but they demonstrated a duty of care to the future of the young boys; of course, it helped that the first team was improving and playing attractive football.

That period of success was finally crowned with the prize which had been coveted for so long; after finishing second in four of the first five seasons after the War, United finally won the Division One title in 1952, scoring 95 goals in the process. This was perceived by most as the culmination of the years of hard work rather than the start of a glittering period; the first team was ageing, and, at a shareholders' meeting that year, Busby delivered an incredible statement that the club had at least £200,000 worth of talent beyond the first team. When you consider that the British transfer record at the time was £34,500 – set when Jackie Sewell moved to Sheffield Wednesday – it was quite a proclamation which understandably dominated the headlines the following day.

The idea of developing a team through the club, with the intention of young players coming through to play for the first team, was not a new one. It had initially been attributed to James Gibson and Walter Crickmer.

The club had previously suffered through a number of controversial and unsuccessful years and their difficulties included a debt that they still owed for the development of Old Trafford. It was Gibson's intention to develop a team of local players but it is unclear – and there is no way of ever knowing for certain – whether this was a matter of necessity or the creative wisdom of a visionary.

When Scott Duncan resigned as manager in 1937, Walter Crickmer assumed those responsibilities for the second time, and he also effectively became everything else; manager of the reserve team, as well as being employed as Secretary, which was his actual official position. In 1938 Crickmer and Gibson established the MUJACs, which would eventually evolve into the youth team.

These events are significant when it comes to establishing the appropriate credit. While we cannot then give Busby and Murphy the acknowledgement of creation we can at least ascertain a few things that seem reasonable.

Busby demanded absolute control when he was offered the position of manager; he wanted to take control of training, to select the team, and to be responsible for signing and selling players. He secured himself a five year contract when he was initially offered three, after explaining the changes he had in mind would take that long to bear fruit. With that in mind it has to be said that his vision absolutely tallied with that of Gibson and Crickmer, for the results which followed seem only too logical. And so, with all of these things in mind, it is worth remembering that as much credit as Murphy deserves and as much as will be attributed to him in the forthcoming pages, he was working under the instruction of Busby.

Park is in no doubt where the majority of the kudos should be placed. "I would say that Walter Crickmer set the strategy in place and I'd say that when Jimmy Murphy was there, he was in charge of all of it," he says. "I think Busby's involvement in that side of it would be when a player was going to sign his contract. When they needed the big guns, Busby and Murphy would drive to get the player signed, as happened with Duncan Edwards. Other than that it was the Jimmy Murphy show."

That much is evidenced by how the youth team played. Whilst adopting the attacking identity to mimic the first team, the influence of Murphy was increasingly obvious. "I'd definitely say

MEETING MATT

that Jimmy was responsible for the style of play," insists Park. "He was a very constructive wing-half as a footballer; aggressive, gritty, but he could play, and had tremendous leadership qualities, as was illustrated by the career he had. For the young players he almost had a Pied Piper quality to him…here was this guy who was half sergeant major and half friendly uncle; the kids loved him and trusted him."

Busby backed up this view and revealed how their relationship worked. "He (Jimmy) was the man who would help me create a pattern that would run right through the several teams of players from fifteen years of age upwards to the first team," he said. "Almost at once we seemed to fit. On the face of it we may have seemed like opposites. He may have looked more excitable, more ebullient than I, though he has always shunned publicity. He may have seemed a physically tougher player and character than I, though he was as much at home with Chopin on the pianoforte as with the science of hard, uncompromising but clean tackling. But as unlike poles attract, if unlike poles we were, we attracted.

"Our ideas were similar and from this understanding, my conception of a creche, a nursery, then a school with a curriculum of playing and character standards and my overall search for a pattern that would facilitate the interchanging of players from one team to another – from all these were born what eventually were known as the Busby Babes.

"Jimmy would always give a straightforward opinion. He was a no/yes-man. But once having made a point he would accept that mine was the decision. He was forthright with never a suggestion of usurping my position…if he judged a player I found that his judgements almost always confirmed mine.

"He was invaluable in training boys but his value did not rest there. He could tackle the established players with the same conviction and enthusiasm…of course, I poked my nose in wherever I could. It was many years before I decided I no longer had the breath to show those young players that I could still do a bit."

Perhaps nobody, even the two men themselves, could predict just how successful the next five years would be.

CHAPTER | THREE
RECRUITING THE BABES

"Jimmy was waxing lyrical about Duncan [Edwards]. 'We've a great player here, left foot, right foot, he's magnificent in the air, he beats men with lightning pace and he scores goals. When I knock the rough edges off him he'll be some player!'" – Sir Alex Ferguson

Ten minutes. That is how long Jimmy Murphy said it took to identify a player of genuine talent. He was able to tell if a player wasn't good enough in a much quicker time. Principally, and modestly, Jimmy put it all down to what he described as a lifetime of experience.

First and foremost Jimmy had only a small, handpicked number of regional scouts, scouts he deemed as experts, whose opinion he trusted implicitly. Sometimes, no further opinion is required. In the case of Duncan Edwards, who is probably the most famous and romantic name of all of the Babes, Murphy explained that he only had to see the youngster kick the ball once.

In recent Manchester United history – or at least recent enough to include the entirety of Sir Alex Ferguson's reign – there are enough examples of odd twists of fate which led to a signing or two which may have otherwise been unexpected.

When attempts to sign Patrick Kluivert and Gabriel Batistuta were unsuccessful in 1998, Ferguson signed Dwight Yorke, who had an immediately successful impact. Better still is the example of Eric Cantona, who was signed only after Leeds United manager Howard Wilkinson made an enquiry to sign Denis Irwin.

Even better still is the story of how United signed Edwards. Matt Busby was interested in a youngster named Alec Farrall – Farrall was a schoolboy international and Busby's friend Joe Mercer was the coach of the Schoolboys. Mercer told Busby with regret that Farrall wanted to join Everton but there was another player who he should sign. That player was Duncan Edwards of Dudley.

Edwards had been recommended to Busby as a 12-year-old back in 1948. When it became clear that he had continued to develop at the expected pace, Busby deployed Murphy, Bert Whalley and Joe Armstrong, as well as Reg Priest, United's scout in the area. Busby even went to see the youngster play himself. Upon witnessing him, Murphy proclaimed he had seen a 'genius' and said that the club 'must move mountains' to sign him.

Edwards' local team Wolverhampton Wanderers were keen and that move would have made sense; United, however, had the appeal of being the 'glamour' side of the country with their terrific footballing side which had just won the FA Cup.

RECRUITING THE BABES

However, Edwards had a reputation of his own and it wasn't just Wolves and United who were courting him; just about every club in the First Division were making their own subtle overtures and promises of handsome signing-on fees once the boy turned fifteen. It inevitably became the fiercest battle for a schoolboy signature of its time and, even after Busby had made a personal visit to the Edwards' family home, United were still concerned that the player may choose to join Bolton Wanderers, who thought they had an ace card in the fact that Duncan's cousin, Dennis Stevens, was a schoolboy player there.

When Reg Priest heard that Bolton were making a serious effort to sign him, he made a telephone call to Murphy to advise him that he needed to act fast. Unbeknown to Reg, earlier that day United had already made an attempt to close the deal. Bert Whalley had set off for the Midlands but his car broke down; he had to hitch-hike a lift back home to Manchester.

Bert arrived back at Old Trafford in the wee hours and Jimmy, having taken the phone call, arranged for a car to be hired – the pair were on the road to the Midlands. They arrived at 3.30am and convinced Duncan's parents to permit them to speak to their son; only to be told by Duncan that he had already been won over by Busby. So, the journey wasn't quite as urgent as it seemed it might have been! Nonetheless, Jimmy made good on the trip and secured Duncan's signature there and then. Jimmy later reckoned that in travelling expenses and meals, signing Duncan must have come at a cost of £100, but he countered that by saying by 1968 standards, he would have been worth at least £200,000. (The record by this point was set by Leicester City, who paid £150,000 for Allan Clarke).

Convincing Bobby Charlton to sign depended a little more on the personal touch. Joe Armstrong returned to Manchester, on the evening of the same day he'd travelled up to the North East, and reported to Murphy. "We had to peer through the mist but what I saw was enough for me," he said. "This boy is going to be a world beater."

That was good enough for Jimmy, who believed in Joe's judgement implicitly, despite the fact that the scout had never played the game professionally. For Jimmy, it was in fact that detachment which helped Armstrong's eye. He had a wonderful nous for spotting the kind of young player Murphy would be looking for. Young Robert Charlton was a player walking in a daunting shadow of his own, as nephew of Jim, John (known as Jack) and George Milburn, all top-class footballers under the family name.

Charlton would later go on record as saying that he felt his performance on the frozen pitch was ordinary at best, but Armstrong introduced himself straight away. "I would like to know if you would like to play for Manchester United when you leave school this summer," Armstrong said to the young boy. Charlton – who had listened to the radio as United won the 1948 FA Cup final – gave the scout his word that he would.

As Football Association rules prohibited clubs from signing young players until after the final schoolboy international of the season, Armstrong, Murphy and United just had to hope that the fact they had made the first approach would stand them in good stead. Charlton became as keenly desired as Duncan Edwards had been; no fewer than eighteen clubs made offers to sign the young player, and Charlton recalled that sometimes he would come home to find two scouts from different clubs talking to his parents.

Jimmy travelled to Ashington where he spoke at length with Bob Charlton Sr, who voiced reservations about his son moving away from home; expressing concerns that United's recent success might mean his young boy would either get lost in the shuffle or be 'blinded by the glamour.'

"Mr Charlton," replied Jimmy. "My father worked down the pit like you. When I became an £8 a week first-teamer, I was able to save enough so my father could leave the coal face for good. If I never had another thing out of football, that precious moment when I could get my father out of the pit was worth it." The human touch worked. Bobby's father was impressed by the morals of the man sitting opposite him and asked his son if he would like to sign for Manchester United. The boy had already made up his mind. Jimmy attributed that decision to the respect Bobby had for Joe but there is no telling just how helpful or crucial Jimmy's personal intervention was.

It was Jimmy who met Bobby after he got the train to Manchester later that summer, and Jimmy who accompanied him in a taxi to digs run by Mrs Watson, one of the club's preferred landladies.

"Bobby tells so many great stories about Jimmy. One of my favourites is when Jimmy and Joe Armstrong picked him up to drive him to Manchester when he was just fifteen years of age," says Sir Alex Ferguson.

"Jimmy was waxing lyrical about Duncan: 'We've a great player here, left foot, right foot, he's magnificent in the air…he beats men with lightning pace and he scores goals…and when I knock the rough edges off him he'll be some player!'"

Attention to detail and Jimmy's personal touch were also instrumental in the acquisition of Wilf McGuinness.

"I admit to having a Manchester City leaning when I was a lad of about thirteen or fourteen – well, because Old Trafford had been bombed, there was only really Maine Road where we could go and watch the football for both clubs," McGuinness says. "But

JIMMY MURPHY

when it came to where I was going to play my football, when I had to make a choice when I was fifteen, then it was a different story and there was only one club. United had the history with the Youth Cup but to me they also seemed to be making ordinary players look great. Bobby Charlton looked every bit the world beater he would become and I thought that if they could do that with him, as the captain of England Schoolboys, they would be able to do something great with me too. It was the right decision – it was a wonderful life at United, just marvellous.

"All the big clubs were after me as I was captain of the national schoolboys but United really went to an effort. They discovered I went to a Catholic school, Mount Carmel, where I was taught by James Mulligan, the headmaster and sportsmaster. Jimmy learned of this and came to see my mother at our local church to try and convince them to have me sign for United. They were bartering terms on the church grounds and at one point Jimmy exclaimed, 'Jesus Christ was sold for fifty pieces of silver!' and stormed off. He knew what would get to the family. I can't say I paid much attention to it.

"My first meeting with him was at our house. I was very impressed with him; his reputation went before him, as he was in charge of the Welsh team. I liked the way he would cut to the chase and not try too hard to impress, like a lot of the other clubs did. 'We've got Bobby Charlton who you've played with for England so you'll have a pal there!' was as friendly as he got. Jimmy would say 'I want to make you, but I can break you, and that part is up to you.' He commanded an instant respect. Matt was a God, Jimmy was a hard man and Bert had the gentle touch.

"Jimmy was a wonderful coach. Matt had such an aura which was helped with the way he conducted himself, he was always polite, he'd always invite your parents in to have a chat about how you were getting on. Jimmy wouldn't go around the houses like that, he'd be much more direct. 'You come here, sit down, you should be doing this, you need to be doing more of that!' Bert would then wait quietly in the wings and if he thought Jimmy had been a little harsh or abrasive he would come up to us and say, 'Don't take it to heart, don't worry, he's saying it because he loves you!' I worked for Richardson Textiles in Manchester city centre and the owners were good friends with Matt and Jimmy, so the gaffer there would always let me off early if I needed to get off."

The story goes that Jimmy took Wilf along to watch United batter Wolves 7-1 in the FA Youth Cup and asked him: "Don't you want to be a part of that?" By this time, Murphy's own reputation was proving to be just as alluring as anything else.

"There were three people I credit with developing me as a player; Matt Busby, Jimmy Murphy and Bert Whalley," Wilf recalls. "But the one who made sure we didn't fail was Jimmy. I was a right-half for the England schoolboys, which made sense because I was right-footed, but United wanted me to play left-half as well which meant I had to practice on my left-hand side.

"Jimmy had me with a ball outside the ground at the Stretford End. 'Right foot, left foot, right foot, left foot, and I'll come and tell you when to stop.' I enjoyed it at first and then a few hours passed – it got to half past one, and I realised he'd forgotten all about me! When he eventually did come out later that afternoon, he exclaimed in disbelief, 'What are you doing? You should have finished ages ago!' Despite that, I knew he was proud that not only had I done what he asked, but I'd gone above and beyond. I think he appreciated that dedication. I think that my extra training had endeared myself to Jimmy and I became one of his favourites. I think I played a bit like him and so he enjoyed that." Murphy's own account of the same story reveals that that was the moment when he realised McGuinness had a tough spirit which would help set him apart.

There can be two sides to introducing a player into a successful team. In some, it can be a natural progression, as in the case of McGuinness. For others, they can have concern; such a daunting proposition can cause self-doubt. Tommy Taylor might not have been a schoolboy footballer, but the then 21-year-old Barnsley forward carried the profile of a young, strong player who would fit nicely into United's plans, and so, his acquisition became a matter of priority for Busby and Murphy.

Jimmy felt that if there was a fault to be found within Tommy Taylor's make-up, it was that he initially didn't know if he could handle the step up from Barnsley to Manchester United. Busby used his charm to win over the shy Taylor and even negotiated the transfer fee to be £29,999 in order to lessen the pressure on the reserved young man. In Taylor, United had acquired a player who Murphy felt was the finishing touch to 'the most fantastic array of young footballers ever assembled at one club…the soon-to-be world famous Busby Babes.'

In the case of Roger Byrne, you can sense the pride in his words when Jimmy explained how management insight shaped his future in the game. "Roger, a Manchester lad, had found it so hard to get a game of soccer on National Service that he had switched, with great success, to playing rugby," said Jimmy.

"Once out of the Services, Roger came back to soccer and at Old Trafford we experimented until we found his speed and positional play suited the full-back position. Over the years we have always gone in for this policy of switching until a boy found his rightful place; this was especially true during 1953, 1954 and

RECRUITING THE BABES

1955 as the United team was re-fashioned into a combination of youngsters who were to stagger English and European football."

Taylor had enough of a background in League football that Busby and Murphy were assured in their own judgement that he would be a success. Murphy admitted that there could be borderline cases; it wasn't always easy to determine who would be a success because there were a number of talented schoolboys who fell away for a number of reasons. The most infamous of these, a real Murphy favourite, was a youngster called Alick Jeffrey, who Jimmy described as 'the most sensational schoolboy forward' he had ever seen.

"Dad just loved the game and would be so enthusiastic about all sorts of players, it didn't matter who they played for," says his son Nick. "Dad used to call Alick Jeffrey the 'English Pele'; he saw him play loads of times when he was a kid. He really wanted him at United. Unfortunately Alick broke his legs and never played at the level he should have but it goes to show just how far-reaching Dad's knowledge was."

Murphy was clinical and clear-headed on the attributes he wanted to see in his players and yet could be sympathetic when someone struggled. Jimmy recalled one occasion when there was a player (unnamed, out of respect) who he knew was not going to make the grade. In an instance which would foreshadow some of his later reservations about being a manager in his own right, Jimmy hadn't the heart to tell the player he wouldn't make it.

When he finally plucked up the courage to tell him, the player turned up for training with a new pair of boots, excitedly saying: "Look at these Mr Murphy, maybe they will help me improve." Jimmy allowed the boy to remain at the club for another year, more through pity than affection for the boy's enthusiasm; at the end of that year, the boy himself accepted he wasn't good enough.

JIMMY MURPHY

The primary quality Jimmy looked for in a goalkeeper was confidence. This was why Harry Gregg was such a successful complement to the vibrant 'Babes' when he signed, because that confidence helped to define a presence which Murphy felt was vital to goalkeepers in order for them to look unbeatable.

Although he wouldn't entirely dismiss the idea of a shorter goalkeeper, he would ideally want them to be above six feet tall, so as to help that presence and identity. Another area where Murphy was critical and keenly observant when it came to goalkeepers was their handling; if they made a mistake while he was watching, he would meticulously watch them in future to see if that was what he described as a 'temporary lapse or a fatal fault.'

He ideally wanted to see a player who had good anticipation skills and quick reflexes but arguably just as important as any other attribute, he wanted a goalkeeper to be powerful; another point to underline just how important he thought it was that a team should have confidence in their last line of defence.

Throughout the 1950s and 1960s the sport progressed so much, and positional and tactical approaches were modified so much, that it seemed like certain positions became obsolete whilst others changed meaning altogether.

'Full-back' is the most perfect example of a definition which effectively once meant a player in the centre of defence and evolved to mean the wide player in the back-line. In the late 1960s, when Murphy was still coaching, the modern term for a full-back was a very new thing, but he showed himself to have a tremendous prescience. He felt that the best full-backs would be players blessed with balance and speed (both speed on the ball, and speed of recovery, for their responsibilities would include overlapping the wide players in midfield). He felt that tackling, whilst still important, was not the most crucial skill a full-back should have; if the full-back had good anticipation and was quick enough, his opponent may be minded to have to mark him rather than attack himself. Due to its relatively recent introduction into the game, it was therefore difficult to identify players who were natural in the position, though Murphy was a big champion of the way Roger Byrne adapted to the position.

For central defenders, Murphy again liked tall players, though his most desired skill in this area was a player who was a capable of 'springing like a gymnast.' Dominance, much like it would be in the goalkeeping area, was a plus, and another preferred quality of his centre-halves was their balance and ability to read the game. He explained that it was through intelligent interceptions rather than tackles, that most attacks were prevented.

There are a number of names for the role that exists just in front of the defence and just behind the midfield; these early days of the 'sweeper' meant it could apply to a player in this position just as it could apply to one who sat behind the defence. Generally, it would be the best all-round player in the team who would play this role and Murphy felt that this position was the evolution of either the attacking or defensive wing-half. Over time, this had become less the marauding style of Duncan Edwards, and more the intelligent disciplined style of Nobby Stiles, who Jimmy described as the 'perfect' sweeper due to his temperament and neat and tidy work ethic. Again, speed of recovery was seen as a great skill to have in this area, as was the ability to make 'snappy' interceptions.

In his midfielders, Murphy wanted a player whose intelligence of passing was exceptional. "He may be absolutely brilliant on the ball, with a whole repertoire of tricks which may thrill the crowd, but he is no use to his team if his final pass is a bad one," he explained, saying that the ratio must be five or six completed passes to one incomplete; considering that modern standards identify exceptional passing percentages as over 80 per cent, it again paints a picture of a man whose own standards were impeccable in an era that is often portrayed as less technically capable than today's game.

Murphy also stressed that midfielders must be composed and able to hold the ball under pressure from opposition or the crowd. He said he would prefer an 'ice-cold' football brain; for, in his mind, this position was probably the most important or demanding on the pitch. Midfielders were the men who would 'set the machine in motion' and so much was consequently demanded of them, though he would concede to find a player with so many attributes was decidedly rare.

Jimmy expected his players to have a great awareness of their space and the positions of their team-mates, but believed that it was the receiver rather than the passer who was the decisive factor in what made a pass good and effective. The mark of a team playing with confidence was the frequency with which players would make themselves available and demand possession of the ball. It is no surprise, therefore, that players who excelled in command in this area were the ones Jimmy was most excited to watch.

Spacial awareness was a key attribute Jimmy looked for in the position he would describe as the 'secondary link man'; in modern terms, that would be the player who operates in the space between the midfield and the attack. Think of Paul Scholes in the era of 2003-2007; or, for a contemporary reference, Bobby Charlton. Whilst Jimmy did not expect these players to be master of the tackle, he did want them to pressurise their opponents to hopefully make them misplace a pass. Once in possession the player would then instantly look to create an attack and dictate the pace of the game. If such a player could combine these abilities with speed, accurate passing and a powerful shot, you had a potential Charlton on your hands.

It's perhaps owing to the physicality of the game of that era that Jimmy preferred his centre-forwards to be as physically intimidating as his defenders, which was no surprise when you consider the standards he set for his centre-half. After all, how does one consider the qualities of a top-class defender without contemplating the abilities a forward must have to get the better of them? Jimmy felt it was important that teams played with at least two dedicated strikers and one of them should be six foot. He preferred strength and power over 'pretty' feet, and said he would like the forwards to have stamina and good general fitness levels for they would be expected to chase balls around the defence to put pressure on; defending from the front.

For all of this, however, Jimmy was in no doubt whatsoever that the players who had the biggest potential when it came to deciding a game were wingers. He was very specific about the qualities a winger ought to have if they were going to be the players who did decide games, and the answer is not so surprising. He listed speed, courage and accuracy of crosses as vital attacking strengths but also said that wingers must have the speed and stamina to chase back when defending. He was a stickler for the point of accuracy, and would be frustrated at players who were over-deliberate without an end product.

Murphy's opinions provide a fascinating insight into how, for all the talk of how modern football has changed, so many of the same principles still remain and apply.

If a midfield prospect came up with all of the desired qualities, this would be a gem, but such gems were exceedingly rare, so it was the job of the coaching staff to develop these rough diamonds and perhaps identify the best complementary abilities in order to create a successful team. And, in this developmental stage, it became increasingly obvious that the influence of Murphy was crucial.

Many young players came and went and did not make the grade at Old Trafford, but all were thankful for the opportunity, not to mention the honesty with which they had been treated. What Busby and Murphy demanded in return for the opportunity was a willingness to listen and learn, and an application of effort. If a youngster was leaving Old Trafford without a footballing career they at least went with the benefit of these lessons and this went a long way to helping to rubber-stamp the reputation the club was quickly earning.

Putting these foundation stones in place was time-consuming and came at a personal cost to Murphy.

"We had a big family but he left a lot of that to my mother," says Nick, Jimmy's youngest son. "He spent so much time at United, I believe that if he didn't have a family he would have had a bed down at Old Trafford, he loved it so much. He'd bring some of the young players back to ours, it'd often be the case that they'd sleep over. I'm not sure why he did it, he never talked about why, though looking back at the bigger picture it seems obvious that it just meant that much to him and he was keen on having a family atmosphere at the club."

With such commitment, it's only natural, then, that even Jimmy's son's earliest memories have United at the centre. "My earliest recollections of Dad are of him putting the coal on in the fire in the morning, coming in and out of the room with a cigarette in his mouth," recalls Nick. "But my actual earliest memories of spending time with him are of going down to Old Trafford with Dad on a Sunday morning. It was a bit of overtime,

RECRUITING THE BABES

he didn't get paid for it, he'd just go down there for the love of the place really.

"We'd get the bus down to the ground and I can remember walking down the car park...that area of Stretford always seemed dark and grey, but as we'd approach the ground on a Sunday morning, there would be a washing line hanging out of the ground towards the rail station, and all of the red shirts and white shorts would be hanging out to dry on it. The colour was vivid and marvellous, it really brightened the place up.

"I'd run around under the stands at Old Trafford...there was something special about the club and I never really could put my finger on what it was but in recent years I've come to believe that my perception was that way because of how much dedication Dad showed the club. He spent his life devoted to that place. What fella would go back to work on a Sunday morning just to be around the place?"

Jimmy had an old tiny hut beneath one of the stands which came to be known as his 'office', and he would look forward to lunchtimes where he would sit with Bert and Joe as well as any combination of Tom Curry, Arthur Powell, and/or Bill Inglis, and talk football even more.

More often than not, though, Jimmy would be found on the grass at the Cliff or the local YMCA ground, wearing a comfortable tracksuit, barking passionate orders to a group of young players who hung on his every word. The early struggles did not dampen his enthusiasm; possibly because he was so grateful to have the opportunity. Jimmy had effectively been forced to retire from playing, and he always feared that it would be difficult for him to make a career for himself, particularly within football.

Make no mistake. Murphy loved training, he loved the day-to-day activities and relished the opportunity to have a positive influence on the life of young men. He was very much a practical coach; he preferred most of his training exercises to be done with the football, when many other coaches of the time would develop entire coaching routines without the ball. His major emphasis in training was on ball movement; tricks and dribbling were all well and good, but Murphy would yell from the sidelines for every player to pass the ball because the ball 'moved faster on its own'. "Doing the simple thing takes years of practice," he said, and again, he would be the first person to demonstrate how hard his charges ought to be working; he would often be the standard bearer, sweating profusely due to the energy he put into his sessions.

'There was also a harshness to his tuition,' Bobby Charlton recalled in his autobiography. 'Frequently he would stop a practice session and berate you for doing something he considered stupid, an over-ambitious pass or some showy dwelling on the ball which surrendered possession.'

In being that standard bearer, Jimmy often found himself to be the 'bad cop', with Bert Whalley there to give the gentle hand. It was a similar situation between Murphy and Busby. "Murphy would be in your face screaming 'What are you doing?!' whereas Matt would be more diplomatic," says Wilf.

Though Murphy wore what seemed, at times, to be a permanent frown, he couldn't have been more approachable and had a tremendous sense of humour. He loved the banter with his colleagues and loving winding up the young players. He could be tough – and usually was – but it was all done with the benefit of the player in mind. Never was an act committed with any maliciousness, for his goal was to prepare footballers capable of playing for Manchester United.

The likes of Duncan Edwards and Tommy Taylor might

RECRUITING THE BABES

have been born to wear a red shirt but the preceding years saw a number of young men try and fail to establish themselves as players worthy of representing Manchester United.

By early 1952, there was more than enough quality on display to know that the shared vision at the club was going to pay some dividends.

CHAPTER | FOUR

STAR MAKER

"It was a great thrill to spot the spark of genius in a youngster and carefully cultivate it until he shines. It's fascinating to watch the development of youngsters. Some mature according to plan, others who are equally promising fade and drop out" – Jimmy Murphy

The summer of 1947 was the first that Murphy could start a full new year with his own ideas in mind. The transition at Central League level wasn't smooth. Results suffered; United suffered seven defeats before Christmas. Things improved but United did not win the Central League, nor did anyone from the second string make the step up. Murphy acknowledged that in order to make progress, it meant the standard of players in the youth team must improve.

What made things most difficult of all was the lack of truly competitive games for United's young players. Murphy attempted to resolve this headache by taking them on the road; killing two birds with one stone as, of course, he was then able to run the rule over some talented young boys in other areas of the country. It enabled him to firmly stamp his identity on the young United hopefuls. This suggestion is furthered by the fact that United's senior team were playing football that had global appeal; they had been invited to play in Canada and North America at the end of the 1949/50 season, and so Matt Busby was solely focussing on the senior set-up.

"I think that the youth team absolutely mirrored Jimmy Murphy when it came to how they played football," says United youth historian Tony Park. "Jimmy had a fine reputation as a footballer but he was defined by how tough he was as a wing-half, the grittiness, the determination, never knowing when he was beaten…I suppose he could be a bit dirty, but he was a very good player. When you looked at the most notable players coming through the youth system, Duncan Edwards, Nobby Stiles, Wilf McGuinness, all of them were in the Murphy mould."

Just as Busby had been mesmerised by the sight of Murphy on foreign shores, so too had the Welshman been influenced by a British coach overseas. Whilst on a day off in France at the end of his international career as a player, Murphy learned that the Austrian international team was training nearby. They were led by Jimmy Hogan, who Murphy was familiar with from Hogan's days as a Fulham player. Murphy was astounded to see Hogan conducting training with the ball; it was not only rare, it was revolutionary.

"We never saw (the ball) from Saturday to the next," Jimmy would later remark, referring to the training sessions at West Brom. Murphy would later say that this was the first time he'd ever seen an actual football coach at work and he was keen to learn more, so he hung around and introduced himself to Hogan.

From this moment, a friendship was formed. For once in his long career, Murphy was the disciple, keen to engage and absorb as much knowledge as he could. Hogan had coached in Hungary and played with attacking centre-halves. In one of their many conversations, Hogan told Murphy he believed that continental soccer was on the verge of a huge shift which would see many European countries surpass their British counterparts as they embraced these new ideas.

At the time, Murphy was disbelieving, but by the late 1940s, it was clear from the emergence of the Hungarians that Hogan was absolutely correct. (And, it is worth pointing out that this was still some time before the 1953 'Game of the Century' which made the philosophy one that was widely accepted as a successful one). It made Murphy even more of a convert to Hogan's ways and it was without apology that he adopted the same approach when he arrived at Old Trafford. "Mastery of the ball and of the simple way of doing things were the basis of football," Murphy later said. "I used a lot of Jimmy Hogan's ideas when I joined Matt Busby at Manchester United. He was a very influential coach."

Jimmy's best way of observing whether the kids were ready for first team football was to put them into Central League action; this was not always the ideal solution for teenagers, as the team at that time was still comprised of disgruntled senior players not trained in the Murphy way and not particularly convinced that this relatively new man knew the best thing for them. Charlie Mitten, a senior player whose appearances in the reserves came when he was dropped from the first team, was one such example.

Brian Birch and Frank Clempson were two teenagers who were given chances in the reserves and then the first team without really establishing themselves, while Jeff Whitefoot was a young player who had more about him. Much was hoped and expected for Whitefoot; in April 1950, at the age of sixteen years and 105 days, he made his debut against Portsmouth.

Murphy was keen – insistent, even – to give the youngsters as many opportunities as he was able to and this had an obvious impact on results, which were inconsistent. In the 1949/50 campaign, United lost seventeen Central League games. There was a winter period where they didn't score a goal in four games, but this did nothing to stop Murphy persevering.

That season Roger Byrne was a fixture in the side while Mark Jones and Dennis Viollet saw plenty of game time (the former more than the latter). Viollet wouldn't even sign professional terms until the summer at the end of that season. They had the talent, but the game lacked the infrastructure for Murphy's approach to pay the dividends he was confident it would. He had the courage in his conviction to believe that the mixed results in the Central League were, in the short term at least, a necessary evil in order to best help his long-term ambitions. While he was still instructed to conduct scouting for senior players, a *Daily Express* feature from September, 18th 1950, said: 'Manchester United, determined to rebuild the old blue-print team, have a patrol of scouts making an all-Britain search for inside forwards. Patrol leader is assistant Jimmy Murphy' – the Welshman was dedicating every working minute to his job.

There is no doubt that in the 1950/51 season he believed he saw a breakthrough. The Central League team regularly fielded Byrne, Jones, Viollet and Birch, while Jackie Blanchflower and Ronnie Cope were also given runs in the side. Birch scored, and most of them played, in the Lancashire Senior Cup Final in May 1951, which United won 2-1 against Bury to end another relatively inconsistent season with glory. They had failed to win any of their opening five Central League games, losing three, but by the end of the campaign, Murphy was proud and encouraged by the progress the younger players had made, and the experience they had gained. United were also encouraged by the announcement from the Football Association that from the 1952/53 season, the FA Youth Challenge Cup – a competition for clubs, rather than counties – would begin.

By the time the domestic authorities had caught up to speed, however, United's ambitions were greater again. On November 11th, 1952 – still, remember, before Hungary's infamous visit to Wembley – United travelled to Belgium to play Austria Wien. Friendly games against foreign opposition were usually reserved for the close-season; this game was officially in memory of John Langenus, a world-famous Belgian referee who had officiated in over 80 international matches (United were awarded a trophy for their 1-0 win). A crowd of 50,000 was in attendance and tickets were going for a princely sum on the black market.

If it is a push to say that Manchester United were sole pioneers for British football in terms of striving to get a regulated European competition, it is certainly fair to say they were amongst the clubs championing and actively engaging in the cause. This extended to the youth team; United would compete in the Blue Star tournament in Switzerland which was held each May. In fact, success in the competition would make the club synonymous with it.

It seemed as if the gods of fate had conspired to align perfectly to showcase the fruit of Murphy's labour with the commencement of the FA Youth Cup. There was nothing altogether convincing in United's form in the Central League to justify Busby's boast in the summer of 1952 about the quality in reserve. The reserve side had suffered a run of four defeats in five games in the latter part of the season. But Jackie Blanchflower, Mark Jones, Jeff Whitefoot,

JIMMY MURPHY

Brian Birch and Frank Clemson – players of differing ability, it must be said – were all fledgling stars given a handful of chances and so, were already on Busby's radar.

By that point, of course, they had already gone through the school of hard knocks which was the Jimmy Murphy University of Football; an eye-opening and uncompromising educational system which promised to make any young boy who had the application into a star. As with everything else in his approach at Manchester United, the standards that he set for others were based on the standards he aimed to set and represent himself.

Jimmy would get the train from Whalley Range, where he lived, to London Road (which is now Manchester Piccadilly Station). From there he would get the train to Old Trafford. He would always dress smartly in a suit and tie before changing into a comfortable tracksuit at the club. "It was thanks to Mum that he was always well-dressed," says Nick. "She bought his clothes, she dressed him…if it was down to Dad he would probably have left the house in his slippers!"

"Jimmy took all of the training and that's completely understandable," says Sir Alex Ferguson. "There are certain qualities you look for when you have an assistant, the qualities I always look for – enthusiasm, loyalty, trust and his work ethic. When Matt picked him after seeing him conduct the army drill in Italy it must have been an instant reaction. There must have been something which stuck out about Jimmy Murphy."

It was not uncommon that Jimmy would work seventy hour weeks; he was known to even work eighty hour weeks many times. His official start would be nine o'clock every morning, training with the full time professionals. Whereas the young players idolised him, the older, more experienced ones, did not care for his aggressive nature.

Of course, this was because there was a natural impasse; these senior professionals had not been raised in the 'Murphy' way and so the Central League represented something else entirely than a step on the path to the promised land. This was exactly the opposite for them, and their disappointment at not being in the first team was exacerbated by the vociferous nature of the diminutive Welshman.

Following afternoons of remedial teaching, Jimmy was at the Cliff from 6pm on Tuesdays and Thursdays, working the youngsters through their paces. After training, Jimmy would always go for a couple of pints until last orders at eleven; he'd be home for half past, before retiring to bed in preparation for another full day's work.

On the evenings when he wasn't coaching, he would be out running the rule over opponents, looking at potential new recruits, and sometimes even maybe a combination of the two. The most time he would spend at home would be on Sundays and even then football played a prominent part. Though he would always be home for Sunday lunch – usually at 2.30pm – and then with his family for the rest of that day, he would have done so via a couple of pints at the Quadrant pub near Old Trafford Cricket Ground. He'd go there after spending some time enjoying a whiskey with Matt, Bert, and the physiotherapist Ted Dalton at Old Trafford, following his attendance at Mass every Sunday morning.

His standards were as identifiable as his routine, but there was no resting on his laurels. The stories of Charlton being told to practice his passing and McGuinness being sent to work on his weaker foot are complemented by a similar story from John Doherty, one of the players Murphy had particularly high hopes for, who was put through a laborious exercise in ball recovery after hitting what Jimmy felt had been the wrong pass. It wouldn't be so bad – United's reserves had not only won in that game, they'd beaten Blackpool 9-1!

"Jimmy was a winner and wanted that for everyone," Wilf McGuinness says. "He had a particular way of putting pressure on you to perform. He'd tell you that he made you, and when it came to matchday, you should be better than your opponent. 'If you're not better than him, it's your own fault', and 'If he's playing well, then you're not, your first job is stop him', and 'You're not feeding your forwards!' It didn't stop him being critical, that was the bare minimum of expectation."

Long before Murphy's fearsome reputation was established, his tactical foresight was being praised by peers. In the Saturday December 30th, 1950 edition of the *Sheffield Telegraph*, Doug Witcomb, the 32-year-old Sheffield Wednesday wing-half and Welsh international, was asked 'to supply four New Year resolutions which may prove beneficial to footballers.'

Number one on the list – *to master the throw-in*. 'This is one of my pet subjects,' Doug wrote. 'I've given the throw-in a lot of thought since I got constructive ideas about it from Jimmy Murphy – now Manchester United's assistant-manager – when he played with me in the West Bromwich team before I moved to Hillsborough. Some tacticians forget that there is no counter-move to a throw-in that is well practised and applied intelligently. There must be understanding between wing-half, inside forward, and winger. Speed in taking the throw-in does not always give a better chance of the desired result: even speed will fail if there is a lack of understanding of moves and positions by which the open space can be created.'

Certainly, in more recent years, Murphy's coaching approach has been evaluated and assessed as being far ahead of its time.

The book *The Birth Of The Babes,* written by Tony Whelan – a youth player at United and as of 2017 the assistant academy coach – was dedicated to the memory of Jimmy Murphy with the following remark: 'Without Whom.'

In it, Whelan highlights Jimmy's contribution. He says: 'Murphy was an outstanding coach and motivator of young players and was a major reason why the club's youth policy in the 1950s was so successful.'

Whelan says that the Tuesday and Thursday evening training routines were crucial for the young players. 'These were extremely important sessions in which a good deal of vital instruction took place. The coaching was extremely dynamic, led by Jimmy Murphy.' What was so dynamic about it? 'Murphy did a lot of coaching during a game, stopping it from time to time to make a point,' Whelan wrote. 'This is called *freezing the play* in modern coaching practice. This once again demonstrates the fact that Murphy's approach to coaching was ahead of its time.'

This wasn't the only area where Murphy excelled. 'Shadow play is quite a formal coaching technique and its use by Murphy and Whalley dispels the long pervading myth that United players did everything by instinct or intuition,' said Whelan 'Murphy placed great emphasis on the ability to pass the ball properly with the correct accuracy and weight. There was clearly a lot of intensive coaching going on… Jimmy Murphy was a tremendous coach in every sense of the meaning of that word. He was well organised, extremely knowledgeable, and very passionate about the game. His contribution to the success of Manchester United's youth policy in the 1950s is inestimable.'

John Doherty, youth team player at the time, concurred with all the above.'You couldn't put a price on what Jimmy Murphy did for United,' he said in his 2005 book *The Insider's Guide to Manchester*

United. 'Matt was the first-team supremo, the personality, the one who was always interviewed. Jimmy was always the quiet assassin in the background, picking up the pieces, shooting 'em down, building 'em up, teaching the lads how the game should be played. The media thought it was revolutionary when they found out that the Brazilians played shadow football, but when I was a kid at United, we were playing it when nobody else knew what it was. When anyone asked why we did it – and plenty did – Jimmy would explain that if we passed and moved enough it would become second nature, we'd all know where our mates were going to be without thinking… It would be impossible for me to overstate the influence of Jimmy Murphy on the Busby Babes.'

Two prominent members of the AFMUP (the Association of Former Manchester United Players), Jimmy Elms and Alan Wardle, were reserve and youth team players in the late '50s and early '60s. "He made you think about the game," says Elms, a comment Wardle agrees with. "Jimmy would be the one telling us things like the left winger was useless on his right foot, so we should show him inside," Alan said. "Nobody had ever thought about things in that way before."

Let it be repeated that Murphy felt the greatest value in football came in the precise and consistently successful application of the simple things. Murphy believed it was often in these seemingly mundane areas that the critical difference between success and failure lay. His point about throw-ins may have been seen as pernickety, but years later, it would come home to roost.

Bobby Charlton had enjoyed a successful introduction into the first team. He had scored ten goals in 14 league games since being introduced into the team – 12 in 17 appearances in all competitions – yet, despite being the next big thing, the young forward began the 1957/58 season in the reserves. He scored in a 5-1 win over Blackburn on the opening day of the Central League season and then scored again in a 4-3 win at Manchester City in front of almost 13,000 spectators, yet couldn't get a spot in the first team. It was a real test of character for the youngster and it all came to a head in a Central League game against Bolton on September 14th. United were winning 2-1. Late in the game, Charlton took a throw-in, but threw it into the field rather than down the touchline. Bolton subsequently gained possession and scored to earn a 2-2 result. "Jimmy gave me a terrible roasting," Charlton said of Murphy's post-match reaction in the dressing room. "I was embarrassed in front of the other players. But I never threw a ball across the pitch in that situation again. It was a lesson in professionalism and even though this was a Central League match, they all mattered to Jimmy."

The Charlton lecture was an example of how high the standards were set at the time. Murphy knew that setbacks in football were inevitable and was proactive about turning them into positive lessons. His reaction may have been aggressive but his intention was well-meaning. And, by the summer of 1951, Murphy felt confident enough to inform Busby that the work he and Whalley had been doing was beginning to reap dividends.

It was enough for the manager to keep his nerve, even if pressure was beginning to gather from outside the club. Even in a record created to document Murphy's contribution it would be folly to suggest he had any meaningful or divine influence over the team which won the Football League Championship in 1952. Certainly, the pair were singing from the same hymn sheet as far as some of those basic footballing principles went.

"Sometimes, people might think that in paying reverence to Jimmy we're placing him above Matt, but that's not the case, we simply want to pay credit to the work that Jimmy did," says Wilf McGuinness. "I don't think either Matt or Jimmy could have done as good a job as the other did if their roles were reversed in the situation they were in at Manchester United."

Whilst we are appropriating praise, the importance of Bert Whalley to this set-up cannot be understated. "Bert and Jimmy were like brothers," Bobby Charlton said in Eamon Dunphy's *A Strange Kind Of Glory*. "You never seemed to talk to one without the other. Bert would do the general things and Jimmy would pick out the young players they thought were important."

If they were the main men as far as the kids were concerned, then it shouldn't be missed that they would start every day in heavy and serious conversation about training with the first-team coaches Tom Curry and Bill Inglis, discussing ideas and philosophies, and the coaching sessions of the day for certain individuals. Arthur Powell – who was in charge of the groundstaff – would also participate in these conversations.

"Jimmy Murphy and Bert Whalley were like father figures to us young players," Dennis Viollet later said. He noted that by this time, the youngsters being introduced into the first team had already been nicknamed the 'Busby Babes' by Tom Jackson of the *Manchester Evening News*.

"Matt Busby would be seen now and again training with the youngsters or the first team but he was very tied up with running the club so the main coaching was done by Jimmy and Bert. They would spend hours and bags of patience and understanding with us kids.

"Bert was like a kindly uncle whereas Jimmy could be gruff, strict, and had a no-nonsense approach. He would play hell with us when he thought we needed it, then he would give us a little sugar. By that I mean he would put his arm around your shoulder and quietly explain what he wanted you to do…Jimmy Murphy made me the footballer I became."

Murphy understood his role. It was to prepare players for the Manchester United first team. The scouts would find talent, and Murphy saw it as his vocation that his responsibility was to instil a sense of composure and maturity in a player.

Murphy went on record to state his belief that natural ability – usually – only went so far. "It was a great thrill to spot the spark of genius in a youngster and carefully cultivate it until he shines," he said. "It's fascinating to watch the development of youngsters. Some mature according to plan…others, who are equally promising, inexplicably fade and drop out of the game. A few reach their best so late and so slowly that you almost give up on them in despair. Nevertheless, there are the odd one or two footballers who are so obviously thoroughbreds that you can place complete faith in them."

Just having the talent wasn't a guarantee that the more talented boys would always win. As recalled by Charlton in his book *The Manchester United Years*, Murphy said: "They don't, you know, Bobby. They don't when they fail to understand there are two sides to the game – and only one of them is about how well you play. Just as important is how you stop the other fellow playing to his own strengths. You can stop people playing if you mark them well enough – and it doesn't matter who they are.

"So you have to learn two basics: you have to learn how to mark someone, and avoid being marked yourself. You have to know how to steal a vital yard with a little dummy and shimmy and hit the ball quickly and on target.

"You have to shout so that you can help a team-mate get out of trouble – you always have to be available to receive the ball, and that is only valuable when you let your team-mates know where you are…if you want to be on the field but you don't want to play, really play, you stand next to the man who is marking you. Better still, you go behind him. You will never get a kick.

"If you do want a kick, if you want to truly influence a game and show people you're a serious professional and not someone just playing at it, you've got to find yourself space. You've got to work your balls off."

CHAPTER | FIVE

GOLDEN APPLES

"I'm an Edwards fanatic. It's a fact. He was the most complete footballer I'd ever, ever seen. He had strength, power in both feet, he hit forty and fifty yard balls with consummate ease" – Jimmy Murphy

The FA Youth Cup was taken seriously by all clubs (all who entered it, at least), an official Football Association competition which had been given massive coverage by the press, so was certain to gather some attention as it begun.

It allowed clubs to showcase their under-18 talent and it seemed that Manchester United were showing off when their captain for their inaugural game in the competition, against Leeds United, had only recently turned sixteen-years-old.

There was nothing of a gimmick to be found in young Duncan Edwards, though. The boy had settled into life at Old Trafford with ease. He had established himself as a leader; it wasn't so much that Jimmy Murphy was building a team around him, more that this freakishly gifted and extraordinarily confident lad from the Midlands had made himself the focal point. Having now had some months to work with young Edwards, Murphy was enamoured.

"I could fill a book with stories about Duncan Edwards," Murphy eulogised. On one occasion, in a youth game against Rotherham, Edwards collected the ball, ran past three players and scored from almost thirty yards. Rotherham manager Andy Smailes had been told Edwards' age before kick-off but asked Jimmy again as he couldn't believe what he was seeing. Murphy added: "He can play in the youth competition for the next two years!"

In another game at Bexleyheath, Jimmy recalled how he was heckled by one of the locals. "Where's this great Edwards of yours?!" the supporter mocked and, whilst he was still speaking, Duncan received the ball, turned, and smashed it in the net from fully forty yards. A smug Murphy turned around and said to the supporter: "*That* is Edwards."

"Any manager lucky enough to have him had half a team," Murphy would often say. He wasn't joking. Edwards was a player who could play in any position, yet Murphy recognised that he would be reluctant to have him elsewhere on the pitch. "Duncan Edwards was too valuable a player as a wing-half to become a negative stopper centre-half," he later observed. "I'm an Edwards fanatic. It's a fact. He was the most complete footballer I'd ever, ever seen. He had strength, power in both feet, he hit forty and fifty yard balls with consummate ease."

His quality spoke for itself but Murphy was equally impressed with Edwards' attitude off the pitch. Even as a teenager he was a true professional. Here was a player who already had the entire country talking about him by the time he arrived at Old Trafford.

He was only seventeen years and eight months old when he made his England debut, yet Murphy would be impressed with the way the player would always make time to play with some of the younger players at the Cliff who absolutely idolised him.

Murphy felt he'd found a kindred spirit. He felt Duncan was as obsessed with football as he was. "On and off the field Duncan was an amazing fellow," Jimmy said. "He never smoked nor drank…football to him was not just a living, but it was more a way of life…I suppose listening to records was about the only concession he made to a hobby outside football."

The first time Murphy saw Edwards play, he described him as the greatest thing on two feet; he maintained this opinion until the day Edwards tragically passed away after Munich, and, indeed, until his own dying day. Funny, then, to recall Murphy had told a young Bobby Charlton that the Dudley boy had some rough edges. Perhaps in honour of his memory, he never elaborated on what those rough edges might be, although we are given an indication in a recollection of Don Revie. In 1954, the future Leeds United and England manager was a centre-forward for Manchester City who had become renowned for playing much deeper than other forwards.

On January 14th of that year, Edwards played just his fourteenth senior game for the club, in a Manchester derby at Old Trafford. He had already established a reputation as a player who could run confidently with the ball and, though he was yet to register a senior goal, was encouraged to strike from any range.

However, on this occasion, City were taking advantage of the youngster's inexperience.

They would allow Edwards to surge forward with the ball and based their entire game plan about exploiting the space behind him. Murphy, watching from the sidelines, understood what was happening and went to the touchline to order Edwards to play simpler passes to team-mates who were breaking and in the clear themselves. "Duncan Edwards became a magnificent footballer," recalled Revie, "and it was Jimmy Murphy who helped mould him into the world-class player he became."

That game must count in what Murphy would later describe as the 'handful' of times he saw Edwards robbed of possession. He would speak in glowing terms about Edwards' immensely powerful tackles, which were fair, but fearsome. He had a vivid and distinctive playing style which made him stand out against any player Murphy had ever seen before. Even when leading and giving tributes to the boy posthumously, Murphy took great care and detail to stress that these were not accolades influenced by sentiment.

Edwards had a partner in crime in Eddie Colman, who joined at the same time. The Colman family lived on Archie Street in Orsdall, which, whilst not quite a literal stone's throw from Old Trafford, was close enough to invite the cliché. It gives an idea of just how 'Salford' Colman was to know that Archie Street was the street used in the original opening credits of Coronation Street.

Think of a young boy from a working class Northern family in the 1940s and you have Eddie Colman; cheeky, hyperactive, and sports-mad. He played cricket and football for town and county, though joked that he felt he'd only been selected to play football because the selectors needed to make up the numbers.

That was certainly not the impression Jimmy Murphy and Matt Busby had; Colman played in a game at the Cliff which pitted Salford Boys against Stockport Boys, and immediately, the United men knew they had a player on their hands. Jimmy said he could not believe how this fifteen year old had gone unnoticed and unselected for England schoolboys. Their observations backed up an earlier recommendation from Joe Armstrong, who had said Colman moved like a hula-hula dancer. "He's sensational," Armstrong said. Bert Whalley had reservations about Colman's size but Murphy pulled rank. "Eddie Colman, he only weighed about nine stone wet through, little Eddie," Jimmy later said in the early 1980s. "Tremendous player. Eddie Colman would have been a star today in his own right."

Here was a player who gave whole-hearted performances, was willing to learn, but also liked to be inventive and showcase his creativity. Murphy loved Colman's infectious character and felt that he and Edwards were the perfect partnership at wing-half.

"They complemented each other marvellously," he said. "The best wing-half, or to use the modern terminology, midfield pair, seen for years." If one needs a comparison they can imagine Bryan Robson and Paul Scholes; Robson, as complete a midfielder as you could wish to find, and Scholes, the master creator who was not shy of getting stuck in.

The first ever game in the FA Youth Cup came a little soon for Colman. Edwards, at a similar age, was so advanced, and yet his selection still raised a few eyebrows.

Murphy looked forward to the tie with Leeds United feverishly. He felt the competition was made for him; it was the perfect environment to assess the quality of the work he had done. Sure, the Central League was a tough arena in which his young prodigies may sink or swim, but the FA Youth Cup was a competition they could all play together, minus older professionals perhaps recuperating from injury or out of favour. This was a test for Murphy and Whalley to finally demonstrate their work, to provide some justification for Busby's boast earlier in the year.

Before the game against Leeds at Old Trafford on the afternoon of Wednesday, October 22nd, 1952, Murphy was energetic, speaking about how Yorkshiremen were tight-fisted and how much he hated Yorkshire! Initially, the bile being spewed by Jimmy would stun the young players into silence, each of them listening intently as their coach went through the team telling them what he expected of them.

"You're playing for this shirt, boys," he said, acutely training their concentration in these last moments before they took to the pitch. By the end, all of the boys were fired up and ready to get stuck into Leeds. What an opportunity for Murphy to play up – and live up – to the occasion. That first ever Youth Cup team read, from 1-11: *Gordon Clayton, Bryce Fulton, Paddy Kennedy, Gordon Robbins, Ronnie Cope (C), Duncan Edwards, Noel McFarlane, John Doherty, Eddie Lewis, David Pegg, Albert Scanlon.*

As the youngsters lined up, trainer Arthur Powell pointed to the sideline and said: "By the way, the boss is here watching you," providing one last reminder that this game was being treated very seriously indeed. Sure enough, there was Busby; so, too, were the national press.

On October 31st, 1952, Willie Evans wrote a special report for the *Daily Mirror*, declaring: 'They look good enough for a Cup Final team.' He wrote: 'Matt Busby, The Manchester United manager, says he has a team of young players worth over £100,000. Believe me he's right!'

'Tempted by the Busby bouquet to the boys I took a trip to watch his young stars play. How they played! They really turned out a great performance beating Leeds United Juniors 4-0 in the FA Youth Challenge Cup, and I came away with the conviction that here was the best junior side I have seen for some time. Brentford Juniors held that place before. But this is a case of north scoring one over the south. Indeed, these Manchester

United lads have that same rhythmic, cultured and planned look as the Cup winning side United turned out in 1948. Floodlight training is working wonders for United. Every Thursday evening, they are watched and coached by Jimmy Murphy and Bert Whalley. On Tuesdays, Murphy and Whalley join in the practice matches. The effect was obvious in the game against Leeds Boys.

'Each member of the United side is a former schoolboy star of international, country or town class. Boys like Johnny Doherty, Eddie Lewis, Albert Scanlon showed more than just promise. David Pegg, the former Doncaster and England winger, two Irish lads, Kennedy and McFarlane, and Ronnie Cope, an England centre-half, all shone in this star-stuffed soccer show. It is hard to be outstanding in such a brilliant company. But the lad who was able to do just that was Duncan Edwards, left half, last season's England international skipper. He was great.'

It was Scanlon who earned the right to call himself United's first ever goalscorer in the competition, although there was some debate about whether or not it was intended. There could be no doubt about the next goal, scored by the left-sided David Pegg, playing at inside-forward, before Jack Charlton made himself the topic of a potentially tricky pub quiz question (albeit an obscure one) by notching a goal for Manchester United before Bobby Charlton had even signed for them. The Leeds defender put into his own goal. Scanlon made it four to complete the rout.

Pegg's performance in the game against Leeds was noted by Busby, and within a few weeks, he was being called up to the first team. Pegg, like most other youngsters at the club, held a special affection for Jimmy.

"I played for England Schoolboys and we beat Wales 3-0... Jimmy Murphy always screws up his face when I remind him of this occasion, which is quite often!" Pegg joked. Due to the

JIMMY MURPHY

quality of his left foot, Pegg found himself one of Jimmy's special subjects in training. Pegg would be put through hours of training exercises centred around delivery of crosses.

Murphy was thrilled that the boys had put in such a spectacular performance and United made comfortable work of non-league Nantwich Town in the second round and then Bury to progress further in the competition.

In the meantime, Murphy was on the road, scouting potential talent and forthcoming opposition. In November 1952, Murphy watched a game between an FA XI and an army team which would not have been remarkable in itself if not for the identity of the player who stood out to him. 'Take it from here that Quixall will be in England action against Belgium at Wembley on November 26,' Hackett wrote in his November 6th report for the *Express*.

A Duncan Edwards goal just after half-time saw off Everton as the FA Youth Cup run continued.

Drawn against Barnsley next, the fifth round took place on a day when United's senior team didn't have a game. It meant that the kids could again play at Old Trafford; though, of course, by now, some of the 12,000 who turned up to watch this game would have been familiar with a few of these players who had already made the step up.

The Barnsley boys gave a good account of themselves. It took a goal right on the stroke of half-time to swing this one in Murphy's boys' favour. An Edwards free-kick looked goal-bound but the brave John Doherty got a telling deflection to turn it past the goalkeeper. Barnsley's second-half response, however, was spirited, and they forced an equaliser only for McFarlane and Scanlon to secure a 3-1 win for the hosts. It meant that United's young lads were then drawn against Brentford – the team that

GOLDEN APPLES

Daily Mirror reporter Willie Evans had raved about – in April's semi-final.

Meanwhile, to say the regeneration of the first team had not gone so well would be an understatement. Most can remember the calls from some quarters for Sir Alex Ferguson to be sacked in the summer of 1995, for what they believed was a blunder in management by selling Paul Ince, Mark Hughes and Andrei Kanchelskis, and deciding to promote the young players. Imagine going from champions to finishing eighth. Even David Moyes finished seventh! The criticism in the modern press would have made Busby's position almost untenable.

Edwards made his home debut on April 4th, 1953, though it has to be said this was as much down to injuries as it was his own unstoppable potential. Everyone remembers he was just 16 years and 185 days when he turned out against Cardiff City; it's a conveniently forgotten side note that United lost that game at Old Trafford by four goals to one. Edwards joined the likes of Eddie Lewis, Jeff Whitefoot, Frank Clempson, John Doherty, David Pegg and Jackie Scott as youngsters being brought into the first team, though some had more success than others.

It was hardly a ringing endorsement of the quality United supposedly had in reserve and so their progress in the FA Youth Cup was tracked with a little more scrutiny.

Expectations for a classic encounter against Brentford in the semi-final were high but it was these expectations which weighed heavily on the shoulders of the southern youngsters. United travelled to London for the first leg and won 2-1; the hosts missed a penalty and seemed to freeze at the prospect of facing opponents who came with such a big reputation.

Thus, a United team who were below-par themselves were given something of a let-off; Scanlon continued his fine goalscoring form to score the winner on the night, after McFarlane had scored the equaliser.

Having displayed character to turn the game around, Murphy praised his boys afterwards, singling out Cope and Edwards for their own performances.

What followed in the second leg was an emphatic scoreline that, perhaps for the first time, not only provided substance to the claims within Old Trafford that they had a wonderfully talented group of youngsters, but also propelled them into a position where they appeared dominant. The victory, as impressive and eye-catching as it had been, always came with a caveat which recognised the weakness of the opposition. In that respect, then, the majority of the 5,877 in attendance at Old Trafford on the afternoon of Wednesday, April 15th, came away genuinely excited about the future of their club.

United's 6-0 victory eased them into the final; a two-legged affair with the highly-rated Wolverhampton Wanderers. Every great team needs a great rival and it can be said that the Wolves outfit of the 1950s was one that – at every level – posed a threat to United's hopes for dominance.

In first-team manager Stan Cullis they had a person who had similar ambitions for his own club to the ones Busby and Murphy had; he wanted his team to play entertaining football, he wanted to raise their global profile by playing against some of the most renowned foreign teams, and he wanted to make his team successful by fielding young players developed by the club. Their own route to the final had been just as emphatic as United's. They hadn't conceded a goal and their list of wins along the way read 5-0, 2-0, 5-0, 6-0, 5-0 and 6-0. Those last two results had given them an aggregate semi-final victory of 11-0, and so, this final meeting was one between the two junior sides who had blown away all of their competition and stood toe to toe as undoubtedly the best in the country.

The visitors' side was packed with glittering talent just as highly-rated as some of the United boys. Most of them had represented their country at some level. However, the ninety minutes at Old Trafford showed there was a clear gulf in class. United ran riot, scoring after three minutes, before getting a 3-1 lead by the 16th minute, and eventually winning 7-1. Almost 21,000 supporters witnessed the game and gave the young hopefuls a prolonged and rowdy standing ovation at the end.

Lewis and McFarlane bagged two each while Pegg and Scanlon also notched; young Whelan had a day to remember by grabbing a goal of his own to round off the huge scoreline in the 85th minute. Tom Jackson of the *Manchester Evening News* suggested that these boys could be 'among the elite of First Division football' in three or four years' time. A commentator for the *Wolverhampton Express & Star* was even more generous in his praise. 'This United team, on this day's play, were, without any doubt, the finest youth side I have ever seen. If I thought I was certain of seeing Duncan Edwards give another such polished display as he gave last night, wild horses would not keep me from Molineux.'

Even in the glow of victory Murphy was not one to crow, or seek personal recognition. Instead he observed the nature of football supporters – or the "noisy and unthinking" among them – to demand that success be instant. He paid credit to the patience of Busby and 'his staff', saying fear stifles creativity.

"We just waited, like a gardener waits for his apples to grow," he said. "Managing a football club is similar to being a gardener. You can't rush nature anymore than you can rise young footballers before they are ready for first class soccer."

He conceded, though, that the 'apples' were almost ripe and that every gardener was viewing their orchard with envy. "Of course other clubs had an inkling of what we were about to unleash," he said. "They could not fail to see. Our youth team won the final, beating Wolves, who were our greatest rivals, in this search to find young stars."

United sealed the victory in front of 14,208 fans at Molineux, many of them visiting fans who had been the beneficiary of a special train journey arranged by the club and British Railways. Goals from Lewis and Whelan secured a 2-2 draw on the beautiful sunny day, enough for a 9-3 aggregate victory.

The size of the win, and the plight of United's first team, led to suggestions and hope that the boys were already ready to go in and play senior football, but Murphy urged caution. Of course, Duncan Edwards seemed ready, because he had the right temperament. For players like Colman, and Whelan (who had immediately impressed his new coach), their integration had to be more gradual.

Murphy observed the case of Dennis Viollet, who'd played just a couple of games, and Mark Jones, who had been in the first team picture for three seasons but had played just four, three and two times in seasons '50/51, '51/52 and '52/53 respectively. He said Matt would not ruin the confidence of these young boys by selecting them to play in games where they were either ill-equipped or just not ready in general; this, after all, was the result of six years hard work, and just because there was a feverish excitement about their success in the FA Youth Cup, they shouldn't give way to that excitement and rush the players through, potentially destroying and undermining everything they had worked towards.

That said, it was only natural that these players, having displayed such dominance, would get more chances on a more frequent basis. And, while it seemed as if the 1953 FA Youth Cup Final heralded the start of a new generation, it's interesting to note that Murphy himself declared that the 1952 First Division success was "the birth of the Busby Babes", where most saw that as the crowning glory of the 1948 side and the beginning of the regeneration. In essence, then, Murphy's description was not inaccurate, though it seems a little generous but not altogether surprising; after all, such loyalty was something Murphy was renowned for.

He heaped praise on Busby for his wonderful man-management. Busby, with the help of his coaches, decided to play Johnny Carey regularly as a half back (Carey had some familiarity with the position from earlier in his career), and Roger Byrne from a left winger into a full-back. Carey – who had captained the team to their Wembley success in 1948 – left United in 1953, creating a natural space for Edwards to come into the side.

In the 1953/54 season, Wood, Blanchflower, Viollet, Whitefoot, Roger Byrne and Bill Foulkes ('Murphy' players too old to have played in the FA Youth Cup) had established themselves as regulars, and Edwards made 24 First Division appearances to more or less indicate he had made that transition. Lewis, McFarlane and Pegg were three more players from the youth team who were given a few first team opportunities.

CHAPTER | SIX
LIKE CLOCKWORK

"Among my most treasured possessions is a little beer mug from a small bar in Zurich... even today I pour beer into it and raise it to the memory of the man who taught me everything he knew" – Sir Bobby Charlton

In the summer of 1953, Manchester City made a deliberate and concerted effort to match the exploits of their local rivals. They went public and bold with their boast that they had signed six schoolboys from the Manchester Boys team. By this point, however, United were only concerned in signing the best.

Murphy had been sufficiently convinced by then to make his young players staples of his Central League team. Particularly in the latter half of the 1953/54 Central League campaign, the team sheet would regularly include the likes of Clayton, Jones, Whelan, Lewis, McFarlane and Pegg. 'Across the city, Manchester United are quietly building reserve strength,' wrote

JIMMY MURPHY

sports journalist Joe Humphreys. "Wilf McGuinness, England Boys' international and captain of Manchester Boys, will start his career towards stardom at Old Trafford. He is one of the new boys Jimmy Murphy, the United coach, has in his school.'

The FA Youth Cup triumph – and, more than that, the style in which it was achieved – had propelled Murphy into a nationally renowned spotter and developer of talent. His opinion was respected, and, it seemed, highly sought, as a feature from the October 17th edition of the Yorkshire Evening Post showed. The Post ran a feature on Tom Finney's recently released book Football Round The World which referred to 'Jimmy Murphy, ex-international and chief scout for Manchester United – and the man who has one of the biggest back-stage football reputations in the game today.'

The graduation of some younger players meant there were spaces up for grabs in United's FA Youth Cup team. McGuinness and Bobby Charlton were the star additions, whilst Ivan Beswick and Alan Rhodes came into the side with slightly less fanfare at full-back. Brian Lowry and Sammy Chapman were also newcomers, while Clayton, Colman, Edwards and Pegg kept their place. The defence of the Cup began at Everton; an Eddie Colman goal decided the 1-0 affair. Further victories over Wrexham, Rotherham United and a semi-final triumph against Murphy's former club West Bromwich Albion lined up a return final against Wolves.

It is worth deviating from the script here to reference a fascinating letter which gives a tremendous insight into the relationship between the players and coaches. The name of Bryce Fulton might not ring a bell to any but the most hardened Manchester United fanatical; and even then, you would have to be a completist. Fulton was a full-back in the Youth Cup team in the first season; in 1957, he moved to Plymouth Argyle, where he had a successful Football League career. His name is of interest in this record because of a handwritten letter which was sent to him by Bert Whalley in March of 1954.

Fulton had been called up for National Service and Whalley's three page letter to him indicated that the club had checked to make sure he arrived safely. Bryce had forgotten his boots and Whalley suggested that the youngster get a new pair to break in; he also wrote that the full-back may be needed for reserve football, so he should either report to Old Trafford on time for the coach, or he should phone the club giving plenty of notice that he wouldn't be available. Whalley concluded his letter by bringing Fulton up to date with the exploits of his colleagues. 'Glad to say things are pretty good here,' he added. 'I hope you are still growing and putting on weight. All the best, your sincere pal, Bert. P.S. Jimmy sends his best wishes.'

Fulton was back at the club in the 1954/55 season and enjoyed probably his best year as a regular in the Central League side, playing 24 times. There are plenty of household names who established their reputation as world stars in these seasons, dozens of players who went through 'the system'. That Whalley and Murphy would concentrate their attention on a player they probably knew wouldn't 'make it' at United just goes to show their overall approach and relationship with the squad. Nobody was treated differently and, in almost every case which presents itself, the boys were treated as family.

Wolves were keen to settle the score from the previous year's final. Just as in 1953, Murphy was left to curse wretched luck on the eve of the final when goalkeeper Gordon Clayton suffered a broken wrist. However, his replacement, Tony Hawksworth, had already made an appearance in the Central League, and had been selected for England Boys. It was a blow, but it could have been worse. As it transpired, Murphy's headache in the first half would have been with his outfield players. Duncan Edwards scored after five minutes but the visitors were not lying down. For arguably the first time in two seasons, Murphy saw the commitment levels of his boys matched and arguably bettered; it caught the Red Devils by surprise, and Wolves took a 3-1 lead at half-time.

It would become humorous anecdote material in the future and there was certainly more than one occasion it could have been sourced – both Charlton and Nobby Stiles have told variations of the same story, and Murphy himself has, too – but for the first time in the FA Youth Cup, Manchester United unapologetically turned to their ace card.

The reluctance to push Edwards into a position further forward, in its own way, speaks volumes about Murphy's instructions and hopes for his team. He wanted them to play the beautiful game and that would ideally involve Edwards in the middle as the conductor of the most beautiful soccer symphony; however, in the pursuit of victory, you can't help but feel Murphy was almost apologetic as he told Edwards to play as a centre-forward in the second half.

United grabbed a quick penalty and a thunderous Edwards header made it 3-3. Still, Wolves came back, and through John Fallon's 30 yarder, made it 4-3. David Pegg (who scored the penalty) grabbed the second equaliser, to make it 4-4 at full-time. It preserved United's unbeaten record in the competition but made Wolves favourites to exact revenge at Molineux.

If Murphy's teachings had stood the young players in good stead before, then they were crucial in navigating an incredibly tall task which awaited them at Molineux. The crowd of 28,651 was as big as most First Division attendances United had played

LIKE CLOCKWORK

in front of that season. It was natural that the occasion would get to one side more than the other and it played into United's hands as the young Wolves players seemed too anxious to play in their usual style. Whereas at Old Trafford, they had played without the weight of expectation, and caught United cold, here, they were favourites, and failed to live up to their supporters' high hopes.

For what it's worth, this was not a vintage United performance either; they were less impressive in both legs of this final than they had been the previous year. Call it experience, call it endurance, call it class eventually telling; Murphy's men were celebrating a second successive FA Youth Cup triumph after Pegg's penalty gave them a slender 1-0 win.

It was obvious that these players could not remain the preserve of the Youth side forevermore. Evolution and time would take care of that. But without a doubt, Murphy adored his time with the young players, and was well and truly in his element in the mid-1950s. Working alongside people who he trusted, under a boss he adored, and seeing the hard work actually paying off, there could have been no greater period for him.

As well as the back-to-back Youth Cup wins, the unity and togetherness was beginning to show some signs of results in the Central League. Whelan, McFarlane, Lewis, Pegg and Doherty combined to give the reserve side a formidable forward line. Mark Jones continued to show his committed professionalism as one of the main members of the Central League side for the fourth year running.

United blew away Derby and Chesterfield 6-1 and 5-1 respectively, in the opening games of the '54/55 reserve season. On fifteen occasions they scored three goals or more. In the first six games of 1955, they won and kept clean sheets – no mean feat when considering the state of winter pitches. It was, however, the FA Youth Cup again where United's greatest success would be found.

Clayton was a veritable veteran at this level and a player who exemplified Murphy's approach to his young charges. Edwards, who had been there with Clayton at the start of this FA Youth Cup adventure, was at the other end of the footballing spectrum, and would achieve full senior international honours by the end of this season. Clayton, however, would only make a solitary senior appearance for the United first team, but his presence in the squad was down to Murphy's love for the group and his loyalty to the young boys.

Clayton would leave the club in 1959 and return a decade or so later when Wilf McGuinness hired him as a scout, but nobody could deny him his own little, but important, part in United's history as the goalkeeper in these early Youth Cup triumphs. Nor should it be forgotten that he played a role in the acquisition of one of the best players in the club's history.

For this story, we should rewind a couple of years, to September 17th, 1952. Clayton had started the season as first choice for the reserves; things had started well, with a 1-0 win at Blackburn, but they went downhill fast. On the September afternoon in question, United came up against a fearsome forward in the shape of Tommy Taylor. Taylor made himself a nuisance throughout, constantly charging in on Clayton, making his afternoon a misery. The hat-trick Taylor grabbed to earn his team a 3-0 win was nothing compared to the physical mark he was leaving on the 15-year-old stopper.

Albert Scanlon, twelfth man on the day, remembered that he didn't know whether to be amused or terrified by Murphy's reaction on watching the Taylor show. "He was annoyed at our lads for letting Tommy treat them with such disdain and allowing him three goals," Scanlon said. "Very few teams or players did that to us in those days. Murphy was screaming out instructions to our lads, it was comical really, but I dare not laugh openly.

"At the end of the game Jimmy flew out of the dugout like a rat up a sewer, out on the pitch…he grabbed hold of Gordon Clayton. 'Son, what did you make of their centre-forward?' I could tell that he didn't know how to answer. 'Oh, he wasn't bad Jimmy.' Jimmy's face was a picture. 'Not bad, not fucking bad?! Well, he fucking knocked you all over the area and you let him get away with it, he scored three fucking goals and you tell me he's not bad!' Coming back to Manchester on the coach, Jimmy was in his usual seat near the front. He had a contented look on his face." The following morning, Murphy found Busby to inform him of the player he'd seen. By the end of the season, Taylor was at Old Trafford.

Busby told a fantastic tale about how he and Jimmy went to Yorkshire to conclude the signing.

"I had sent Jimmy to see him play," Busby said, "He reported. So I went to see him play for Barnsley against Birmingham. After half an hour I had seen enough. He was the boy to complete my pattern. Other clubs were interested. So Jimmy and I stayed in a pub in the Barnsley area for two days and nights, trying to keep hidden. For a breath of fresh air we would slip in my car out into the countryside. One afternoon we decided to pass a couple of hours in the cinema. We know one manager at least was in the district trying to sign Tommy. So Jimmy tupped the girl who collected our tickets and asked her to let us know if a tall fellow wearing a trilby and a fawn overcoat came in. Sure enough, a few minutes later, along she came and pointed. It was our friend all right. We sat back and enjoyed the film." That tall fellow was

JIMMY MURPHY

Cardiff City manager Cyril Spiers. As Roger MacDonald wrote in his book Manchester United In Europe: 'Busby and Murphy spent four tense days in negotiations at Barnsley, playing cat and mouse with the Cardiff City manager, Cyril Spiers.'

Taylor – like Edwards – would enjoy career highs that Clayton could only have dreamed of, but he was an extremely dependable squad member who Murphy was very fond of nonetheless, and first choice in the youth team, as United sought to successfully defend their Youth Cup trophy for the second time. By now, however, Pegg and Scanlon – both such reliable players in terms of both form and goals – were too old to participate, so Murphy had to field a new look forward line which included Kenny Morgans and Seamus 'Shay' Brennan. Brennan scored twice, with Colman and Ken Adams scoring the other two in a resounding 4-1 win over Liverpool to set up a showdown with Manchester City. City hosted their game underneath the floodlights at Maine Road, yet it was a surprise that the game went ahead at all, such was the denseness of the fog. City wouldn't have minded; the conditions served as a leveller, and they took the lead through a goal from Peter Lamb.

What followed was one of those infamous Duncan Edwards stories. At half-time, Murphy was frustrated that he couldn't see, and therefore was unable to give advice as to how his team could turn it around. United trailed one-nil. For once, the Welshman was unable to make any of his trademark fiery criticisms.

"Don't worry, all will be well," Edwards, his young leader – back in the side after missing the Anfield game – reassured him. The young wing-half scored twice in the second half to win the game. Almost seven thousand were in attendance for an occasion that was remembered more for this wonderful anecdote than it was the memory of anyone who could actually claim to have witnessed

Edwards score either of his goals. It's a story that, had it not been recorded in history, people would find difficult to believe, such is the extent to which it adds to the player's legend. More fascinating is the fact that the game was originally postponed from its date the previous week due to a waterlogged pitch; had it taken place then, Edwards would have been unavailable.

It was Edwards who once again played a pivotal role in helping United to another final. After defeating Barnsley, Sheffield Wednesday and Plymouth Argyle, Murphy's young stars faced a daunting challenge against Chelsea in the semi-final. Despite going a goal behind, they took a 2-1 lead on to the home leg. With the tie finely balanced at 1-1 on the night, Edwards, surrounded by a number of blue shirts, ran, jumped, and drove a header into the net. The final aggregate score was Edwards (and Manchester United) 4, Chelsea 2.

Awaiting Murphy and United in the final were West Bromwich Albion, in a repeat of the semi-final from the previous year. In front of 16,696 at Old Trafford, on the occasion it mattered most, United's boys finally did deliver a performance worthy of their collective reputation, triumphing 7-1 over the two legs.

United had fulfilled one part of Busby's 1952 boast. They had quality in reserve that was now finding its way into the first team. Could they fulfil their supposed potential to become the £200,000 crop of talent Busby had suggested? Again, it seems a strange concept to think that this suggestion could even be measured; United's kids were not going anywhere, and so, what price does one put on such a player? That summer, Eddie Firmani's £35,000 move from Charlton Athletic to Sampdoria broke the British transfer record. £200,000 may have looked a conservative estimate just three years after the comment was said.

When Eddie Colman made his senior debut in November, to

partner Edwards at wing-half, his emergence forced the eventual departure of fellow youth product Jeff Whitefoot. Colman, though, had simply made himself undroppable, after a run in the Central League in the preceding weeks when it was obvious he was too good for that level.

Murphy and Whalley could barely have expected how the year would have panned out; Colman and Edwards were just two players who had taken the step up and were impressing in the First Division; Bill Foulkes, Geoff Bent, Ian Greaves, Jackie Blanchflower, Freddie Goodwin, Wilf McGuinness, Mark Jones, John Doherty, Eddie Lewis, David Pegg, Albert Scanlon, Jackie Scott, Dennis Viollet and Liam Whelan all played their part in the senior team.

"It came on just like clockwork," said Murphy. "It was wonderful. They all fitted in the Old Trafford groove, our own products, our own future stars, and quite a few of them came into the first team at a very young age indeed."

The creation of almost every great senior footballing team can be traced back to a catalyst. Supporters can still remember the opening day of the 1995/96 season, where Sir Alex Ferguson played six youth players in a 3-1 defeat to Aston Villa. However, you would probably have to travel back to a League Cup game against Port Vale in the autumn of 1994 when Ferguson played a team so wet behind the ears that it provoked a complaint in the House of Commons.

In late October 1953, Aston Villa were ironically the opponents again; this time, United won 1-0 at Old Trafford, but the performance was described as 'the season's worst' by one journalist. It had been suggested on that Saturday evening that Busby had told directors: "Something must be done, and I'm going to do it. I must be drastic, and make big changes. Even

LIKE CLOCKWORK

if everyone calls me crazy. I intend making the move which is going to make or break Manchester United."

If this seemed like an over-reaction after a below-par victory then it's worth pointing out that following that 1952 League Championship, United's form had been dreadful; they had been flirting with the relegation spaces as soon as the autumn of the following season and recovered only to finish eighth. They had won none of their opening eight league games of the 1953/54 season.

The reputation of the Old Trafford youngsters may have been gathering pace for a while, but it is fair to say that the major transition from Busby's first great side to the 'Babes' took place over the winter of that campaign.

A staggering seventeen players from Murphy's school were now part of the first team squad, with Tommy Taylor, the player who had impressed him so much at Barnsley, leading from the front as top goalscorer.

You could also add the name of Roger Byrne to those; at 25, Byrne was a senior player, and though still very much a 'Busby Babe', he had not been indoctrinated in the Jimmy Murphy way. Nobby Stiles would later observe in his autobiography After The Ball that Byrne was the one member of the squad who would challenge Busby and Murphy; the one who would not just automatically accept the word of his coaches at gospel. This is rather ironic, seeing as he was one of the players who benefitted most from their wisdom.

Byrne's conversion from winger to left-back was one of their major successes, Murphy felt; so much so that he absolutely supported Busby's decision to make Byrne the captain, and, further, felt that he could have played a part in England sides that would have made a serious challenge for the World Cup.

Murphy went on record to praise Byrne's performances against Tom Finney and Stanley Matthews, praising his intelligent decision making.

Those eighteen 'Babes' (with Byrne, Foulkes, Edwards, Colman, Pegg and Viollet all players who could say they were automatic first choices) stormed the First Division. In all competitions, fifty goals were scored by players who had come through United's youth system. United suffered just one defeat in the League after the turn of the year. It was a remarkable and spectacular triumph. Only Byrne and Johnny Berry remained from the team which had won the First Division in 1952. "The fruits of our labours at the training ground and Old Trafford itself brought a rich harvest in season 1955/56," Murphy later said.

It was not only the senior side who enjoyed fantastic results. Manchester United's success in the First Division and Central League in the 1955/56 season was of course complemented by a fourth consecutive FA Youth Cup victory.

Even those who didn't make so many appearances for the senior side – Bent, McGuinness, Whelan, Scanlon, Doherty and Greaves, for example – were now consistently playing in the Central League. As, of course, did one player whose name has been conspicuous by its absence in these lists: Bobby Charlton.

Charlton was the star pupil in the reserve side, scoring 37 times in 37 games (including six in a home win over West Brom on April 2nd, 1956) as the stiffs, with scorelines of 7-1, 6-2, 7-1, 5-0, 5-1, 6-1, 7-1, 5-2 and 8-0 as emphasis (as well as a handful of four goal hauls), won the Central League in their own incredible style.

Yet Jimmy never rested on his laurels. Charlton may well have been the star name but he recalled being told he had to act as linesman in amateur matches on days when he wasn't playing – to help refine his footballing intelligence. Here was a coach who left no stone unturned. If – as in the case of Charlton – it seemed a lost cause trying to teach him to tackle, well, then Murphy would impress on a player that they ought to compensate by improving their awareness and their ability to find their own space. This would not mean they were allowed to shirk their responsibilities in terms of pressing opponents, but, it would at least mean that they should provide themselves as an 'out' for a player who had the ball and needed a pass.

Jimmy would tell Bobby that he must shoot at every opportunity, saying that he would be forgiven by supporters for shooting and missing, but maybe not for not taking the chance. And, in order to make sure he was best prepared, hours and hours of practice must be put in, just for that one chance which might present itself on a Saturday afternoon.

That preparation would begin on a Sunday, running through what went wrong the day before; a process that may have seemed laborious for youngsters who wanted time off, but, more often than not, if you were that youngster summoned to Old Trafford, it generally meant something positive. It meant that Murphy saw incredible potential in you. Charlton recalled that often, after Sunday practice, Jimmy would take him to the pub and talk football. He said that he loved to talk about different players, to compare them and the technique they used. Knowing Murphy, there was probably some lesson in there, some pearl of wisdom he was hoping the kid, whoever they may be, might pick up, though it does seem just as likely that on these days of relaxation, Jimmy was just talking about something he had a great passion for with somebody he had great affection for.

These kind of stories and recollections were prominent in Manchester United's early trips to Zurich to participate in the

JIMMY MURPHY

Blue Star tournament. As the club sought to make a global stamp, the idea of sending their youth team to play in a prestigious international competition such as this one just made sense. And so at the end of the 1953/54 season, Murphy and his staff took their players over to stay in the Stoller Hotel, which would become known as their traditional home for the tournament.

A squad of Beswick, Charlton, Clayton, Colman, Edwards, Fulton, Hawksworth, Harrop, Lewis, Littler, McGuinness, Pearce, Pegg, Rhodes, Scanlon and Whelan would be representing United in their first competitive games on the continent. Perhaps it is no surprise that United qualified from their group. Indeed, they got to the final and did so without conceding a goal. When they faced host nation Red Star Zurich in the final, they had saved their best performance, winning 4-0. Edwards scored a hat-trick and Scanlon got the other.

This was a fantastic accolade for all the youngsters but the name who featured in all those mid-'50s' trips to Switzerland was Charlton. He was in the team that lost in the final to Genoa the following year; in the squad that finished fifth in 1956, and the star name, scoring four on the way to another triumph in 1957.

When Charlton looked back on those trips, it was spending time in the company of Jimmy, rather than on the football pitch, that remained the most vivid memory. 'There was always a bonus in the company of Jimmy Murphy, though; always a feeling of excitement about the game – and the fact that you had been picked out for so much of his attention,' Bobby said in his autobiography. 'It is the reason why among my most treasured possessions is a little beer mug from a small bar across the street from the Stoller Hotel in Zurich. It was Jimmy's unofficial headquarters each year when we played in the youth tournament. If anyone needed Jimmy, we knew where to find him – but in my case, if a game wasn't imminent, I would probably be in his company anyway. Even today, I pour beer into the mug and raise it to the memory of the man who taught me everything he knew.'

Paul McGuinness, Wilf's son, is well-versed in stories of this tournament. "Jimmy would travel to Switzerland with the club for the Blue Stars tournament every May and as soon as he'd get there he'd take up residence in the Flora Pub which was across from the hotel they'd stay at," he says. "The players knew that if they wanted some advice or just to talk football with Jimmy that's where they'd find him, but he'd keep them for hours talking about the game."

For Charlton, the first year sticks out. "The most memorable occasion was when we played in 1954 – the year of Switzerland's World Cup," he said, remembering the time that he went to a Catholic mass with Arthur Powell. "So I went with Arthur and knelt down and said my prayers, something for which I hadn't had a lot of practice. I prayed hardest that we would win the tournament – that would please Jimmy Murphy, and maybe he would give me a little peace – but there was also a prayer of thanks, for so many memories that I knew would never die."

Perhaps Edwards was the most gifted player Murphy ever coached. But no player better benefitted from his teachings than Charlton.

No player demonstrated the virtue of patience and hard work and a constant dedication to self-improvement in quite the same way. Long term, it would perhaps be no surprise that Charlton would – for a long time – be United's record appearance maker.

CHAPTER | SEVEN

THE GREATEST

"Jimmy had me up against the wall; I'm not kidding, I thought he was going to knock the living daylights out of me. 'Look son, I don't mind you doing what you did,' he said, 'but don't bloody well get caught!'" – David Gaskell

In the autumn of 1956, Bobby Charlton was making his debut for Manchester United against Charlton Athletic. At the same time as his name was becoming widely known, so too was that of his mentor. Jimmy Murphy was just about the worst-kept secret in soccer at this point.

The FA Youth Cup successes had been one thing, but the subsequent progress of the players in the Manchester United team had been quite another. United's success was clearly not an overnight one, and yet, the speed in which these youngsters had acclimatised to top level football made it seem as though it was.

This fact had not been lost on the Welsh Football Association, who approached Jimmy and asked him if he would like the

JIMMY MURPHY

manager's job of the national team. Welsh football had fallen on hard times since Jimmy's playing days, and though they had a collection of talented players – John Charles being the prime example – they also had a number of players coming towards the end of their careers.

The offer of the Welsh FA made it clear just how deeply the work Jimmy had done in Manchester was respected; never before had the national team manager been a full time position, and, after careful deliberation with Matt Busby, Murphy decided he would take the job. Busby himself had already given his aide a symbolic new role; in 1955, Jimmy had been appointed as 'assistant manager', though at that point, his role remained unchanged but for the title.

United had recently started their first ever European Cup campaign, defeating Belgian side Anderlecht in the second leg of their first round tie by a score of 10-0 at Maine Road. There were no shortage of plaudits heading United's way and no hyperbole spared when it came to assessing their quality.

United's run at the start of the 1956/57 season had been incredible. They won thirteen of their first fifteen games, drawing the other two, but it was the number of goals scored which drew most attention. This was a team scoring three or four goals wherever they went and, going into the European Cup game against Borussia Dortmund, they had won their previous seven games, scoring a staggering twenty five goals in the process.

As Dortmund came into town, *Daily Mirror* journalists Frank McGhee and Archie Ledbrooke attended hoping for a spectacle to justify their planned column for the following day and they weren't disappointed.

McGhee and Ledbrooke wrote: 'Manchester United are the greatest team and the greatest club in the world. THEY are

THE GREATEST

the reigning champions of English soccer. THEY are a model for every other club in the League. THEY are unbeaten in twenty-six successive League games, stretching back to last January. THEY haven't been beaten at home since March, 1955. Their supporters have forgotten what defeat tastes like. And last night they beat Borussia Dortmund, the German champions, 3-2 in the European Cup.'

The two journalists were given rare access to the inner workings of what they called 'the greatest soccer talent factory in the world' and they started by grilling Busby on the secret ingredients of United's success.

'GREATEST TEAM IN THE WORLD'
Daily Mirror, October 16th, 1956

Manager Matt Busby, the Scottish genius who presides over the glass and chrome luxury of Old Trafford, gave us facilities no other reporters have ever had. He talked to us of his scouting and training methods, of strategy and tactics, and past success and future aims. He handed us over to assistant manager Jimmy Murphy and chief coach Bert Whalley. We saw these men, the back-room boys who have achieved so much, in action.

"Manchester United," Busby said, "have not got to the top by accident. It has been done by years of planning." Busby's first public statement as manager was: "I am determined that United shall provide the great football public of Manchester with the best possible in the game. It is my intention to develop young players".

"It goes right-back to 1928 when I was a youngster myself," said Busby, his craggy keen-eyed face thoughtful, one strong hand brushing through sparse hair the colour of sand sprinkled with snow.

JIMMY MURPHY

"I was seventeen and a bit and just started playing for Manchester City. I have never forgotten the tremendous pride I felt in being part of a great club. It is a feeling you can only experience as a kid. And it is a feeling, an outlook on life, that I want from all my lads. I want them to be proud of Manchester United, just as much as I want United to be proud of them."

United started looking for youngsters from the day he took over. They were ploughing and sowing for the years of harvest. And the years of harvest are with us now. Yet they were sparked off in a moment of black despair.

"The worst moment of my football life," said Busby. It was in season 1953/54 when United were right down at the wrong end of the League table. Angry fans were reminding Busby of his proud boast that he had youngsters worth hundreds of thousands of pounds on the books. Busby still sweats when he thinks of the gamble. "I didn't want to bring them into a losing team," he told us. "I didn't want to risk ruining them, breaking their hearts, but I finally faced it. It had to be done. I told the kids not to worry about results. I told them to try and play football. I needn't have worried. They were magnificent. We finished FOURTH in the table, fifth the next season and last year we were CHAMPIONS."

Then he handed out this blazing message: "Manchester United were great last season. They have been great this season. Yet the best is still to come." How good will Manchester United be at their peak? Busby had no hesitation. "As good as they were two weeks ago when they beat the Belgian champions Anderlecht 10-0. That was the greatest display of football I have ever seen. They had all the skill in the world, all the confidence in the world, all the ruthlessness in the world. They played as I've always dreamed they could."

United, the team that every club dreams of being, have been criticised lately for cockiness and over-confidence. They stroll out *like young lions to toy with the opposition before chewing them up. Busby is the man to blame – or praise. "I want them to be confident," he said. "I want them to be arrogant. I want them to tell themselves that they are better than anyone else. Because they are, you know."*

But he also admitted there is another valid reason for their superb displays: Every man in the team knows that there is a youngster in the reserves, breathing down his neck, yearning for the chance to do better. Some of these youngsters are going to feel strong enough to one day insist on first team football.

The 'best team in the world' defeated Dortmund in the first leg by a narrow 3-2 scoreline, drawing the return in Germany to qualify for the quarter-final against Athletic Bilbao.

It seemed as if Murphy was omnipresent in those days, though it is almost certainly rather the case that his exploits had made him a distinctive and recognisable individual, as opposed to before, where he would have quite easily been able to sit in attendance at a game and go unnoticed. Now, Manchester United's assistant coach was the one getting the headlines after games between two completely separate First Division clubs.

Norman Wynne was at Hillsborough reporting for the *Express* on Sheffield Wednesday's 4-1 win over Tottenham Hotspur on November 18th, 1956 and noted Murphy in the crowd. 'THE SPY SAYS…SPURS HAD AN OFF DAY,' Wynne featured as the headline for his piece. 'Manchester United coach Jimmy Murphy went *spying* on Spurs for next week's battle of the giants…Spurs v. United at White Hart-lane. He was not misled by the humbling of the title challengers. "Spurs must have had an off day. They can do better than this," he told me.'

Meanwhile, United's defence of the FA Youth Cup was already underway again. United played Huddersfield Town in the second round, where they would come up against a player who would represent them with distinction. Busby was in attendance and Murphy said that it was clear from the offset that they were playing against a 'one man' team. That man – or boy – was Denis Law.

Murphy said that both he and Busby were astonished by the forward's performance. He was impressed by the effort put in by the 'skinny straw-haired' lad – but not so impressed that he would go easy on his own team. In a story that echoes that which Gordon Clayton tells about Tommy Taylor, United's goalkeeper on the day, David Gaskell – who had already made his first team debut, called up as an emergency goalkeeper for the Charity Shield earlier that month – recalls that Murphy was livid that his team had allowed Law to score. "We were leading the game easily – we had a hell of a side – and Denis Law scored a goal against me," Gaskell said. "It was a great goal to be fair, so I gave him a sporting thumbs up. I had another run-in with Jimmy afterwards, who said that it wasn't my place to offer congratulations to the opposition – or, words to that effect, anyway! He gave me a right bollocking as you can well imagine."

Gaskell was used to Murphy getting on his back. "Jimmy was manager of the second team, the reserves, but it was still a team filled with international players," he says. "I was only sixteen and a bit – I thought I was the bee's knees.

"I remember a game we played down at Derby County and of course in those days there was little protection so their centre-forward was kicking the hell out of me. We were leading one-nil going in to the last few minutes…I saw an opportunity to get my own back when I had the ball, so I followed through on a kick and whacked their striker up in their air. The referee saw it and gave a penalty. It finished one all and when the game finished I went off the pitch slowly to be one of the last in. As soon as I got into the changing room Jimmy had me up against the wall; I'm not kidding, I thought he was going to knock the living daylights out of me. 'Look son, I don't mind you doing what you did,' he said, 'but don't bloody well get caught!' That was my first actual personal interaction with him! Despite that bumpy start I got on famously with him. Later on he said to me: 'Son, I know you're only young, but you've got to look after yourself. Get your retaliation in first! Let them know that you're around and you won't be knocked down.'"

Though there was no dedicated goalkeeping training as we know it today, Gaskell insists that Murphy did more than most: "He would give simple directions; he would say that even if I thought I couldn't get the ball, that shouldn't stop me trying to dive for it anyway, as one day it would be the effort that would make the difference."

United did win that Huddersfield tie, 4-2; Huddersfield had gone two goals up, and a report in the *Hudaersfield Examiner* observed: 'An interval pep talk by former Welsh international Jimmy Murphy worked wonders.' Dawson scored twice; he repeated the trick in the next round to help his team defeat Sunderland 3-1.

It was a case of 'Dawson at the double' once again, taking his tally in that season's competition to a remarkable eleven, as United played against Everton in the fourth round on Wednesday, February 6th, 1957. On this occasion, Murphy had to settle for a draw and a replay, before making a mad dash to Old Trafford to watch United take on Athletic Bilbao in the second leg of their tie that evening.

United had lost the first leg 5-3, and Murphy remarked that 'there was a time' when there was a concern that the team would be stranded there because of heavy snowfall. Amidst a blanket of white, Jimmy recalled the final minutes of that game in Northern Spain.

"There are goals that stay imprinted in the mind for all time, and this was one of them," he said. "Manchester United were being hustled out of the European Cup, losing 5-2 with only a few minutes to play when Whelan picked up the ball in his own half of the field, cutting through the slush from the right he beat five opponents with brilliance and strength, then cut in for goal, hammering the ball into the top left hand of the net from the edge of the penalty area as the Bilbao keeper Carmelo started to come out. How that boy had the strength to draw breath let alone draw his boot back to shoot after that 40 yard run I will never know. But that goal kept us in the European Cup."

It certainly did prove to be a defining moment; United triumphed 3-0 at Old Trafford to overturn the deficit on an evening which still ranks as one of the most incredible in the club's European history. It was incomprehensible that in exactly twelve months' time, Manchester United would suffer its darkest day.

Murphy took training for a few days the following week as Busby flew to Germany to discover who United's opponents in the semi-final of the European Cup would be after the dramatic tie with Athletic Bilbao.

On top of this, Murphy still found time to be present for the FA Youth Cup fourth round replay with Everton which the youngsters won 5-2. Immediately after the game, Murphy was concentrating on Bournemouth in the FA Cup.

United's trip to Bournemouth was eventful. The tie captured the imagination of the public and was aired by the BBC to an audience of approximately one million viewers. The Babes were

THE GREATEST

up against it when Mark Jones suffered a knee ligament injury after just ten minutes; in these days before substitutions, United were forced to play on with ten men. And Bournemouth reacted accordingly; their crowd sensed another giant-killing, and when they were given a half-time lead by striker Brian Bedford, they had every right to feel optimistic.

United's class told – the composure spread through the side by the cool head of captain Roger Byrne was given special praise by Frank McGhee of the *Daily Mirror*, though it was Johnny Berry whose two goals turned the game in the visitors' favour. The second – from the penalty spot – was disputed after Cherries defender Joe Brown insisted he didn't handle the ball. Replays showed that he did, if, albeit, accidentally. Afterwards, Murphy spoke of his relief and pride. "I rate this a greater achievement than giving Bilbao two goals start and a beating in the European Cup," he quipped, while Busby concurred, calling it the toughest match of the season.

A few days later, in March, Busby and Murphy went to the City Ground to watch the FA Cup quarter final replay between Nottingham Forest and Birmingham City – with United scheduled to play the winners. It was an event which was almost marred by tragedy as a lorry backed into a gate where five thousand people were trapped in the car park outside the ground.

Amongst that crowd were United's manager and assistant. 'Women cried. Children screamed in terror. And men shouted angrily for officers to resign as a crowd of thousands, packed tightly together, swayed and rocked and pushed and shoved outside the Nottingham Forest football ground yesterday afternoon… there will be an official inquiry into the cause of these disgraceful scenes today,' wrote McGhee for the *Mirror*.

'I saw several fans risk serious injury by scaling the eighteen

JIMMY MURPHY

foot wall surrounding the ground,' McGhee continued. 'I saw hundreds more try to force two huge double gates which could have let in the crowd in a matter of minutes. They were prevented by someone inside the ground backing a lorry up against the gap and sealing it. I saw a mounted policeman try to drive a wedge through the crowd, only to find himself and his sweating horse hemmed in on all sides, unable to move. Among those kept back for a time were Matt Busby, manager of Manchester United, who play the winners of yesterday's tie, his assistant Jimmy Murphy, and the first citizen of Nottingham, Alderman William Cox, Lord Mayor of the City.'

Thankfully, Murphy and Busby escaped unscathed. Talk of United's treble hopes was dominating even regional press from Yorkshire. Journalist Fred Walters wrote an article in the Saturday, March 9th edition of the *Sheffield Star's 'Green 'Un* which said: 'Manchester United are in line for a treble – League, FA Cup, and European Cup. There is no doubt about it that Matt Busby and his henchman, Jimmy Murphy, have the best playing staff of any club in Britain.'

On the afternoon of the FA Cup semi-final (where United would face Birmingham at Hillsborough), Jimmy was at Old Trafford, taking charge of his young players in the quarter-final of the Youth Cup. Despite that senior game, over 12,500 supporters turned up for the kids' match against Blackburn Rovers. They were rewarded with a fantastic display. Dawson got his customary two goals with English, Hunter, Lawton and Morgans getting the others in a 6-0 win.

Any recollection of Murphy at this time paints the picture of a man absolutely loving life. And with good reason. Here was a man who not only lived and breathed football as a hobby, he was able to work in the game for a living, and had carved out a reputation

THE GREATEST

– whether or not he was fully aware of it – as one of the greatest contemporary football minds. The boys he had carefully crafted from precocious school-leavers to First Division winners and now, to most, the backbone of the best team in world football, were on the cusp of footballing greatness. "Manchester United were on a crusade," he was to say later. "We had a wonderful spirit of adventure."

Murphy's enthusiasm was felt all through the club. "Jimmy would take part in all of the five-a-sides; he was very much involved with the lads and even though I never saw him play as a professional, I could certainly tell that the reputation he had was well-earned by how he played in these games!" laughs David Gaskell. "It would be very much a case of playing until his team scored or won; occasionally some of us would fix it just so we could get away!

"The Welsh side he was managing was pretty decent and if it was coming up to international week he would have us play mini-internationals in training; the Welsh lads in one team, the English lads in another, the Scottish boys and so on. He was so competitive and tried to inspire that competitive streak in us as players too…He was a typical Welshman, extremely passionate; he was diminutive but he was a very physical man and would stress to us in the defence that we had to be men and get the first kick in; I remember him often screaming at Billy Foulkes that very phrase.

"Jimmy was so fiery; so passionate. He was a great motivator and he liked a tipple; he'd bring his whiskey down to the changing room, say his speech and then go and have a little drink. He and Matt were like chalk and cheese but Jimmy knew how to light the fire. He would be spitting feathers, effing and blinding. He was a lot like Bill Shankly in that respect."

Stories of Jimmy joining in training are common. On many occasions he would do it to make a point to a certain player, or to go in hard to test a youngster's temperament, but generally, he would join in just because he loved playing. "Training stories of Jimmy Murphy are legion," Busby said. "One I cherish concerns Jimmy in action against one of our younger players. Training has to be realistic. It is no use being gentle in practice games. That would be bad practice for the ferocious reality. This time Jimmy went across the lad with a blatant foul and the lad landed him on his backside. 'Sorry Mr Murphy,' said the lad, and Jimmy said, 'Come here. Don't let me hear you say sorry again. I fouled you. You were quite right.'"

Busby's recollection is elaborated upon by Jimmy Jr. "He was called 'Tapper' because he used to kick his opponents," he says. "Peter Doherty, the former Manchester City player – in my father's opinion, the greatest player they ever had – would say that when he played against Dad, he would wear two pairs of shin pads – two for his shins, and two on his calves!

"He took this into his coaching; Bert would be in one half of the pitch. Bert – a real gentleman, a Methodist preacher – would give the players gentle encouragement. 'Unlucky there!' Dad would be kicking them – especially Bobby. 'Pass the fucking ball!' Mark Pearson was a tough, tough lad. In one training session he knocked into my Dad and nudged him over the touchline. 'Oh Jimmy,' he said, 'I'm so sorry.' My Dad's response – 'Brilliant that Mark, but watch yourself next time!' He enjoyed it, but was warning him he'd get him back."

Manchester United were physical, dominant and clinical; it was almost as if they had become fully fledged experienced professionals as soon as they were in the first team. Of course, that isn't quite the case, as some had found their way into the side gradually, but the way that so many of these late teenagers and early 20-somethings had become the premier side in the country defied all expectations. They stormed to a second consecutive First Division title, ending on 64 points at a time when it was still two points for a win. Had this been three points for a win, they would have set a club record 92 points, which has only been matched once since (in 1994).

It would be negligent to understate the importance of Murphy in the success of Manchester United in 1956 and 1957. The story would take a profound turn in the years to come but in the days pre-Munich, it could — indeed should — be argued, that he was as responsible as anybody for the creation of the club's best ever team. They attacked and entertained in precisely the way that Busby had demanded, and with the arrogance and swagger he called for, but they also performed with a tenacity and aggression which was undeniably Murphy's hallmark.

"Matt was the architect. Bert Whalley laid the foundations and my dad was the master builder," says Jimmy Jr. "Between them, they created a magnificent mansion and if it's even bigger today, then that is down in no small part to what my Dad achieved immediately after Munich."

At this time, Murphy remained dedicated to the players of tomorrow. While the senior team prepared for its ultimate task — Real Madrid — Jimmy was down at the Dell, seeing his boys get a 5-2 win over Southampton to take into the second leg of the FA Youth Cup semi-final.

United lost that second leg, but progressed thanks to another Dawson brace in a 3-2 defeat. It was a landmark night, and not only because it was Manchester United's first ever Youth Cup loss, after forty four ties without being defeated.

The rebuilding of Old Trafford had been continuing over the

years and that season, floodlights had been installed; it meant that the Athletic Bilbao game was the last time they would have to play a home game at Maine Road, and it also meant that for the first time, United would be able to play a youth game at Old Trafford underneath the lights. The result on the day would have been a disappointment for Murphy, but Southampton were proud that the watching Busby came into their dressing room afterwards and gave them a sporting congratulations.

And so, with the place in two cup finals booked – the senior and youth equivalent of the FA Cup – Busby and Murphy prepared for the biggest test of their career yet.

Real Madrid's 1956 win of the inaugural competition left the rest of the continent in no doubt who were the team to beat. Jimmy later described the Real Madrid side of that era as "the yardstick which every great team measures itself against" and they relished the opportunity to take on the Spanish giants.

Madrid had glittering stars all over the pitch, and the brightest of them all was arguably Alfredo di Stefano. United had a plan for the Argentine-born forward, in the shape of 5ft 7 inches tall Salford wing-half Eddie Colman. "For all his skill on the ball, few people realised there was no better tackler in the game… Eddie was so beautifully balanced and mobile that when the time came to play Real Madrid in the European Cup, everyone was surprised to find that Eddie Colman was given the job of marking Alfredo di Stefano," Murphy said. The plan worked for an hour in the Bernabeu, but United's youngsters were themselves hit with the sort of two goal hammer-blow they had so often dished out to opponents. It seemed as if they had found a lifeline when Tommy Taylor scored with eight minutes to go, but Madrid scored less than a minute later to take a 3-1 lead to Old Trafford.

THE GREATEST

Murphy noticed the pattern and would later go on record as saying that he was sure the players' inexperience at that level was what ultimately cost them. Bobby Charlton admitted it had been a learning curve. "I was a midfielder still learning my trade under the prompting of Jimmy Murphy and maybe it was a benefit of that education, or simply that di Stefano made the game seem so simple, but I understood everything that he was doing," he said.

The naivety seemed to play a part in the second leg, too, as Madrid stormed into a half-time lead of 2-0, to lead 5-1 on aggregate; the sort of scoreline United's young starlets were used to being on the right end of. Their second-half response, whilst ultimately in vain, was heroic nonetheless. Taylor and Charlton scored to equalise in what Murphy described as one of the bravest United performances in Europe, recalling "the great display of pulling two goals back against Real Madrid in the same year when the Spanish Masters had coolly snatched a two goal lead at Old Trafford."

And yet, defeat it was, with the small consolation that Dennis Viollet, a Busby Babe, had ended as the top scorer in his first year playing in the European Cup. The treble hopes, so near yet so far, were extinguished, with United now having to regroup and reinvigorate themselves for the FA Cup final against Aston Villa.

Conveniently for United, the first leg of the Youth Cup final was also in London, as they travelled to West Ham. The Hammers' programme was curiously sporting, wishing United all the best for Saturday 'in their efforts to complete the greatest *double* in modern English football.' A great spectacle was served up in front of 15,000 supporters at Upton Park. 'Manchester United's big, bustling youth team showed at Upton Park on Thursday the sort of class that can keep the Old Trafford club on top for years to come,' said a report in the *West Ham Express* of United's victory. 'They played some brilliant football to beat West Ham Colts 3-2 in the first leg of the FA Youth Cup final.'

Youth was very much the buzzword for the showpiece of the season that Saturday; United fielded the youngest FA Cup final team of all time against Aston Villa.

Before they were able to get into their stride, Busby's game-plan had been well and truly hampered, when Villa forward Peter McParland charged in on goalkeeper Ray Wood. Wood had to be stretchered off, forcing Jackie Blanchflower to play in goal. McParland rubbed salt into the wound with two second half goals; the first of which, Wood might have expected to have had a decent effort of saving. United pulled a goal back with seven minutes to go – a masterful, floating header from Taylor from an Edwards corner – and Wood hastily returned to goal to see out the game, but the damage was done, and Villa held on to win the Cup. "I am absolutely certain that we would have won the double but for that unfortunate incident," Jimmy later said.

Despite the anti-climatic way the '56/57 season ended for the seniors, there was the sizeable silver lining of the FA Youth Cup final second leg. By the thirty minute mark, United were 3-0 up, with the destiny of the Cup as good as decided. All that was left was for a second half display from Dawson to get his name amongst the goals, and he did so with two strikes to round off another resounding victory for Manchester United and Murphy.

Thus concluded a remarkable run of results for United in the competition. They would go all out for a sixth consecutive win in 1958, yet circumstances beyond anybody's control were set to have a devastating impact on United's hopes of success.

Were it not for this, how long would Murphy have been able to prolong this run of results? Another five years? Another ten? Might it have ended anyway, even if Munich had not happened, and had resources not been so stretched? How many of the class of '57 could have gone on to establish themselves as regular first team players had they had the benefit of the same dedicated coaching and patience; had they not been thrust into a situation in which nobody could have expected anything of them. It is like most footballing what-ifs, open to objective and subjective debate.

In recent years, Chelsea have achieved similar results. They defeated Manchester City in the final in 2015 2016, 2017; this gives you the kind of impression of the sort of resources required, even at that level, to achieve sustained success.

Then again, what is success? For Chelsea, it will represent a record, but nobody can present a convincing argument that any player from any of their successes so far has carved out a successful first team career at the club (or, top flight career away from the club), which, after all, should be the objective of any youth team. As a quick comparison, it is interesting to note the millions and millions that have been spent without achieving anywhere near the same sort of success achieved by Murphy and Whalley. Then again, few clubs have; even Barcelona and Ajax were not able to boast as many youth products in their senior squad as Manchester United were able to in 1957. What those clubs do have are European Cups to cement the legacy of their own incredible youth system.

United's 1957 side would come to be remembered for a potential untold; unfulfilled.

Part Two

"For unto Thy Faithful, O Lord, life is changed, not taken away, and the abode of this earthly sojourn being dissolved, an eternal dwelling is prepared in Heaven."

Preface,
Mass for the Dead.

8. Munich

9. United Spirit

10. A Proud Man

11. World Class

CHAPTER | EIGHT

MUNICH

"These were the darkest days of my football life, and they passed in a blur. But something which remains crystal clear is the almost superhuman strength and resilience of Jimmy Murphy, as he took on the gargantuan task of keeping Manchester United afloat" – Bill Foulkes

The mood at the Cliff on the morning of Thursday, February 6th, 1958, was very much 'routine'. Domestic form had picked up in recent weeks, at just the right time, considering that top of the table Wolverhampton Wanderers were Manchester United's next opponents in the league. Bolton had been walloped 7-2 and Busby's men had left for Belgrade having performed exceptionally at Highbury in a 5-4 win which would become forever known – arguably, at least – as the Babes' most famous game on British soil.

Back in Lower Broughton, those players left at United had gone through their paces before a sombre looking Bill Inglis and

JIMMY MURPHY

Arthur Powell came into the dressing room and stood before them. Nobby Stiles was part of this group and described how Inglis' words did not sink in.

The plane had crashed.

Inglis told the boys to leave for home and to call into the club in the morning. Powell stood silent.

Once left to their own devices the junior players had a bit of a joke. "We'd been laughing about this crash back in the dressing room, saying maybe somebody had broken a leg, maybe the big chance for one of us had come," Stiles recalled. He got the bus into town, and saw a newspaper seller with a copy of the *Evening Chronicle*. The faces of Geoff Bent, Roger Byrne, Eddie Colman, Mark Jones, David Pegg, Tommy Taylor and Liam Whelan were on the front of it. The front page said those players were dead; Stiles said he felt sick, and rushed home, hopeful that his parents would tell him somebody had got it wrong.

Somehow, the news had escaped Jimmy Murphy's taxi-driver (though, in fairness, the news was still filtering through, as it was still only coming up to 4pm). The driver recognised his passenger. By now, everybody did.

"Looks like we might win the European Cup this year, Mr. Murphy," the driver said. Jimmy nodded politely and smiled. He was proud of what the team had done and believed they had learned from their lessons of the previous season but he hated the idea of making such forecasts and predictions, for they only served to make fools of those who had made them.

Jimmy's mind was mostly on his friend, Matt. Busby had recently undergone an operation on his legs and Murphy was amazed that he had shown such dedication to the job that he had gone to Belgrade. Jimmy didn't even note his own dedication – he hadn't even gone home after the Wales game. Straight to Old

MUNICH

Trafford to plan for Saturday. He was eager to get back to work. Excited, even. He remembered taking the stairs to his office two at a time. In his haste, he almost ignored the voice of Busby's secretary calling him.

"I got to the office and went past Alma George, who was our secretary then…there seemed to be nobody there, the boss wasn't there, it was strange," Jimmy recalled. "No-one around at all. I had a drink and gave Alma a drink.

"She said, 'Haven't you heard Jimmy?'

"I said, 'Heard about what?'

"'The plane has crashed.'"

"It never struck me at all. She said it again. I had another drink. I took that second one quickly. She said it again and she started to cry. And then it struck me very vividly. I thought, 'God, no… the last thing I would have ever thought of was a plane crash. I went into my office and cried for about twenty minutes. I couldn't realise it. Half of those players you'd brought up, more or less lived with…it was very difficult."

Jimmy rushed to his office and started to make phone calls, to the police, to the BBC, to the newspapers and journalists he knew. The news was brutal and unrelenting.

The accident had occurred at Munich-Reim Airport. The plane had stopped in Germany to refuel and failed on two take-off attempts. On the third, the plane failed to take off through the slush, and crashed through a fence at the end of the runway before the left wing was torn completely off after hitting a house.

The names of those players who were already confirmed as dead were relayed to him. The names of Tom Curry and Walter Crickmer followed. As did that of Bert Whalley; Jimmy's best friend.

Busby was gravely ill, and fighting for his life. So too was

JIMMY MURPHY

Duncan Edwards. Others were in a critical condition. "I was like a man living through a nightmare waiting to wake up," Jimmy said. "I locked the door, put my head on the desk and wept like a child." He received some phone calls of his own. Nobby Stiles' father informed Jimmy that he had a car for whenever he may need it. That generous offer would be much appreciated in the forthcoming days and weeks.

Elsewhere, the Murphy family had been in a state of genuine panic, however brief. At the time Jimmy Jnr was a fifteen year old schoolboy making his way home from St. Bede's College and he heard about the disaster from the late editions of the evening newspapers on the way home. "My mother threw her hands up in horror," he recalls. "She was saying, 'Oh dear God, your father, your father's on the plane!' I must confess that in the initial shock the same thought went through my head. Once I'd gathered my thoughts and remembered he'd been with Wales, I calmed my mother down and assured her he'd gone to Cardiff and would be home any minute."

That wouldn't be the case. Jimmy didn't sleep; he remained in his office throughout the night, waiting for news, and sitting, catatonic, with a bottle of whiskey and his bag of oranges. The bottle was full when he arrived back at Old Trafford. It was empty, twelve hours later at 4am, when Jimmy left to go back home. It was probably only the allure of more whiskey back at College Road that influenced that decision.

"He talks about losing those hours where he went into the office and drunk a bottle of whiskey and had a cry," says Jimmy Jr. "He went in and came out of the office as a different man. He had remarkable inner strength."

He was just about able to make the plane later that day to Munich, with family of the victims, including Busby's wife Jean

MUNICH

and his daughter and son. He knew how tentative Matt's hold on life was, and when they arrived at the Rechts der Isar hospital in the Haidhausen area of Munich, Germany, Jean, Sheena and Sandy went to Matt. As they had landed at the airport, Jimmy shuddered as he observed the remnants of the wreckage which were still present.

Howard Johnson and Anne Lloyd, reporting from Munich for the *Daily Mirror*, shared how Jimmy had travelled with his colleagues' families. 'Earlier in the day Matt, a Roman Catholic, had been given the last rites by a priest,' they wrote. 'And he did not know tonight that his red-haired wife Jean had arrived in Munich…she had to be supported by her son Sandy, and assistant team manager Mr. Jim Murphy, who had flown in with the relatives.'

Bill Foulkes remembered Jimmy arriving amidst the chaos. Foulkes and Harry Gregg had been amongst the luckiest, to escape with no major injury. "Sooner or later – I can't remember when exactly – Jimmy Murphy appeared on the scene," Foulkes said in his autobiography.

Matt lay in an oxygen tent; a few feet away lay Edwards. Here was the player Jimmy had travelled to Dudley in the wee hours to sign. The boy wonder who had been the subject of so many great tales already for Jimmy in such a short career. The most recent of those had been the past November.

"There was an infamous team talk he gave his Wales players ahead of facing England," Jimmy Jr says. "Of course he was familiar with a few England players. 'Roger Byrne, very good, but he prefers to jockey for the ball rather than tackle, so come on his inside. Tommy Taylor, you've got to stop him heading the ball, so we need two of you to get near him…'

"The inside-right, Reg Davies popped up. 'What about me

Jimmy, you haven't told me what I've got to do,' he asked. 'Who are you playing against?' Dad replied. 'Duncan Edwards.' Dad quipped: 'Keep out of his way – I don't want you getting hurt!'"

That same boy, destined without question to become England's greatest player – if he wasn't already – was now in perilous danger, slipping in and out of consciousness.

Jimmy was initially hesitant but was approached by one of the sisters. In her limited use of English, she was able to tell Jimmy that Duncan, between gasps of breath, had been asking for a watch. He was insistent it had been stolen; the sister had tried to reassure him that he was wearing no watch when he was brought in. One of the rescue team had found the watch and given it her; she passed it to Jimmy. It was beyond repair.

In a heartbreaking scene, Jimmy went to Duncan's bedside, and put the watch back onto his wrist. Feeling the touch, Duncan's eyes flickered, and showed recognition of who was with him. Duncan struggled to speak, so Jimmy moved closely towards his mouth so he could hear.

"I sat with him a while, and then he turned his head, it was the saddest thing I've ever seen or been a part of," Jimmy said. "He turned and said, 'Oh it's you Jimmy.' I said 'yes'. I had to put my head to his mouth. He said, 'What time's kick off tomorrow?'"

Jimmy told him, with a desperately sad smile and tears falling down his cheeks. "Get stuck in," Duncan whispered. The boy slipped back out of consciousness while Jimmy held his hand. "You've got your watch back, Duncan," he said.

Harry Gregg recalled the same moment. Gregg explained that because Duncan had been conscious and talking – for however brief a moment – when they left Munich, his death was particularly shocking for the club.

Gregg had walked around the beds of the injured with the

MUNICH

Chief Surgeon, Professor Georg Maurer, who told him that he expected Jackie Blanchflower and Albert Scanlon would be alright, and then he felt Matt Busby and Duncan Edwards were strong enough to pull through, before the pair visited Johnny Berry. "I am not God," Maurer told Gregg, giving the impression that Berry was the most likely to pass away. "During our last visit Duncan had briefly come round, asking Jimmy what time kick-off was," Gregg recalled. "With his eyes welling up, Jimmy told him: 'Three o'clock, son.' Duncan said: 'Get stuck in!' then lapsed back into a state of unconsciousness."

Jimmy moved from Duncan's bedside and went into the corridor, where he found a stairwell; he sat on the stairs and cried. "Clearly he was horrendously shaken, utterly demoralised, but he put on a brave show and tried to joke for our benefit," said Foulkes. "I remember going out to the toilet and seeing poor Jimmy sitting up all hunched up on the stairs, his head in his hands as if his world had crumbled about him. The shock to him must have been monumental. He had missed the trip to Belgrade cause he had been away in charge of Wales for a World Cup qualifier. These boys were like sons to him and now so many of them were snatched away."

Albert Scanlon remembered stirring back into consciousness. He said: "I woke up again later in Munich to hear a voice saying: 'Albert Scanlon will never play football again.' Jimmy Murphy came in and I was crying and I told him what I had heard. He said: 'That's not true, Albert, you are all right.' Given that it came from Jimmy, it was enough for me."

Later, Jimmy went to spend time with Matt; Busby was unable to speak, but recognised his old friend, and the pair held hands.

That evening, Jimmy went to the Regina Hotel with Harry Gregg and Foulkes. Harry and Bill arrived after Jimmy, and when they got there, Harry said he would take the stairs while Bill took the lift. As he reached the top, he heard and then saw Jimmy with his hands bunched up around his head again, hysterically, deeply sobbing.

Matt had been moved into a private ward but remained in an oxygen tent. He was considered too ill to be told about the tragic news; he was only able to understand he had been in an accident. It was thought that any further shock may prove fatal. Jimmy visited his friend and held his hand tightly. Matt signalled that he wanted to speak, so Jimmy bent low to hear. "Keep the flag flying Jimmy. Keep things going until I get back."

With those words, Jimmy pledged to begin the rebuilding of Manchester United. How? Well, that was a significant question that he had no answer for.

"I have seen the boys," Jimmy told the press. "Limbs and hearts may be broken, but the spirit remains. Their message is that the club is not dead. Manchester United lives on.

"My boss and my greatest friend, Matt Busby, would want me to tell you that the Red Devils will survive this. We have a motto at Old Trafford which means 'Work and Wisdom'. The work of the country's finest players, and the wisdom of the country's finest manager have made the club what we were. It is going to be a long, long struggle, but together we hope to be back 'there again'. And we know that they will be back. They have to be, because they are the greatest."

'The glory of Manchester United is not so much in their trophies but in the way they won them,' wrote Bob Pennington of the *Express* on Friday, February 7th, 1958. 'For this is the club that always moved one jump ahead of its rivals. And English football was always the better for United's enterprise. The enterprise began in 1945 when Matt Busby was signed and given complete power. His ideas appeared revolutionary to some of football's elder statesmen. But as the glory years rolled along, everyone tried to copy him. Busby changed the club that was in danger of slumping to Division Three before the war into the greatest soccer academy in history. He realised that the cheque-book methods that brought honour to Herbert Chapman's Arsenal were over. And he launched a youth policy, backed by a nationwide talent recruiting staff headed by his lieutenant, Jimmy Murphy.'

Pennington spoke fondly of United's accomplishments but ended his piece with a poignant and significant message: 'If they could give football one last message I believe it would be: "Don't let this put the clock back ten years. Go on making Europe and the world smaller – and football greater."'

The FA postponed United's home game against Wolves on February 8th. Programmes for that game had already been printed and the team read: Gregg, Foulkes, Byrne, Colman, Jones, Edwards, Morgans, Charlton, Taylor, Viollet, Scanlon. Pennington's words on the day after the disaster (written, it should be added, on the day of it) may have been filled with emotion – it was all well and good to speak of defiance, and continuing in the memory of those who had gone – but it goes without saying that over that weekend the future of Manchester United was in doubt.

Elsewhere, others chose not to think about what may be, and simply offered condolences for what was undoubtedly the most horrific tragedy to afflict a British sporting team.

Reporter Harry Langton compiled tributes from around the world. From Torino, secretary Gino Giusto (whose club suffered a similar tragedy in 1949): "The hearts of all Italians go out to Manchester United. We know what it means. We went through the torture and hell of a similar catastrophe." Real Madrid manager Antonio Calderon said: "This is one of the best teams in the world and the world will mourn their losses." United's opponents in the European Cup, Red Star Belgrade, issued the statement: "We will propose to the European Cup organisers that Manchester United be awarded the honorary title of 1958 Champions."

After column inches had been dedicated to the deceased and the country awaited news of those who were still critically injured, the Saturday newspapers speculated just if and how Manchester United might progress once Jimmy returned from Munich.

A statement to the press for Saturday, February 8th from chairman Harold Hardman underlined the club's intentions: "We will undertake our full League, FA Cup, and European Cup commitments as soon as it is humanly possible to do so. We have a duty to the public and a duty to football. We shall carry on even if it means we are heavily defeated."

'If Manchester United had to play this afternoon, they could send out a side with eight players of First Division experience,' Bob Pennington noted for the *Express*, as he explained that in David Gaskell, United had 'one of the greatest goalkeeping discoveries in the country' and Freddie Goodwin and Wilf McGuinness were 'wing-halves who would walk into nearly any other First Division side.'

'This will give you an idea of the incredible reserves of talent still available to Jimmy Murphy, who will now command the Busby Babes,' Pennington wrote. 'Assistant manager Murphy is left with only two players comparatively uninjured – £23,000 Irish international goalkeeper Harry Gregg and England right-back Billy Foulkes…it is probable that Murphy will give his youngsters a chance to show their ability before seeking the co-operation of other clubs in the signing of experienced players.'

MUNICH

A report from Munich on Saturday listed the players United had available. These included Foulkes, Gregg, Viollet, Morgans, Charlton, and Brennan. "We have 20 youngsters, too," Murphy said. "But they are all amateurs and we cannot consider them."

"We must also forget, for the present, all those lads here in hospital – even chaps like Billy Foulkes and Harry Gregg, who escaped from the crash uninjured. Reaction is bound to hit them, as it will surely hit the others. Doctors can't say when any of these players in the crash will be fit to play again – and I wouldn't like to guess."

The newspaper report painted the picture of Murphy's dilemma: 'In hotel room 610, long after most of the other guests had gone to bed, Jimmy Murphy, United's backroom boy, now the only senior official left active, stayed on, wrestling with his problem. The rebirth of a great club was being planned. But even Jimmy Murphy, who never gives up easily, finally had to say: "What a mess we're in…" and go to bed, to think all over again.'

Still, that didn't stop clubs who were already keen to offer assistance in United's hour of need. 'Blackpool were the first club to offer to loan players to United,' Pennington wrote. 'Sheffield Wednesday, the team United are due to meet in a fifth round FA Cup tie next Saturday, have also offered to loan Don Gibson, their wing-half, who is a son-in-law of Matt Busby. Will the cup clash with Sheffield Wednesday be postponed? United could not say last night. They will hold a board meeting when their assistant manager Jimmy Murphy returns from Germany, where he flew last night to wait at the bedside of manager Busby and his injured stars.'

Following Murphy's meeting with Busby, he was at least emboldened enough to speak to the press. Headlines read: 'I PROMISE: RED DEVILS WILL BE BACK!' and Jimmy, writing a column for the *Express* in his own words, said: 'The Red Devils will rise again. It took Matt Busby, Bert Whalley and myself 12 years to produce the 1958 Red Devils. It was long, tiring, hard work. But we succeeded. We reached a perfect system. We had the best set-up in football. It will again be a long, tiring job to rebuild the Red Devils.

'This time we have to start practically from scratch. But we'll do it. Just sketching through the players we have left, it is obvious we shall need more to help us fulfil our commitments this season. But where are our type of players? You just don't go out and buy them. You find them, nurture them, coach them, live with them, play with them.

'As soon as I return to Manchester I will confer with our chairman, Harold Hardman, and his directors, to decide our future action. At the moment I'm so confused, so tired, so sad, I can't think clearly. I haven't slept for three days. Cigarettes have kept me going.

'But this I do know. United was and will again be a great club. We have the greatest club spirit in the world. Everybody was a boss in his own right. Everybody respected everybody else. We had a job to do and we used to pool our ideas. Ultimately and invariably we come up with the right solutions. And always backed by wonderful co-operation from the board.

'Apart from having such a wonderful side which became world renowned, we had a unique, happy, *holiday camp* atmosphere at Old Trafford. We were all friends.

'We insisted on 100 per cent plus and we got it. Our wonderful system was organised and led by my dear friend Matt, and I'm not forgetting my very good friend Bert Whalley or dear old Tom Curry. Or our ever-energetic backroom boy Walter Crickmer, who carried out his office duties as smoothly as we carried out our soccer duties. Matt, thank God, is improving at the moment. Slowly, but he is improving. So we will have his spirit with us. Mercifully, too, we have assistant secretary Les Olive. There is none better than him.

'The future? It will be a long, hard struggle. But the game must go on in tribute to all members of our staff who have left us and who did their job so nobly and so proudly to make Manchester United one of the foremost in the soccer world. Matt, I pray, will soon be back. Soon the world-famous partnership of Busby and Murphy will be reunited. Soon we will be working together again for the greatest club in the world.'

A defiant message no doubt.

But on the same day Murphy had confided to the press: "Our plight is worse even than I thought. I can't see at the moment how we can pick a team for any sort of football."

As he travelled back to Manchester by train on the Rhinegold Express with Foulkes and Gregg, Jimmy sat numb, wondering just how he might be able to put a team together.

'In the immediate aftermath of Munich, I travelled back to England overland with Bill and Harry Gregg,' a quote from Jimmy reads towards the back of Foulkes' autobiography. 'Quite understandably, both men were showing signs of panic claustrophobia on the train, and it is an immense tribute to their strength of character that – despite all they had been through – they were playing an FA Cup tie in only a little more than a week's time.'

Foulkes recalled that difficult journey home. "After one more visit to the hospital, when things were beginning to look blacker than ever for some of the badly injured, Jimmy Murphy decided wisely that we would be better off at home," he said.

"He was brilliant, telling us not to bother about football. But we all knew that, sometime soon, we would have to start thinking

JIMMY MURPHY

about the future of Manchester United. Unbelievably the airline officials were stupid enough to ask us to fly back to Manchester at their expense. My reaction was unequivocal. I told them they would never get me in a stinking plane again. But, as it turned out, it was just as bad on the train…I know it was an illusion but we seemed to be travelling for days, Harry, Jimmy and I in one compartment.

"In Holland a little Chinaman passed us in the corridor and Jimmy, doing his utmost to cheer us up, said that we had better sign him on. We might need him! In fact, there was a lot of truth in that little joke. Obviously, on the way home we gave some thought to the future and Jimmy told me that I would have to be captain for the next match. He didn't ask me, he just told me."

United's returning players made their feelings on travel known to the press. On Monday, February 10th, the *Express* reported: "'We will never fly again,' say Manchester United players Harry Gregg and Billy Foulkes. Jimmy Murphy, the club's assistant manager, takes a different view. "Air transport," he says, "is absolutely vital in modern football." He has wisely overcome his immediate emotional reaction against air travel after the crash.'

"Dad didn't shirk away from the fact that they would have to fly," Jimmy Jr. says. "He had a job to do. He did enjoy his trips abroad."

In those ongoing conversations through the Alps, the players had, however, reassured Jimmy they were ready to answer the call to play football.

Another report in the *Express* that Monday bore the headline 'BUSBY CRASH BOYS ASK TO PLAY.' Frank Palmer, reporting from Munich, wrote that Gregg and Foulkes had declared themselves fit for action. 'Jimmy Murphy said: "It's a great relief to know that the boys feel like this. They will have a complete medical check-up when we get home on Wednesday. If they come through that then there's no reason why they shouldn't be in."'

'Gregg and Foulkes leave Munich tomorrow by boat train with Mr. Murphy,' wrote Palmer. 'They plan to meet their wives in London on Wednesday morning and then go on to Manchester. Their wives went to London on Saturday expecting them to arrive today. But plans were changed when Jimmy Murphy asked the two players to stay on and help him in Munich.'

The *Daily Mirror* reported a more direct message from Murphy, and that was an emotional insistence that he too was ready to lead his team into battle.

'Manchester United WILL play their Fifth Round FA Cup tie against Sheffield Wednesday on Saturday,' wrote a *Mirror* sport reporter. 'That was the dramatic message from Jimmy Murphy, United's assistant team manager, in Munich last night. It came after the club's directors had talked by telephone to Jimmy about the possibility of turning out a team at Old Trafford.

'Jimmy, who earlier had been told by his injured boss Matt Busby, "Go to it – it is in your hands," told the directors: "We can field a team. Whatever happens Manchester United will be on the field again on Saturday. It may not be the strongest side but it will have all the Busby spirit."

'He then outlined his plans for picking a team, naming the players who would come in from the reserves to take the place of those killed and injured in the tragic air crash. United have six vital days in which to lick a team into shape to meet Wednesday. All available players have been ordered to report at Old Trafford today to recommence training. Mr. Murphy will be leaving Munich to return to Manchester by train this morning. This then is the start of United's fight back.'

JIMMY MURPHY

The trio arrived back in London amidst a press circus. "The trip home was a nightmare, for both Harry and Bill showed signs of panic and claustrophobia unless I kept a window open in our train compartment," Jimmy said. "The speed of the train followed by the crush of people who wanted to speak to them when we reached London made both players jittery, so instead of taking a train I hired a taxi to take us from London to Manchester."

Jimmy was frustrated by the attention. "There are a lot of pictures of Dad coming back on the train with Harry Gregg and Bill Foulkes," says Jimmy Jr. "You can tell that they're vacant, that their expressions are put on. One of the journalists was at my Dad. 'Jimmy, Jimmy, have you got a quote for us?' he said. 'Yes, if you don't get out of the way, I'll piss on your shoes!'"

Jimmy made sure the players were safely home with their families before going back to Whalley Range to be with his own family. It was clear that the commencing days and weeks were going to be very difficult indeed. "The mood at home was different," admits Jimmy Jr. "That was partly because he was there even less; I didn't think it was humanly possible to work more than what he was, but somehow he did.

"Amidst all that, there were all the funerals he had to attend. He went to Bert's funeral and I know that was a particularly tough experience for him, with Bert having gone to Munich instead of him. I see Bert's daughter once a year and I always cry as soon as I lay eyes on her. There were the moments of privacy which I witnessed fleetingly but, even in front of the family, he tried to keep a brave face and a strong front. We didn't generally witness any of his vulnerability."

However, there were moments, when Jimmy felt he was alone, that the mask would slip, as Jimmy Jr recalls: "Although he swore a lot and would bully people in his job, Dad was a deeply religious man and a regular churchgoer. I have haunting, vivid memories in the weeks after Munich, memories of passing my father's bedroom and seeing him kneeled by the edge of the bed, praying, in floods of tears."

He believes that his father would not have wanted the responsibility he had been given.

"There's no doubt in my mind that he didn't want the job, but equally, I have no doubt that he was the driving force for keeping the club running," he says. "Dad was a natural number two but he was thrust into a position where he was Matt's right-hand man. It's too simple to say he was the assistant; Dad was doing so much.

"Dad had the responsibility of making the telephone call to the Whelan family to tell them their son had died. I only found that out a few years ago, just after the 50th anniversary. Dad had called them from Munich to inform them of the tragic news and he said: 'Your son will never be forgotten by this football club.' He had contrasting public and private reactions but his public reactions ensured that the club kept going and it shaped the identity of the club forevermore from that point."

Nick also recalls that his father was home even less than before. "I was ten when Munich happened," he says. "My strongest recollection from that time was that he was never home. I was too young to comprehend what had happened, too young to understand what death was…I was coming out of school and someone told me.

"I was told that Mum fainted when she heard the news. I just knew that Dad was needed. It seemed like he was there, and then he wasn't for a long period of time…I mean, I knew he came home, but we never saw him. And I know he slept at the ground a few times as well. He had so much to do…the football was a big enough job on its own but people forget that the secretary died in the disaster and so there was an incredible amount of backroom things to be doing. My sister and one of my brothers were down in the offices opening the mail and dealing with the donations. And, of course, he had to organise the funerals.

"I don't know how he did it. As I've got older that question, 'how?' is one I've asked myself so many times and I really have never found an answer."

"He was always a religious man and he never changed. If anything, I think his faith helped him get through the tragedy, it helped to give him the strength to do what he did," Nick says. "I would go to church with him every Saturday and he went to confession every week, and it never changed in his later years, so I have to think that it gave him comfort in those dark hours. He always had a set of rosary beads in his pocket and he found comfort in that. Dad had a crucifix and a set of rosary beads with the figure on it and he rubbed it flat, saying his prayers, walking up and down the garden. I inherited it from him and had it for years before misplacing it. I wish I knew where it was because people don't believe me that he actually did rub it flat."

"Unquestionably these were the darkest days of my footballing life, and they passed in a blur," said Foulkes. "But something which remains crystal clear from that period is the almost superhuman strength and resilience of Jimmy Murphy, as he took on the gargantuan task of keeping Manchester United afloat."

On the same day that Jimmy, Billy and Harry arrived back in Manchester, so too did the bodies of those who had died in the crash. Police estimated that more than a quarter of a million lined the streets to pay their respect as the procession of cars carrying the coffins travelled from the airport to Old Trafford.

"I walked past the gym and brushed away the tears," Jimmy

Early years: A team picture with Pentre Boys Club in 1921. Jimmy is pictured to the left of the boy holding the ball. *Right:* A Welsh schoolboy international

Playing days: *(Above, second from left)* in West Brom colours and *(left)* a newspaper team line-up. Right: playing the organ

Duty and pleasure: *(Centre, with ball at feet)* running the army team where a friendship with Matt Busby led to a job offer and *(above)* a match programme from the time

Like brothers: Two pictures *(left and below)* of Jimmy with Bert Whalley – the close friend and United colleague who would take his place on the ill-fated trip to Belgrade

The teacher: An early training photograph *(left)* featuring Bobby Charlton.
Above right: Words of advice for Duncan Edwards, Liam Whelan and Dennis Viollet

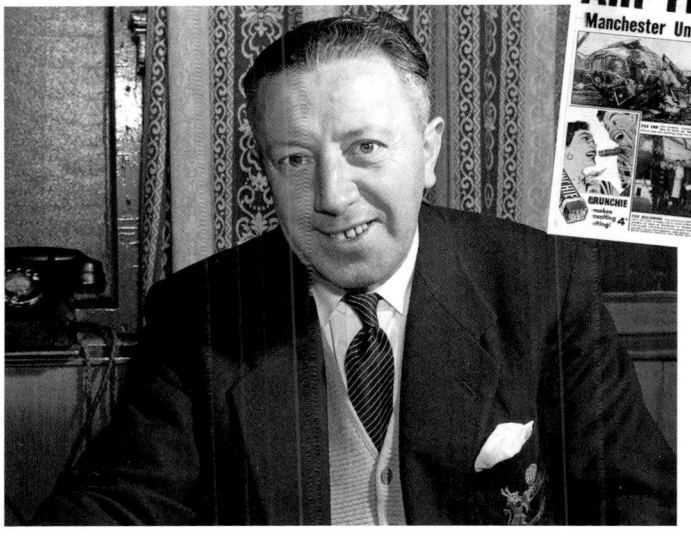

It takes two: Matt Busby entrusted Jimmy with the role of nurturing an exciting new generation of young talent

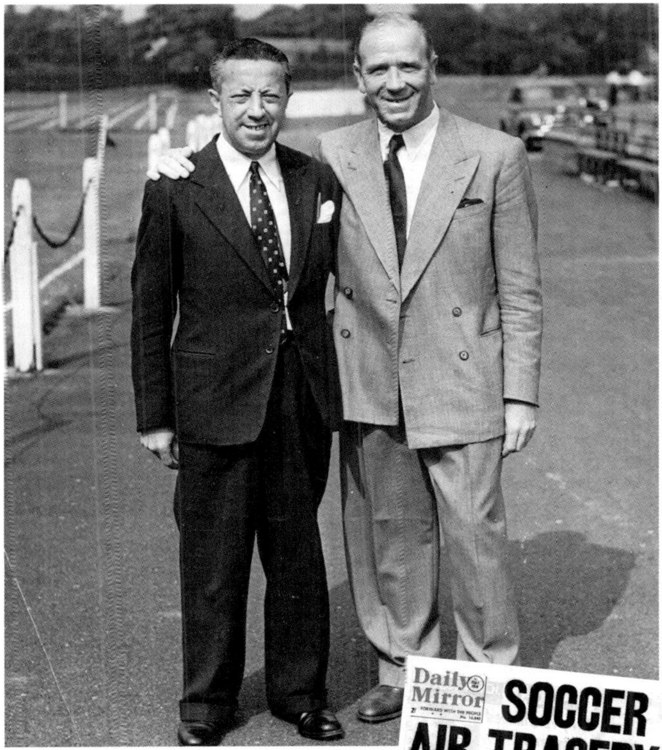

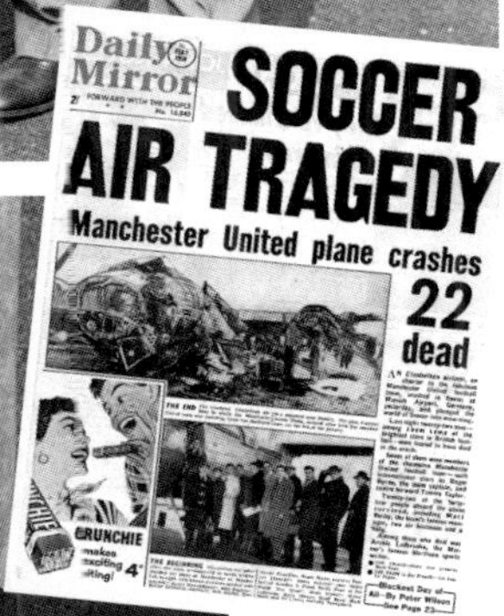
Daily Mirror

SOCCER AIR TRAGEDY

Manchester United plane crashes

22 dead

Smiling through the pain: A photo of Jimmy immediately after the tragedy – putting on a brave face for the cameras

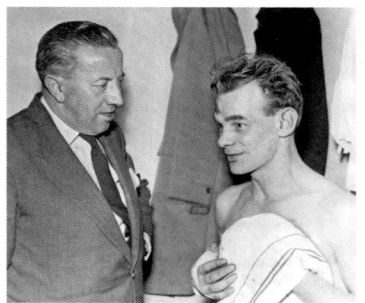

Welcome return: *(Above)* Jimmy and Harry Gregg are surrounded by press and police as they return to England after the Munich disaster. *Above left:* In the dressing room with Ernie Taylor in March, 1958

In charge: Keeping an eye on a training session in March, 1958 as United battled through the aftermath of the disaster

Personal touch: Hard work and attention to detail were classic Jimmy hallmarks. Here he talks things through with *(left)* young keeper Gordon Clayton and *(above)* Wilf McGuinness

Rebuilding the future: With Bobby Charlton and Ernie Taylor in late February, 1958

On our way to Wembley: Jimmy with his 1958 FA Cup final squad prior to training at Blackpool

Happy family: *(Below)* With the Wales squad in 1963 and *(below right)* with Ivor Allchurch, Roy Vernon and John Charles

Inner circle: *(Left)* A training pitch discussion with Matt Busby and Jack Crompton in August, 1961. *Right:* Denis Law puts pen to paper on a contract in 1962

The new breed: Pre-season 1964 at Old Trafford and Murphy and Busby line up with a talented squad that included a young George Best

Toasting success: Raising a glass to the league title triumph of 1965

Cream of Europe: With Matt Busby and the players ahead of extra time in the 1968 European Cup final against Benfica at Wembley which United would go on to win 4-1

All smiles: *(Left)* Lining up for an FA Cup press shot with Matt Busby and Martin Edwards. *Above:* Enjoying a drink in ater years with Dennis Viollet and Kenny Morgans

United spirit: With Matt Busby and some famous names in 1973

Friends reunited: One of the last pictures of Jimmy and Sir Matt Busby together
Image: Courtesy of Frank Wilson

Recognition: *(Below)* Rising young stars of the future join with Sir Bobby Charlton and other key figures to open the club's new Jimmy Murphy Centre

Legacy: Wes Brown wins the Jimmy Murphy Memorial Award in 1999 and a bust at the club shows that Jimmy's contribution to Manchester United will always be remembered

MUNICH

said in later years. "That had been the worst nightmare of all… when the victims were brought back from Munich. The boys who had been so full of life, laughing and joking and playing ball in that same gym, now they lay in their coffins.

"I can talk about it now, I couldn't then. For I knew in my heart that Roger Byrne, Tommy Taylor, David Pegg, Duncan Edwards, Eddie Colman, Bill Whelan, Mark Jones and Geoff Bent would have been proud of the way their team mates played their hearts out to make sure that Manchester United did not die in the aftermath of Munich."

The following morning, one by one, the coffins were removed from the Old Trafford gymnasium as hearses collected them to take the boys to their families.

*****

Back at Old Trafford, Jimmy met with club chairman Harold Hardman and other board members. "You have got to keep it going, Jimmy," Harold told him. "The club must go on."

Jimmy admitted he felt as if he was going out of his mind, that he didn't know where to begin. He described himself as a 'football technocrat', someone who just wanted to speak about the game, whereas Busby was a remarkable figurehead, able to cope confidently with the intense pressure of public relations the role of Manchester United demands, and thus, the assurance of sound judgement and experience in that pressure.

It was Busby who was used to dealing with dressing room politics; Jimmy had been blissfully disengaged from the internal politics of the summer of 1948, when the squad threatened to revolt because they felt the club had short-changed them with a bonus for winning the FA Cup. That time the tension became so heated that it affected the first performances of the following season. Busby would not be moved. It didn't matter what they had been told from players from other clubs. This was Manchester United. Jimmy was more than happy to deal with less political matters.

"Jimmy hated some of the jobs in football," said Bobby Charlton. "He was happy to work in the rain and the wind, hour after hour, with some young player he thought of as a real prospect, but he could not bear to tell a player that, in the end, he had failed his test as a professional.

"That, he said, was a manager's job. Jimmy didn't want to hire or fire, he didn't want to impart news that he knew would cast a shadow over a young person's life. He was a teacher, a passionate and sometimes unscrupulous motivator, but if you wanted somebody to do the nitty and the gritty and the dirty of the manager's job you had to look elsewhere.

"The problem, though, was that United couldn't do that when Matt Busby lingered between life and death. Murphy was Busby's right arm and now that limb had come into play. It did so magnificently. The background enforcer stepped into the harshest of light."

Jimmy's first task was to call Joe Armstrong and ask him to compile a complete list of available players. He despaired at the results. The players showed plenty of promise but they were at least two years of schooling away from being suitably prepared for First Division football. Despite all of the reporting to the contrary, Jimmy went on record to say that only Nottingham Forest and Liverpool contacted him personally to offer players.

"I remember him saying that he would have to find a trainer, before anything else, now that Tom Curry was gone," Foulkes said. "I suggested Jack Crompton, United's former goalkeeper, who I knew was doing a very good job for Luton Town at that time....

"Jimmy was a firecracker of a motivator who lifted men by his sheer passion, but he was an articulate fellow, too, a cute psychologist in his own way, and well-loved by all of us. In the past he had been the perfect foil for Matt, the two of them bouncing ideas off each other as they attempted to get the best out of an exceptionally talented squad of players. Now he found himself in sole charge of a team which was far from first-rate and, despite the crushingly tragic circumstances, the weight of expectation must have been immense."

The news which greeted Jimmy as he returned to England on February 11th was not of reinforcements but instead of more bad news – Wilf McGuinness, certain to be one of the most crucial players to be relied upon, was said to be ruled out for the season when he was diagnosed with cartilage trouble.

Seeing what was available to him (or not) in terms of playing and coaching staff, Murphy knew his declaration that United would be able to face Sheffield Wednesday was his heart speaking and not his head.

Bill Holden reported for the *Daily Mirror* that United had requested a postponement for the Cup game. 'Stricken Manchester United's four directors drafted an urgent appeal to the Football Association last night after a crisis meeting lasting for nearly four hours,' Holden wrote. 'They are asking for rules to be waived to help them sign players they need to get a team together...United chiefs will hold another top-level conference today when Jimmy Murphy, assistant manager, returns from Munich.'

Whilst Murphy scratched his head for players who may be suitable or available – Liverpool chairman Tom Williams having added the caveat that his offer didn't extend to the very best players, of course – some players decided to make themselves available.

Desmond Hackett reported 'NOW PUSKAS WANTS TO HELP UNITED' in his *Express* column. 'The Hungarian immortals of soccer, Ferenc Puskas, Zoltan Cziborh and Sandor Kocsis yesterday phoned from Vienna offering aid without price to broken champions Manchester United,' Hackett wrote.

'It is an offer that again dims the eye, another gesture warmly, bravely emphasising that football at heart remains a sport the world over…Manchester United will say: "Bless you for your kindness, but no thank you. We will fight on the best way we can. It will be a struggle, but then, we have struggled before." And Manchester United will have the same heartfelt reply to the many generous offers of help they have received.

'Of course, they will buy when they think it is necessary. They have bought before, and bought boldly and wisely. But first they will test the babes who are really still babes, young, eager kids, from Matt Busby's thoughtfully housed creche.

'These boys were training yesterday. Looking on was one of the old boys, international full-back Johnny Aston. He was one of the early glory boys of the Matt Busby boom, until ill-health made him quit football. Johnny Aston said: "The playing spirit of these boys is as high as it was at the end of the war. Our ground was blitzed, but you know what a recovery we made then. The family spirit of Manchester United lives on. It will pull them through." Amen to that, Johnny Aston.'

After the Hungarian football revolution of 1956 prompted talk that all the great home-based players would find clubs abroad, Jimmy had immediately suggested to Matt and the board that they should sign the best of them all, Ferenc Puskas. However, the only non-British passport holders at Old Trafford in those days were players from the Republic of Ireland. Whether Busby or the board found it a bit too daring for their liking, the recommendations appeared to fall on deaf ears.

Then, when the situation seemed to present itself, Murphy admitted that he gave serious consideration to signing Puskas but the acting manager was caught in two minds. He was approached by a third party offering not only Puskas but Czibor and Kocsis as well.

The first obstacle was the staggeringly prohibitive financial arrangement, despite the suggestion that they would play without pay. That United's maximum wage at the time was £17 a week was only half the issue. It is believed they would have pushed to their limit of £20 a week but it seemed like a fruitless exercise when it transpired that the contract Puskas eventually signed with Real Madrid was worth a reported £800 a week.

The added complications with the FA's stance on foreign players – even if they were to make an exception in Puskas' case – meant that altogether, the process of bringing Puskas to Old Trafford was a potential financial and bureaucratic nightmare at a time Murphy needed fewer headaches, not more.

Added to this, all three players were serving a FIFA ban because they had refused to return to Hungary after the 1956 uprising. The final major setback on the transfer was Jimmy's absolute reluctance to go against everything he and Matt had worked so hard to build. They had built a team of British players who fought so valiantly and impressively for Manchester United and even if a solution could be found that would have permitted them to bring Puskas in. Murphy went on record to state he felt it would be a 'negation' of all of the work the club had done.

'What happens to Manchester United now? Can they ever

regain the greatness of the last decade?' wrote journalist Arthur Walmsley, before concluding, 'Murphy will keep United moving. Murphy, if he has to, is good enough to do it alone…At the start, Murphy will have to do three men's jobs – his own, Matt Busby's and Bert Whalley's.'

On the evening of February 12th, Murphy had shared his reservations on that theory, telling the press: "I shall be very surprised if any of the boys who survived the crash play again this season. They seem fit enough, but the shock will take some time to get over." It had been an exhausting day physically and emotionally for Jimmy; he attended the funeral of David Pegg in Doncaster after participating in an emergency board meeting. The club released an official statement afterwards saying that Jimmy had been 'authorised to make enquiries regarding certain players.'

Murphy made moves to sign two players he was familiar with, through the Welsh set-up, Mel Charles and Cliff Jones, who both played for Swansea City.

United were told that Charles was unavailable, while Jones – a tremendous prospect in any situation – was valued by the Swans at £35,000. At that price, United could not proceed with the deal, and Jones went to Tottenham that February instead, where he fulfilled his own potential as a world-class winger.

In Jones, Murphy had identified a player he would have wanted at United anyway. The previous year the winger had scored a hat-trick for the national side against Northern Ireland. Jones recalled Murphy approaching him after the game. He said: "As I stepped out of the bath Jimmy came over to me. 'Turn around boyo,' he said. 'I always said when a Welsh player scored a hat-trick while I was in charge of the team I would kiss his arse! And he kissed mine amidst a chorus of giggles and shouting."

MUNICH

Incidentally, Murphy received a telephone call from John Charles – the more well-known brother of Mel – who said that he only wished he could help. John, however, was contracted to Juventus for another year, and would have caused United to have similar financial headaches to the ones they would have had if they had pursued Puskas.

*****

It was a new name identified as the man at the top of Murphy's wanted list on the morning of February 13. It seemed the message of sentiment didn't quite reach Roker Park; or, if it did, their own need trumped United's.

'Ernie Taylor, England and Blackpool inside right, will be asked to sign for Manchester United today – but Sunderland have made an offer for him too,' reported Bob Pennington. 'Others under discussion on the list compiled by United's assistant manager, Jimmy Murphy, are Jim Iley of Spurs; Mel Charles, of Swansea; Jeff Whitefoot, of Grimsby; and Laurie Hughes, of Liverpool – all half-backs.'

It was perhaps being faced with the temptation of Puskas which refined Jimmy's resolve and helped him identify, more clearly, the players he wished to bring in to help United's cause. British players. But more than that, underdogs, who perhaps had something to prove of their own.

Peter McParland had scored the goals which won the FA Cup final for Aston Villa the previous year but Murphy reckoned that Stan Crowther was the heartbeat behind the victory. Likewise, the 1953 FA Cup final may have been famous for Stanley Matthews' contribution, but Murphy's view was that it wasn't Matthews who deserved the credit, nor was it even hat-trick

JIMMY MURPHY

scorer Stan Mortensen, but in fact little Ernie Taylor, who was the best player in a thrilling final. Here were personalities much like Jimmy's own; almost reluctant heroes, men who were willing to put in the hard yards for the greater good.

Taylor had other ideas, however. After learning of Sunderland's interest, the 32-year-old wanted to move back to his native north-east to wind down his career. That seemed to be it as far as the transfer was concerned, until, for the second time in a couple of years, Paddy McGrath found himself an important part of an important moment in United's history. Jimmy mentioned the idea to Paddy, who then told him he happened to be a good friend of Ernie's. This friendship did not guarantee Ernie would sign for United but Paddy did agree to at least attempt to facilitate a meeting between him and Jimmy. Paddy pleaded with Ernie, explaining the dire straits United were in and how much he was wanted, and in a meeting over a beer at Jimmy's Old Trafford office, Taylor signed that day. He moved to Sunderland later in 1958 after helping United in their hour of need.

Foulkes, however, told a slightly different story. 'Jimmy and I went to Blackpool to talk to veteran schemer Ernie Taylor, who had recently experienced his own tragedy with the loss of his seven-year-old son in a car accident,' he said in his autobiography. 'His wife said she was glad we had arrived because he needed taking out of himself and it was obvious straight away that he was keen to join us.'

The Whitefoot rumour was a peculiar one; he had only just left the club the previous year to join Grimsby Town. "After Munich there were rumours that he might re-sign, and when assistant boss Jimmy Murphy mentioned it to me I told him it was a marvellous idea, but it never happened," said Foulkes.

Jimmy did listen to the suggestion of Jack Crompton and

made an approach to Luton. 'Manchester United stand-in chief Jimmy Murphy made his second major capture within 24 hours last night when he took Jack Crompton, United's Cup-winning goalkeeper, back to Old Trafford to the key job of trainer-coach,' reported the *Daily Express* on February 15th. 'Crompton's engagement is the first administrative move by United as they fight back after the Munich air disaster, in which they lost both trainer Tom Curry and coach Bert Whalley.'

Later in the same column Bob Pennington wrote: 'Jimmy Murphy gave his henchmen this briefing last night on the eve of the fifth round of the FA Cup: "Go out and find two Cup men – a left winger and a left-half ready to play for us against Sheffield Wednesday next week." Playing outside the Cup spotlight today, somewhere in Britain, are two men who could be plunged into United's team of survivors to meet Sheffield in the postponed tie at Old Trafford on Wednesday night. Murphy will train with his boys at their ground this morning before leaving on his secret mission. "Must it be secret?" I asked Murphy last night. "Surely you need not fear rivalry from other clubs." "We do not FEAR rivalry," said Murphy. "But this is still a highly competitive business. And we are not looking for Third Division reserves or lads who might make it in a year or so."' Pennington listed Alex Govan, the Birmingham winger, Jackie Henderson of Portsmouth and Spurs' £16,000 priced left-half Jim Iley, although the London club were apparently willing to drop their price for United.

All of these players were scouted on the weekend of February 15th. Jimmy Murphy would spend some of the time scouting but first and foremost, he arranged – and participated in – a practice match at Old Trafford. This twenty minute each-way game was as much to observe how Gregg and Foulkes were coping as it was to run the rule over new players. Ernie Taylor was given a chance to play alongside his new team-mates.

After the quick game, Murphy met with the directors to talk about transfer plans, before going to watch Burnley play against Luton Town, and specifically, England international winger Brian Pilkington.

Burnley were angry at the idea and their chairman made an astonishing public outburst. Journalist Terence Elliott reported: 'Chairman Bob Lord made a slashing attack on *people who think clubs should give away their star players to Manchester United.* "Some people have got hold of the wrong idea," said Mr. Lord. "Of course clubs will help United. But not in the extent of parting with star players. Surely we are not expected to help United win the League, the European Cup, the FA Cup and the Central League? I don't want to be unfair or unkind in any way but clubs still have a duty to themselves. Football is a big business. With all our sympathy and sorrow we just mustn't let this thing get out of focus. Help? Certainly. But star players? It cannot be done."'

The comments were ill-timed, coming as they did on the day of the memorial service for those who died in the disaster. It was a no for Pilkington, though the *Daily Express* suggested that all was not lost with Murphy's scouting mission – Reg Pearce, the Luton left-half, was apparently a target for United, as well as Sunderland. '(Former Luton boss Jack) Crompton can confirm that Pearce is United material – one of the few wing halves in Britain even approaching the stature of Duncan Edwards, now fighting for his life in a Munich hospital,' they reported.

Bill Holden for the *Daily Mirror* reported that it was the coincidental timing of Luton's trip to Turf Moor which alerted Murphy to the thought of bringing Crompton back. 'When Luton's game against Burnley is over this afternoon,

MUNICH

he (Crompton) will hurry to Manchester to talk over United's plans with assistant manager Jimmy Murphy for the match on Wednesday. Then all United players will go to Blackpool on Monday for special training. Luton chairman Percy Mitchell wrote to United offering any help his club could give after the tragic air crash. On his return from Germany, Murphy asked if Crompton was available. The deal was arranged in Manchester where Luton are staying before the Burnley match.'

At the same time, a trial was being run at the Cliff. Young players from the Federation of Youth clubs and the Manchester and District clubs were given an opportunity to impress; of the many that turned out, only 18-year-old John Barker was recruited.

In the days before United were due to play Sheffield Wednesday, Jimmy took the players to Blackpool in order to escape the enormous press scrutiny. Obviously, the press followed, but at least Murphy was in comfortable surroundings.

"Such was the fervour in Manchester itself I had, on the chairman's instructions, to keep the players for long periods out of the way at Blackpool, away from the crowds, away from the feverish anxiety in the city," he said.

Most of the squad – even including the new players who were to be brought in – stayed at the Norbreck for six weeks. For the players left behind in Manchester, it created a clear distinction between the players who would be expected to play. "I didn't go to Blackpool, I was part of the group that was left behind, but we didn't mind, we just got on with it, we knew Jimmy was doing what he had to," said Jimmy Elms. "We didn't think he would go out and buy anyone at first. We all thought we'd get a chance. In one of the newspapers it even said that I was playing. You get excited and obviously then you get disappointed when you realise you won't be playing. It was obvious that for some of us,

JIMMY MURPHY

including me, it was much too soon, and Jimmy did the best thing for the club. I don't think I would have been ready for it."

Foulkes said he felt it was a great decision. "It was imperative to me that I escape the emotional, near-hysterical atmosphere which had built up in Manchester, and although nothing could put the world to rights, Jimmy Murphy offered the best solution possible by taking the fit senior players, plus a collection of youngsters, away to the Norbreck Hotel in Blackpool to prepare somehow for the immediate future," he said.

When the time came to deliver press conferences, there were unfamiliar faces. Alf Clarke and Tom Jackson, the local reporters for the *Chronicle* and *Evening News*, had perished in Munich. So too had Archie Ledbrooke of the *Mirror*, and Frank Swift, the former Manchester City goalkeeper, of the *News of the World*. David Meek assumed the responsibilities of Tom Jackson. The biggest blow for Jimmy was the loss of George Follows, a reporter he considered a genuine friend.

"It was a time that effected everyone," says Jimmy Jr. "David Meek had been a political writer for the *MEN* and had to cover sports after the disaster. He says he cannot go to a swimming pool or sports club without thinking of my father, as Dad used to hold his interviews and conferences with the press at the indoor pool at the Norbreck Hyrdo in Blackpool. The smell of chlorine, David says, was something he forever associated with Dad.

"He says Jimmy was very good with the press. That wasn't the man I knew! The man I knew didn't like the press; that's why the family find it so funny that the building named after my father at Carrington is the one used by the press."

Jimmy may have usually shunned the limelight; he may have hated the idea of speaking with the press. Now, however, he understood it was part of his short-term responsibility, though it stands to reason that his cordial and friendly attitude would probably have been down to the fact that he had bigger problems to worry about. He would avoid most reporters when he saw them at the bar, but, he remained close with Arthur Walmsley. Walmsley had served in India, and so he and Jimmy had common ground; in fact, he became something of a confidante, as Jimmy, unable to sleep, would often take a bottle of whiskey into his friend's room and they would drink until sunrise and talk about their love of different sports, and music, in particular. Despite the comfort in this company, Jimmy later confessed how isolated he felt. "You don't realise, I went through hell," he said. "I came back (from Munich) and had no-one to talk to really…There were plenty of people around, but nobody to talk to about soccer."

Murphy's late-night hotel room visits would become the source of rich anecdotes; young reporter Keith Dewhurst recalled many a night spent in Jimmy's room, while various players and officials of the time spoke with fondness about the time Jimmy had got a hold of them and stayed up all night talking sport.

"We went to one of the former player dinners at Old Trafford in April 2017 where we got talking to Doctor McHugh," Jimmy's grandson Paul said. "He told me this story about them going to Denmark and Granddad knocked on his room at 10pm, inviting himself in with a bottle of whiskey. They talked for hours, drinking and smoking, and Doc McHugh said, 'It's getting a bit smoky in here' so opened the curtains – it was daylight! He spoke to one of the other doctors who said, 'You made a bleeding mistake there – always go to his room, because then at least you can leave!'"

With Bob Lord's words no doubt ringing in his ears (as they would again in a short time), and the welcome isolation of Blackpool, Murphy worked on a strategy alongside Joe Armstrong, Jack Crompton, Bert Inglis and Arthur Powell. How best to move forward? How best to repair the damage? What had gone which could not be replaced? What remained and could not be destroyed?

The answer to the latter question was easy. The bond Murphy had established with his young players was something Manchester United had benefitted from in their wonderful successes. In tragic circumstances, the bond between him and the perished players was frozen in time. The unity that it created for those who were back in Manchester was profound. All were grieving, all were devastated, but all, like Murphy, were running on adrenalin. "Keep the flag flying," Matt had told Jimmy.

Jimmy had motivation and purpose. He didn't ask for this responsibility. He didn't want it. Nor did the players. But they had an inspiration greater than that which could have been provided by any number of professional ambitions. In the end, it wasn't even a choice; this emotionally charged response was the only way Manchester United could survive.

"More than anything, victory for the club was carrying on at all," says McGuinness. "The lads who had died were in our thoughts, it was pointless trying to pretend otherwise, so the best thing we could do was use them as inspiration to play on and achieve the best results we could. Jimmy would say, 'Let's go out and give everything for the lads we lost!' and by embracing it, it helped us get on with things. We were in our own cloud so I suppose it would be difficult for us as young players and young men to have the behaviour of others at the forefront of our mind, but from my recollections, I didn't notice much of a change in Jimmy after the disaster.

"Of course, I'd lost my best pal, Eddie Colman, and the person I was understudy to, Duncan – my thoughts were on the lads we lost and especially those two. He never messed about, he wouldn't say things that weren't true, and you'd get the truth from him and deal with it. He was the best man to stand in for Matt after the tragedy."

Murphy resolved to protect his players at all cost. Here was a man who was already defensive of the young boys he had helped develop into young men, young superstars; he didn't need a lesson in how to conduct himself in that regard. Protection also meant isolation from the media, as much as possible. It meant staying in Blackpool as often as possible in order to increase that sense of communal spirit and resolve.

Resolve was the key word. Survival another. Manchester United prepared for their game against Sheffield Wednesday without any expectation of victory; they didn't even know who would be in their team.

Two days before the game, Murphy took a moment to be frank with the press. "It could hardly be tougher," he admitted. "But then, that's what we have become accustomed to."

Murphy made contact that day (February 17th) with Aston Villa, telephoning them to enquire about Stan Crowther, wing-half. Meanwhile, Jackie Henderson turned down a move to Newcastle, despite repeating his desire to move away from Portsmouth. He was keen to fan the flames of a move to United. "Naturally you could not refuse to go to a club like that," he said.

The evening before the game, Jimmy went from Blackpool to Old Trafford for another meeting with the directors. Transfer plans were discussed, and the topic of the Munich Memorial Fund – to help those affected – was raised. It was after 10pm that Jimmy left the boardroom, to meet reporters waiting outside. "Keep fit you boys," he joked. "I may need one or two of you tomorrow."

On the morning of the game, United's line-up was still not

JIMMY MURPHY

certain. Reg Pearce did what Ernie Taylor didn't, and chose Sunderland instead.

'United assistant manager Jimmy Murphy, who is hunting for players even more desperately than (Sunderland manager Alan) Brown, was hurt by Pearce's refusal to help out the crash-shattered club,' reported journalist Harry Langton. 'But last night Murphy switched to his second-choice left hand – Stan *The Shy Man* Crowther, the England Under-23 cap from Aston Villa. Like Luton, Villa put the question to Crowther: "Will you help United?" and last night Crowther, who starred against them in last year's Cup Final, was considering his answer…

'Worried Manchester United directors talked for four hours last night and still were unable to name their team. Their two top problems are left half and outside-left. Duncan Edwards is seriously ill in Germany and deputy left-half Wilf McGuinness is out with cartilage trouble…If Crowther says "yes" today, United will seek special permission to break the cup-tie and 14-day qualification rules so that he can play tonight. United made one decision – Billy Foulkes, England right-back, becomes the new captain. He may lead out this team: *Gregg, Foulkes, Greaves, Goodwin, Cope, A.N.Other, Webster, Taylor, Dawson, Pearson, Hunter.* United hope to name the definite line-up at lunchtime today.'

Gregg spoke to the press to give a rallying cry ahead of the emotional event. "Out we go tonight on to the Old Trafford pitch for the first match since Munich," he said. "Can we win? I think so. But there are far more important things on the minds of everyone at Old Trafford than forecasting.

"The main job we will be out to do tonight is to show the world that Manchester United will rise again, that we are determined with all our hearts to see that new ambition come true. We not only have to play our hearts out, as we shall do. We older and more experienced players have to set an example. That we are determined to do. And I regard tonight's cup tie against Sheffield Wednesday as a memorial to those boys we so well remember. I am sure that is what it is going to be. And I am sure that goes top for the youngsters who will be stepping out tonight in the red shirts that carry the battle honours of many a far-flung soccer field.

"Since my return home I have had the chance to know better these boys who now carry the banner of Manchester United. I can tell you that in such players as Alec Dawson, Mark Pearson, and in all of them, I find the great enthusiasm, pride and spirit of determination that took United to the heights. Whatever the result tonight they will send a message to manager Matt Busby that will help him on his way to recovery."

The programme for the game against Sheffield Wednesday has its place in history for the sombre blank team listing in the middle (rarer, and perhaps more sombre still, is that programme for the postponed game against Wolverhampton Wanderers from February 8th, listing a team which of course included a number of players who perished in Munich. Only a few were printed). The programme did include a bold headline on its front page. 'UNITED WILL GO ON...' while inside it says 'Our thoughts are constantly with those who still lie in Munich... among them is our dear manager, Matt Busby, and we know that his first concern is always for his players...we recall his words to Jimmy Murphy (assistant manager): "Glad to see you Jimmy, how are the lads? Look after them for me."'

The team that eventually took to the field included, miraculously, Harry Gregg and Bill Foulkes. Ian Greaves, who had been kept out of the Central League by Peter Jones, was in the eleven.

Alex Dawson, the striker from the Youth Cup team for who the word prolific seemed a huge understatement, was thrust into the responsibility of leading the line. Mark Pearson, the equally fantastic player from the previous season's FA Youth Cup success, was given his first team debut without even a handful of Central League games under his belt.

Murphy had been wise with Pearson's and Dawson's footballing education. These two players were destined to be Manchester United stars. They should not have been forced to bear this responsibility. When people assess the damage that Munich did to Manchester United, the impact it had on those back in Salford is often understated. United's long term prospects were sorted. Under Busby's guidance, the Babes would have continued to shine, and the reserve players would be given their opportunity when they were ready. It had already worked that way for five years. But just as their present was destroyed in the crash, much of their future would become burned out by the exposure. Too much, too soon. This was no fault of their own; lesser boys – and that's what they were – would have completely wilted under the pressure. They may not have become the Manchester United legends that their potential projected but the significant role that they played in the club's history is as important as any other and their contribution over the coming weeks after Munich was worthy of being lauded as heroic.

Colin Webster, another kid being given a chance in daunting circumstances, agrees with the point. "Through the circumstances of the crash, these lads were pushed much too quickly into action for the first team and believe me, it was hectic action and very physical in the games following Munich," he said.

In came Webster, Freddie Goodwin, and Ronnie Cope. Ernie Taylor would hopefully provide the experienced head, though

MUNICH

even he would surely struggle on such an unprecedented occasion. Stan Crowther, now he had agreed to join and his clearance had come through, would be there to assist. "I am not keen about leaving the Midlands, but any offer from Manchester United is worth thinking about," the Villa wing-half had said.

On the morning of the game, the United incumbent-manager had a conversation with young Shay Brennan to inform him he would be playing. Brennan was called to see Jimmy at 10.30am.

"I thought he wanted to give me a telling off because I had been seen out in Blackpool the previous night for a couple of pints," Shay said. "I was stunned when I was told I was playing…we went to Davyhulme Golf Club for a pre-match steak and then to Old Trafford. Everyone was just lost in their own thoughts in the dressing room. There are always jokers in a football changing room but nobody was laughing or larking about."

Aside from the fact that Jimmy had a bond with all of his players, he and young Brennan weren't particularly close before this point. Nor were they the best of friends after, really. However, they now shared a bond in the grief and tragedy they were experiencing together. Some years later, the pair would share another emotional moment.

Murphy met Crowther and Villa manager Eric Houghton at Queens Hotel in Manchester at 5pm. The clubs, in the meantime, had agreed a deal, and all that remained was for Jimmy to convince the youngster to sign. "Mr Murphy told me why United wanted me," said Crowther. "In fact, the way he put it, they needed me. He said I could help them start the long climb back…eventually Mr Murphy persuaded me to sign. When I'd done so, I looked at the clock. It was nearly 6.30pm and the match was due to start in an hour."

Crowther's last-minute arrival meant disappointment for Bob

English; English hadn't even been in the Central League game yet was in consideration. "Going back to Manchester on the coach I did think I had a good chance of playing," he said. "Shay Brennan was my best friend at the club at that time and our wives were friends and we both had young children. Shay had a dream game and never looked back – my story was quite the opposite."

After the anxiety and grief of the previous two weeks, Manchester United were ready to play football again.

"Very soon it was clear that Jimmy Murphy, and everyone else at the club, needed one thing to happen more than anything," said Bobby Charlton. "They needed another match, some sense of continuity, some belief that, however haltingly, the club was moving forward from the worst of the grief."

Gregg agreed. 'Jimmy was a tower of strength,' he said in his autobiography, noting that the request that he should play football as soon as he was able was the best thing for his sanity. 'Jimmy was a very fiery Welshman,' he later said. 'His language and mood was frightening. He could have started a war in a convent. I can remember the great Steve Richards, a fine writer. Every month, United would go away to a hotel for four days, and soon after the accident, Jimmy took us in Matt's absence. We were sat having dinner when Steve walked in and said: "Jimmy, could I have a few words? I don't want to disturb you but..." and Jimmy interrupted and said: "Well, what the fuck are you doing here then?!" And they were close friends! Jimmy could laugh with you, cry with you and fight with you...I believe the greatest thing to come out of the disaster was that Jimmy Murphy was with the Welsh team.'

At Davyhulme, as he approached for one final talk with the makeshift Manchester United side, Jimmy took a deep breath and prepared to deliver one of his sermons.

This time, however, he had intended to mimic Matt Busby, to give a calm and analytical view of Sheffield Wednesday. He couldn't do it. In the heat of the moment, he couldn't even bring himself to give a typical rousing Jimmy Murphy special, laying into the Yorkshire team, as no good footballing side had ever come from there, as he had been known to do in the past.

"Play hard for yourselves, play hard for the players who are dead, play hard for those still in hospital, and play hard for the great name of Manchester United!" he said, before emotion got the better of him and he had to stop. Jack Crompton then gave a hearty "Come on lads!" before leading them to get the bus to Old Trafford. Murphy gave a similar speech in the dressing room before kick-off. "I want you to get out there and now I've told you how to beat them, we are going to win this game for the lads, we're going to win it."

Charlton, arriving late to the stadium, sat alongside Murphy as the teams took to the field. The minute's silence before the game was one of the most emotionally charged moments in the entirety of the club's history, if not the most. The only sounds to break the silence were the sobs of those unable to contain their grief.

"Frankly I was astonished by the individual spirit and endeavour that swept us along on a tide of emotion," Murphy remarked about his team's performance. "The players chased every ball, ran themselves to a standstill until they scarcely had the strength to lift their legs after each game, and when they tackled they did so with fanatical zeal."

Manchester United won 3-0 – an early and a late goal from Brennan (his first coming direct from a corner kick), and a third from Alex Dawson six minutes from time, gave the team passage to the quarter-finals on an emotional night. Matt Busby will be proud to call the new Manchester United "MY TEAM"' wrote Frank McGhee for the *Daily Mirror*. 'That is the highest compliment I can pay to the side built on the shattered framework of the famous Busby Babes which played so brilliantly, so bravely, so wonderfully at Old Trafford last night.

'Their victory over Sheffield Wednesday in this fifth-round Cup-tie was more than just another football win. It was a memorial built with skill and courage to the men they mourn and the men who are still in hospital after the Munich disaster. It was all done in a fantastic atmosphere of emotion, drama, excitement and sympathy. This was a night when the only man in the ground who tried to be impartial was referee Alf Bond.

'Nearly 80,000 fans listened in silence as the quiet, unemotional voice read out the names of Manchester United's new team. But when he got to "NO. 6 STAN CROWTHER" there was a great roar from the crowd…but even that was nothing to the fantastic welcome the new United team received when they ran on to the field. It made Wembley Stadium seem like a whispering gallery.

'Although United's players were all heroes, the game provided its own extra special stars. And the brightest of them all was outside-left Seamus Brennan, 20, the boy with an Irish heart and the love of a fight. Outside-left is the position where United were hardest hit, but assistant manager Jimmy Murphy needn't bother now, Brennan is the man for the job.' McGhee also paid special tribute to Crowther. 'Surrounded by strangers, whom he has only known as rivals, he worked harder for United than he did against them in the Cup Final.'

Ernie Taylor did the job he was brought in to do – providing an older, experienced head to guide some of the pups around him, allowing Gregg and Foulkes (despite the latter being named captain) to lead by their prominent example.

MUNICH

Foulkes admitted that the evening had almost been too much for him. "The lads played their hearts out," he said. "They couldn't have given more. I like to think they did it all for our colleagues who died at Munich. I haven't cried since I was a kid, but I cried tonight." So too did Murphy, who was seen walking off the pitch with tears streaming down his face.

Journalist Terence Elliot interviewed Jimmy as he was walking out of the changing room after congratulating the players. "I have just been in tears in our dressing room," Jimmy said. "Because I've just seen something wonderful, which means more than the victory deservedly won.

"We have all been privileged to see the beginning of a great build-up. And now we know that the future has its sunshine. They were tears of joy. I have always said that enthusiasm plus ability can beat anything and this is the greatest day of my life, even after 30 years in football.

"I told the lads before the match: 'Play hard for the lads who have gone, for those who are still in hospital, and for the great name of Manchester United.' For the first time in my life I was not ashamed to find those tears of joy could not be forced back. Matt Busby would have been proud to see these youngsters."

Jimmy was able to use his *Manchester Evening News* column to pay tribute to the scratch side:

Manchester United are back in business…and I am the proudest man in soccer today. The way the boys rallied round and rose so superbly to the occasion against Sheffield Wednesday overwhelmed me. They pulled everything they had out of the bag. Some of the youngsters, who have never played for the first team before, performed like veterans.

Everyone gave of their best. But this was not a chase for personal

JIMMY MURPHY

glory. Your Cup team, the first to rise from the terrible horror of that crash of Munich, were not playing just for themselves. Always at the back of our minds, was the thought of friends once so alive and such fine soccer players, now alas, dead. Also in mind were the sports writers, including Tom Jackson of this newspaper, and the injured men still at Munich who we knew would be expecting much of us… not least the Boss, our dear manager Matt Busby.

The last round of the Cup was fought as a tribute to these people, and we are glad we did not let them down. But what happens now? How will United fare without the inspiration of such a dramatic atmosphere? Those of you who saw us play against Sheffield Wednesday will acknowledge, I hope, that we have some rare talent.

Shay Brennan, who made a sensational debut with two goals and thoroughly deserved them, is only 20, but the real "babe" of the present side is young Mark Pearson. He is 17, but plays ahead of his years. My main worry is the fear that we are bringing these youngsters into League football too fast – but at the moment what else can I do? I know I have had to push two or three of them ahead of their time, and can only hope that the experience doesn't harm their careers.

It is one thing blooding a youngster into a team of experienced men, but quite different to promote a batch of them into faster football, which is liable to upset their natural game. However, Manchester United is fortunate to have this kind of reserve talent. I say fortunate, but really, you know, there is no luck about it.

For although Matt Busby never anticipated a catastrophe like Munich, he always planned ahead and strove to build up a young Central League side who could play for the first team, an "A" team treading on the heels of the Central team, and so on. Now in the real hour of need Matt's policy has paid off and thanks to the years of careful grooming by people like my good friend Bert Whalley,

MUNICH

Manchester United will live on. I am still looking for one or two of the type of players who will fit in with the Old Trafford style of play, but at least we have reserves who will bridge the gap and might even make permanent first-team berths.

So I salute the Boss and hope he is soon back with us. There is a big job of reconstruction ahead and that is our target now. Happily we have rejoining us an old friend – indeed a player for 13 years with us – Jack Crompton. In the desperate hours when I realised that it fell to me and the few club officials spared from the disaster to keep United going, I thought of Jack, who left us 18 months ago to become chief trainer and coach to Luton.

During his stay there Luton have lifted themselves from the dangers of relegation to a place among the leaders of Division 1 – and it's my best Jack can take a fair share of the credit. Training has never been more important than now and it is in good hands again.

Teamwork at Old Trafford begins in the office and we are all dedicated to rebuilding the club. It would have been impossible to carry on without the efficiency of Les Olive, the acting secretary, Joe Armstrong, who is always doing a million jobs at once, Miss Alma George, who has tackled cheerfully the mountains and correspondence and all the others in an ever willing band of volunteers who rallied to United's help.

Finally, I would like to thank the hundreds of kind folk who have written to Old Trafford either letters of sympathy or later messages of congratulations on our Cup win. There are too many to answer, but every letter is deeply appreciated. We shall do our best to make United the GREATEST club in British football AGAIN – out of respect for the memory of past club-mates who would want us, I am sure, to do just that.'

*****

JIMMY MURPHY

Two days after the win, Manchester United were rocked by the news that Duncan Edwards had lost his battle for life.

The news shook Murphy and all of the players, not just because it was Duncan, but because of everything Duncan's fight was beginning to represent. Here was a young man whose courage had now transcended sport and had become a national hope; Duncan Edwards was Manchester United. He had survived and so could the club. But no longer. Charlton described the news as unbearable.

Murphy was still working late into the night at Old Trafford. His mind had been temporarily taken by annoyance at some of the pressmen labelling the boys who had overcome Sheffield Wednesday 'Murphy's Marvels'. He took umbrage with it because he insisted that the man who was the architect of the recovery was still fighting for his life in Munich. It was Busby, Jimmy said, who laid the outline of the youth policy, and it was Matt Busby's foresight which Jimmy was staying faithful to which had proved to be triumphant on the most emotional of occasions.

Shortly after 1.26am on the morning of February 21st, 1958, Jimmy received the telephone call that well and truly knocked any regained wind from his sails. Again, he found himself inconsolable in the early hours.

Murphy had hoped against hope; prayed against all reason that Edwards would not only recover, but be the figurehead around which Manchester United would rebuild their side. He was the symbol of hope; and now, not even the fact that Jimmy believed lesser men may not have fought for as long as Duncan did was enough to give him respite.

For 24 hours Jimmy had held on to that bittersweet victory against Sheffield Wednesday and cruelly even that narrow, thin slice of happiness had been taken from him.

MUNICH

Manchester United had lost a great footballer. Murphy had lost one of his dearest friends, and, just as tragic, a young man he had helped develop into a fine human being; the man who, upon seeing a nervous Nobby Stiles, took his autograph book and passed it around the team. Murphy was not a man for predictions and did not like to speculate, particularly about the dead. But, even at the age of 21, he had seen enough to declare Duncan Edwards the greatest. "This news is the final blow," Jimmy told the press.

Duncan's would be yet another funeral he had to attend. Accompanied by Charlie Stiles, their sons Nobby and Phil would be altar boys at the funerals back in Manchester. These were distressing times which seemed as if they were unrelenting.

*****

Phil Murphy had just had his 18th birthday and found himself suddenly called into help his father at the club.

Phil was a local footballer but he himself admitted he was not ready for the demands of playing for United; he felt he was drafted in because he had a good knowledge of local football that Jimmy could call upon if more players were needed.

"My brother Phil was called into the B team because they didn't have any players," says Jimmy Jr. "He was at Manchester Boys and had played with Nobby Lawton. He wasn't the greatest player but United needed bodies. That's a funny thing about Dad, and the people he surrounded himself with in those difficult days…they might not have been the best, but they were nice people, generous people, real characters. Those were the kind of people Dad liked because he knew they would give their all to the cause. Later on he had a real fondness for Nobby Stiles and that's what I mean, really, Nobby wasn't the best player but he had a commitment, a dedication and a perseverance which endeared him to Dad. He'd go through a bloody brick wall for Dad, he was all heart."

Phil would play alongside Nobby in the B team. Johnny Giles was also in the side. In the post-Munich days they suffered confidence-crushing defeats such as a 5-0 loss to Stockport County. Jimmy, who had the responsibility for picking all of the sides at the club, now found his biggest selection headache was actually getting enough players to make a side that could turn out for the Central League.

It meant Bob English getting a call up to that level, while Johnny Giles also made his debut at that level in the aftermath of Munich. And still, getting eleven players for the first team was a struggle.

All of the team who played against Sheffield Wednesday had been outstanding in their courage but Ronnie Cope stood out more than most; he, and the other star man, Brennan, had picked up slight niggles, but both declared that nothing was going to stop them playing against Nottingham Forest in the next league game a few days later. Pearson suffered a bruised foot on his debut but he too was not going to give up his place. This was a tremendous boost for Jimmy, who was able to name an unchanged side.

The Forest game was a similarly emotional affair to the Wednesday one. The decision had to be taken to open up the gates much earlier than usual because of the amount of people gathering at Old Trafford. The stadium was full by 2.30pm. A short service dedicated to those who had lost their lives preceded the game before a tremendous roar from the 66,123 inside the ground greeted the players onto the pitch. Forest took a first half lead, but in the 75th minute, Dawson scored to earn his team a point.

The 1-1 result was another commendable achievement for Murphy; after the game, he was told that Kenny Morgans and Dennis Viollet felt well enough to return to Manchester. A boost in one sense, though, they had been told in no uncertain terms that their injuries would prevent them from playing for the rest of the season.

One player who was back from Munich and ready to play was Bobby Charlton. United had been drawn to play at West Brom in the quarter-final of the FA Cup and the club were keen to get Charlton some practice beforehand. On Monday, February 24th, Bob Pennington reported for the *Express* that Charlton had declared himself fit. 'Lance-Corporal Bobby Charlton, Manchester United crash survivor, will plead with his Army medical officer this week for permission to make his come-back in two Cup ties within four days. Charlton will return to his battalion in time to play in the RAOC Cup Final, at Didcot, on Wednesday afternoon. Three days later he could line up for Manchester United in their quarter-final cup battle at West Bromwich.'

As it transpired, the Army game was postponed, which meant Charlton's condition could only be assessed in training. His form on a snow-covered pitch proved to United's officials that Charlton was ready but there was a shock when goalkeeper Harry Gregg dashed to hospital for an X-ray on his bruised right hand. The injury was caused when Gregg slipped in some dressing-room horseplay after the practice match. But Gregg returned with the news: "Nothing serious – they say I could play tomorrow if necessary."

Murphy knew it was important to build up strength in depth to deal with any eventuality. To address the problem in the Central League, Murphy had a solution that was certainly outside of the box in its thinking. He approached famous amateur side Bishop Auckland with a view to signing some of their experienced players. Name one was centre-half Bob Hardistry. Hardistry was known to Jimmy; when Busby had coached an Olympic team for Great Britain in 1948, Murphy did some coaching. "Matt, Jimmy and the late Tom Corry all helped us a great deal then," the 37-year-old Hardistry said. "It is good to be able to do something in return."

It was age and experience that Murphy had called for, in Hardistry and his team-mates Warren Bradley and Derek Lewin, who also made the move to Manchester. "I want you in the reserve team even if you just stand around prompting the youngsters," Murphy told Hardistry. And the Welshman told the press: "First I approached Bishop Auckland and their officials were kindness itself. Then I approached the players and their reactions were spontaneous. Grand chaps, all of them. I know they will be a great success with our youngsters, especially Bob Hardistry, an old and respected friend. And Derek Lewin is almost one of the United family, as he has trained with us so often."

With each positive step, though, so too came a blow. Busby finally started to feel slightly better but the hospital staff maintained their stance not to tell him about the disaster; until, that was, he asked a priest how Duncan Edwards was, and the priest, unable to lie, finally told him that his young player had died. He called for Jean; Jean was unable to tell her husband the names. Instead, he asked her to simply nod or shake her head as he spoke the names. He was told about what was happening back in Manchester; that the team had played against Sheffield Wednesday.

Immediately, Matt said he could not carry on. The guilt for him was too much.

MUNICH

In 1973 he said: "The inner voice kept on saying: 'If I had not taken them into Europe those eight Busby Babes and the other victims would be with us still.' And this was not all. The voice admonished: 'I should not have allowed the pilot to make that third attempt at take-off.'

"I was spared, but even if I survived how could I face the loved ones of the lads who were not spared? 'Was I to blame? Was I to blame? Why can't I die?'"

He felt the mental torture he was going through was even worse than the physical pain he was suffering. "I will never go back into football," he would say. This went on for weeks. Jean eventually told him that the boys who had lost their lives would want him to go on; he eventually decided that she was right.

For his part, Jimmy was also weighed down by incredible guilt. He was always haunted by the knowledge that he should have been on the plane, and that Bert had been sitting where he would have been.

Murphy later referred to just one phone call made by Jean – to relay a message from Matt.

"Tell Jimmy I'm delighted. Keep it up."

By then Manchester United had qualified for the FA Cup final; but, by the end of February, there were still some tumultuous weeks to go until that point.

CHAPTER | NINE

UNITED SPIRIT

"He can stick out his jaw and thump his massive fist into a hefty palm and insist: 'If you play for Manchester United you will NEVER shirk a tackle. You will ALWAYS chase a loose ball. No game is EVER considered lost. Get it? And never forget it'"

'MURPHY STEALS FANS' LOYALTY' wrote Bill Holden for the *Daily Mirror* after United's 2-2 FA Cup draw at the Hawthorns. 'Fists clenched, his teeth bared, Jimmy Murphy, current master of Manchester United, stood in the centre of the dressing room at West Bromwich and told his team: "Get out there and fight. Show 'em we don't need any sympathy. Go and win!" And they almost did.

'The brilliant battles these Manchester players are putting up are entirely due to the energetic genius of Murphy, the little Welshman who has worn the Matt Busby mantle since the Munich disaster. He has fashioned a team, which must still be feared, and he is using every trick a lifetime in soccer has taught him. Murphy's tactics began before the game. He took the youngsters out on to the pitch and, waving his hands, made a show of introducing them to the ground. This was their first away match, and he made the 58,000 crowd realise it. Showmanship. But it worked. It sent a buzz of sympathy through the crowd. Then Murphy waited until Albion had taken the field before sending out United. They were greeted with a shattering, deafening roar. From that moment Albion felt as if THEY were playing away.'

One newspaper report said Murphy described the show as "the greatest performance in the history of Manchester United." If it was emotional hyperbole, well, others were buying into it. The game was regarded by *Daily Express* reporter Desmond Hackett as 'The greatest game I have seen.'

Bobby Charlton had an immediate impact, avoiding two rough challenges and showing calmness of mind to provide an assist for Ernie Taylor. The Baggies equalised but Alex Dawson scored just before the interval to send United went in to the half-time break with a 2-1 advantage.

'The second half had United chief Jimmy Murphy covering his eyes in agony as West Bromwich battled with a Wembley brand of courage,' Hackett wrote.

West Brom did get a late equaliser to earn a replay but it seemed as if the change in the calendar from February to March ignited a change in Murphy. Indeed, he reacted angrily when interviewed by Hackett afterwards. 'Jimmy Murphy, the inspired baby-sitter at Matt Busby's creche of wonder babes, is angry', he wrote. 'He is tired, sick tired, of all the talk that Manchester United are trading on the cruel disaster that still saddens every true sporting heart. He is wearied of the innuendos about sympathy for the opposition, of stupid talk that every team that has to take on Manchester United will get no cheers for beating 'a shadow team'.

'In this time of anguish and anger Jimmy Murphy has my sympathy. Jimmy Murphy is a Welshman with the Irish name and a battling defiant spirit to match. He does not like one bit the brutally emphasised opinion that Manchester United fans are suffering from mass hysteria, that they are behaving like those groaning morons who idolise whichever skiffle hero happens to be the noise of the moment.

'Jimmy Murphy told me: "I am not like Matt Busby. Matt could keep quiet even when I knew he was really wild. I cannot keep quiet when I see and hear the players and now the supporters made the victims of cheap criticisms and ridicule. The Manchester United fans have shared our successes. They have been the proudest supporters in the country. Of course they stuck out their chests and boasted that they belonged to Manchester United. We had the good fortune to give them something to boast about. I hope we will be able to carry on making them proud and noisily proud."

'Jimmy Murphy could have said a whole heap more…Nobody has insisted more firmly than Manchester United that they should be permitted to get on with the game and not live on beloved legends or the golden glory of their triumphs…Matt Busby would be proud of his new football fledglings. He would be proud because his great helpmate Jimmy Murphy, the man who refused the highest offices in soccer to stay at Old Trafford, has not pleaded for tears or talent. Perhaps, most of all, he would be proud of his beloved fans. I hope to watch Manchester United replay against West Bromwich on Wednesday night. And I hope that those fans will stand up and cheer like hell.'

Jimmy took some time in his *Evening News* column to emotionally praise the wonderful, mature work done by Ernie Taylor since arriving in such difficult circumstances. 'We don't like picking out individuals at Old Trafford because Manchester United has always been essentially a team – and will always continue, I hope, to put the emphasis on teamwork,' he wrote. 'Ernie Taylor's arrival, however, has been exceptional. He came in our hour of need and the marvellous way in which he has settled down with us shows, I think, that the boys were glad to see him.

'Ernie has been a *natural* at Old Trafford. He plays the type of football we like. With so many youngsters coming into the first team together, it is important that there is someone able to help them playing the right brand of soccer. And anyone who has seen Taylor's careful working of the ball and watched him spraying defence-splitting passes in our last two games will know that he plays football and is no kick-and-run player.

'I also reckon that Stan Crowther was a good buy. This England under-23 half-back is playing himself into the United side with great care, and will soon be a firm favourite at Old Trafford. It was heart-warming the way that Stan joined us too. He was not particularly keen to leave the Midlands – yet in our plight and search for experienced players, he said he would come to Manchester. But then the spirit at Old Trafford has always been something out of this world. The boys have pulled together magnificently. Everything I have asked of them has been met with keenness. When I asked Bobby Charlton to play on the left wing in today's match – which meant a switch from inside right, the position in which he was fast becoming an England prospect – he said: "I will play anywhere you want."

'Another example of Manchester's spirit...I heard when we were at Blackpool Shay Brennan assuring David Meek (the new *Manchester Evening News* United reporter) that United was a great club. Yet this was at the time when I had to tell Shay that Charlton would be playing in his place on the left wing. How many other players would have smiled after scoring two goals in a vital cup game, and then been told that he was being dropped? That is United's spirit for you.'

Supporters turned up in their droves for the replay – a more than capacity crowd were in the stadium and it was estimated that more than thirty thousand more were locked outside. Colin Webster's goal, which secured a 1-0 win one minute from time, sent the home faithful into delirium. "The boys played magnificently," a proud Murphy told the press afterwards. In fairness to him, despite his anger, he had stated he felt a draw from the first game was a fair result. News filtered through to Matt Busby, still convalescing in Munich. Busby had requested that the doctor be late with his nightly sleeping injection so he could learn the result as it happened. "Bang on – wonderful!" he told goalkeeper Alf Wood, who had informed him of the result.

United's victory meant their logic-defying success in this most harrowing of periods remained the story of the country and suddenly the man at the centre of it all – a man who had hitherto taken a welcome back seat – was now finally receiving some well-deserved recognition.

'Jimmy Murphy was the eternal, inspired backroom-boy, the superb supporting cast to the football factory they call Old Trafford,' Hackett wrote in his *Express* column on March 7th. 'That was all 46-year-old Jimmy Murphy wanted to be, just the foreman at the football factory. He was the man in the tracksuit. He turned boys into soccer men.

'Jimmy Murphy had no time for the posed pleasantries and diplomacy of the boardroom, but now, as the man who salvaged the wreckage of a shattered team and moulded them into defiant unbeatables he has to appear in what he calls 'the drawing room'. He endures the back-slaps and the hearty handshakes that are

JIMMY MURPHY

part of the parade of success, but this forthright man Murphy almost hisses as an aside – "Yes, and they would be the first to turn their backs if you flopped."

'That is Murphy the realist. Murphy the Welshman with an Irish name and an Irish fighting fury to match. It was Jimmy Murphy who stored up the treasury of talent that is keeping Manchester United on the glory way. His chief and his friend, Matt Busby, relied upon Jimmy. If Murphy said "sign" then a player was signed. And he watched his nursery of soccer starlets with a mother's devotion and sergeant major's discipline. After all, he was wartime Sergeant Murphy of the Royal Artillery. He can stick out his jaw and thump his massive fist into a hefty palm and insist: "If you play for Manchester United you will NEVER shirk a tackle. You ALWAYS chase a loose ball. No game is EVER considered lost. Get it? And never forget it.'"

Jimmy took to the press to express just how special the game against West Brom had been. He said: "I don't mind admitting I'm flattered to hear the new Manchester United described as 'Murphy's Marvels'. But let's keep a sense of proportion. They're marvels all right, as their tremendous displays since Munich have shown the football world – but they were not made overnight by Murphy.

"I'm no soccer magician. I couldn't even have started to pick up the pieces after the terrible air disaster if Manchester United had not had the richest reservoir of young talent in English soccer. What other club could have carried on in the face of what happened at Munich? Seventeen players out of action, eight of them, tragically, for ever. And ten of the 17 were internationals.

"Yet United have not only carried on, but, as everyone knows, the youngsters have written a page of glory almost without parallel in the history of sport. I like to think I have helped – but believe me,

UNITED SPIRIT

it is really a stupendous triumph for Manchester United's youth policy at Old Trafford, the system that has kept us in the football forefront since the war. For years now we have concentrated on grooming our own youngsters. The management have always been just as concerned about the progress of the fourth and fifth teams as of the league side. We have not hesitated to promote likely lads, however young, and they have seldom let us down. But never has youth been asked to shoulder such responsibility as in the past four weeks. And never has it responded so magnificently!

"Before Munich, we had a First Division-class Central League side, which included no fewer than six capped players. Injuries were no problem. But afterwards, we had to pitchfork THIRD-team players into the electric atmosphere of Cup football – and play them OUT of position!

"Frankly, before that wonderful night, I didn't know where to start. The terrific shock, the journey to Munich with the players' relatives, the horror of seeing these poor boys over there – all took their toll. It was ten days of sheer hell which I pray never to experience again, and which at times made me feel I was losing my sanity. There were so many demands on my time – and so little time. I should have liked to stay over in Germany, but my great friend Matt Busby made me realise the show must go on.

"I have been astonished by the fantastic spirit and individual endeavour that has swept them into the FA Cup semi-final. In a lifetime of football, I have never seen anything like the performance that overcame one of the country's finest footballing sides, West Bromwich, in the 180th minute of an unforgettable Cup clash. These young gladiators have exceeded all expectations – and it is to them that the credit must go. I'm proud of every mother's son of them. I'm proud, too, of the fans who have cheered them on. Their incredible vocal support has almost willed the team to victory, and all I ask is: 'Keep in good voice.' Remember that teenagers need all the encouragement they can get on the field.

"'And I take my hat off to the Old Trafford backroom boys who have kept everything ticking over smoothly in the face of colossal difficulties. That goes for trainer Jack Crompton, thrilled to bits to be back on his old stomping ground, and doing an excellent job with long-serving Bill Inglis. It goes for acting secretary Les Olive, who has worked 14 hours a day since the disaster, and for Miss George, who has worn her fingers to the bone at the typewriter. I'm not forgetting our chief scout, 'Uncle Joe' Armstrong, whose helping hand has been turned in every direction, nor the numerous old stalwarts who rushed voluntarily to our assistance. Everyone has rallied round."

After a short absence, Murphy was able to resume his own column in the *Evening News*. He wrote: 'This week I have written a long letter to Matt Busby – and my word haven't I had something to tell him about,' he said. 'I'm glad we have managed to do well for Matt's sake. It will be a great tonic for him, because he was devoted to Manchester United. In spite of the overwhelmingly tragic end of so many fine players he will be glad to know that we are still in the game and that United lives on. If it is going to help restore Matt to good health all the struggles at Old Trafford will be well worth while. The glamour and excitement of striving for Wembley count for nothing: If only we can have the Boss fit again! He is getting the best possible medical attention at the Rechts des Isar Hospital, Munich, but we at Old Trafford can help I am sure by seeing that the club he worked so hard to make great survives this most dreadful air crash.

'Perhaps we shall even win success again before long. Reaching the cup semi-finals shows we mean business and indicates the tremendous determination of the boys who have responded by giving their all for United. West Bromwich are a fine side – the hardest to beat in the country. They gave us two hard and sporting games, and despite seeing their cup hopes snatched from them in the last seconds of Wednesday's game their players were the first to come into the dressing-room to wish us all the best.'

For the third time in eight days, United faced West Brom, this time in the league on Saturday, March 8th. The game was preceded by an announcement over the public address system by Matt Busby, giving an update on his condition, praising the work of the doctors in Germany and also the team for their efforts. Unsurprisingly, you could have heard a pin drop as that Scottish drawl – weakened, but, unmistakably that of Matt Busby – echoed around Old Trafford.

Vic Buckingham had spoke of heavy score-lines ahead of these games and his words were finally prophetic; the Baggies hitting four goals without reply against the beleaguered Reds, who had been handicapped beyond their already perilous position when Ernie Taylor was forced off for a significant period in the first half. It was the first on-pitch setback since the disaster and probably the first time that United were forced to realise that adrenalin alone was not going to be enough to sustain a First Division Championship challenge. Murphy continued his work that week, signing Tommy Heron, a 21-year-old Scottish left sided defender who showed plenty of promise; he was a player who fitted the United profile in any event.

On March 14th, Murphy trekked to London to see semi-final opponents Fulham play at Leyton Orient. Fulham won 3-1 but barely had to break sweat. 'And that other distinguished guest, Manchester United's acting chief, Jimmy Murphy, had seen little to guide his planning for the cup semi-final against Fulham a week tomorrow…But Murphy, the fox of Old Trafford, was not one to be fooled by this deceptive match. "The dry pitch, high wind and light ball made it difficult for the players and difficult for me," he told me in a boardroom huddle. "But there was still a lot of good football,'" reported Bob Pennington.

The day after, United played at Burnley. Following the angry comments by Clarets' chairman Bob Lord about the supposed interest in winger Brian Pilkington, and given the locality, this fixture was always likely to threaten to be the one which exposed the bitterness which existed in certain circles and was beginning to bubble to the surface.

United were certainly fired up for an aggressive game and gave as good as they got. Burnley forward Alan Shackleton went in aggressively on Harry Gregg, who dropped the ball after making what was described by Derek Wallis of the *Daily Mirror* as a 'wonder save'. Gregg swung around to Shackleton with fists raised but was only warned by the referee. It set the tone for a bad-tempered first half and Mark Pearson was sent off for 'scything' Les Shannon minutes after Stan Crowther was booked. After half-time, Shannon attempted to exact his own retribution with a strong challenge on Bobby Charlton, yards from the touchline where the trainers were sitting. Murphy, Pearson and Crompton jumped off the bench to remonstrate and were given a 'wagging warning finger' by referee E.S. Oxley. United were a goal down by this point, and conceded two more to record a heavy 3-0 loss.

Before the cup replay against West Bromwich Albion, United had been involved – by virtue of the fact that the Babes' result in Belgrade had achieved qualification – in the draw for the semi-finals of the European Cup. Due to the circumstances, no draw was made, and it was decided that United would face the winners of the tie between Borussia Dortmund and AC Milan, who played in cities United could reach by train, boat and road. If this seemed like the logical decision, it didn't go down well with some.

And Burnley chairman Lord now fanned the flames with an undignified slam at United's approach, saying the players were 'running around like Teddy boys', and telling reporters that if United continued to be 'allowed' to play as they were, it would have an impact on the sport itself. "Let this lot run roughshod, and it could upset the whole of organised football," he said. "It looks as if they don't like losing. If Manchester United continue to play like this, they'll lose the sympathy the public have for them. They must remember there are other clubs in football." Desmond Hackett of the *Express* had a considered response. 'If this did turn out to be the hate match that Mr. Lord insists it was, then he must take the blame for stirring up enmity between the players and the supporters. I firmly insist that Mr. Lord is talking cheap nonsense when he accuses Manchester United of being Teddy boys.'

Murphy's public response was anger; however, one of his sons believes this was just the tonic he'd have wanted. "Dad would have enjoyed it when opponents and the press started giving United a bit of needle," Jimmy Jr says. "There were a few local clubs who seemed to resent the sympathy United got after the crash. If Dad would read in the build-up to games that opponents were going to beat us heavily, nothing would motivate him more."

"It was a shameful thing to say," Murphy said at a press conference after the game. "I take the strongest exception to these comments. I must defend my boys against such unwarranted and unworthy attacks." Perhaps understandably, Jimmy was a little more angry than even his initial post-match comments intimated, as Derek Wallis reported for the *Mirror*. 'Acting-manager Murphy, after a long talk with United chairman Harold Hardman at Old Trafford yesterday, told me: "This attack is totally unjustified and we take strong objection to the statement about the players behaving like Teddy boys. Had it not been for that, I would not have bothered to answer this outburst. It is a shocking thing – disgraceful coming from the chairman of a football club.

"I have been in football for thirty years and been on the losing end many times. After the Munich disaster, we did not expect to win a match. All we wanted to do was to keep the flag flying until the end of the season, when we could start to reconstruct. So the question of losing does not enter into it. Since Munich there have been no untoward incidents in any of our matches until now. They have all been played in a sportsmanlike manner."' Murphy later said: "I had to reply on behalf of the boys…I had to defend my players."

Harry Gregg went on to say that Murphy was incensed by the type of attention United were receiving. "He would speak to the press, but if their timing was wrong, if it interfered in him talking to his players, then that particular reporter could expect to be sent away with his ears ringing," he said. "It would be fair to say that Jimmy was anti-establishment and if Matt hadn't resumed control after Munich I reckon World War III would have broken out. If he'd had his way the only people allowed in the boardroom would have been the players."

Lord had suggested he intended to seek further action and he wasn't joking – two days later, Burnley sent a 'letter of protest' to the Football League, specifically about incidents involving Murphy from the weekend's game. 'One of the items on their *protest* agenda is an allegation about a heated scene between Mr.

Murphy and Burnley wing-half Les Shannon in the Burnley dressing-room immediately after the match,' Bob Pennington reported for the *Express* on March 19th.

'Murphy and Shannon were involved in an angry scene during the game. The ball went out of play and Shannon went to get it from the trainers' bench where Murphy was sitting with United's coach, Jack Crompton. There were heated words. Mr. Murphy, it is claimed, *stormed into the Burnley dressing-room* to continue the controversy.' Pennington wrote of how he spoke to Shannon, who remained silent, and also to Lord, who remained indignant.

"I stand by every word I said," Lord insisted. "Quite 80 per cent of the letters I have received are in complete agreement with my views. We at Burnley are as sympathetic as anyone else in football over the Munich crash, but if what you say is right, then you need have no fears about saying it."

Certainly, the mood in Manchester was bemused; why had their team, who had suffered the most terrible fate, suddenly become the victims of such vitriol?

"I remember being confused by it at the time," says Nick Murphy. "People can be dead jealous for the strangest of reasons, and for some reason you can see that sometimes even in today's game. It's as if there was a community that turned against the club. Commentators are critical about United and lenient against other teams that commit the same indiscretions. Marcus Rashford was criticised for diving against Swansea City and everyone went crazy; a day later two Liverpool players dived in the first ten minutes of their game and nobody said a word.

"I can't understand the double standards but I can imagine that Bob Lord going off the way he did was the best thing Dad could have hoped for. It was something that Dad could use for his team talks for the rest of the season."

JIMMY MURPHY

The Bob Lord controversy was a headache Murphy could have done without in preparation for the FA Cup semi-final agianst Fulham at Villa Park. Ernie Taylor was struggling to be fit with Ted Dalton, the 'magic-hands physiotherapist', working urgently on Ernie Taylor's injured leg. "He's all right. He can play," said Dalton.

United were in such short supply for players that the impatient Nobby Stiles was finally given a chance in the Youth Cup team; improbably, the Red Devils won 6-2, even without their star men Dawson and Pearson. Graham Smith – another debutant, and recent recruit – stole the show with the best goal of the game. This relatively minor moment in Manchester United history was the pinnacle for Smith, who had been nicknamed 'Sputnik' by Jimmy after he had hit a shot that went way over the crossbar.

Smith later revealed in Brian Hughes' *Starmaker – The Untold Story* how Murphy had instantly put him at ease when he joined the club. He said: "Jimmy told me how pleased he was that I had signed. This I found difficult to take in. Here was the assistant manager of one of the most famous clubs in the world, making the effort to spend time with a raw inexperienced, and as yet untried youngster."

Ahead of the senior side's game against Fulham, Jimmy used his *Evening News* column to update on the players who had travelled back with him from Germany – he had gone to accompany them on their return. 'I would like to welcome home Ray Wood, Dennis Viollet, and Albert Scanlon from Munich. Dennis has been doing some light training and Albert has been down to Old Trafford although one of his legs is still in plaster. I wish a speedy recovery and look forward to the day when the rest of our boys still at Munich come home. We are also all looking forward to that day when the Boss – Matt Busby – comes back."

United's performances had been understandably stuttering; on occasion, fuelled by emotion and sheer adrenalin, and others, like their most recent league games, disjointed and inconsistent. Journalist Malcolm Brodie, writing for the *Belfast Telegraph*, felt United's show against West Brom was from the latter category. "It was not the glorious United which defeated West Bromwich Albion in the sixth round," he said. "It was a mere skeleton of a once-great side."

Fulham player Johnny Haynes had said in his newspaper column on March 7th, 'Four months ago I walked off the Wembley pitch asking myself: "How does anyone beat a goalkeeper of Harry Gregg's class?" referring to a game where Northern Ireland defeated England by three goals to two. 'Now I am asking myself the question again – how to beat Gregg. We at Fulham have to find the answer if we hope to beat Manchester United in the Cup semi-final at Villa Park on March 22.

'I regard this game as my toughest task in two seasons as captain as Fulham. Any normal semi-final is tough. But this one isn't normal. All the sporting world – bar their opponents – are willing Manchester United on to Wembley and fresh glories. Only Fulham now stand between them and their goal. But we are determined to smash the Cup hopes of Manchester United – to become the villains of Villa Park, even though we risk the title *most hated club in soccer* for doing so.

'I am among the great admirers of United – the old and the new. I cheered when I heard they had beaten West Bromwich… [but] every player in every team is breaking his heart to get to Wembley and not one would dream of pulling out of a tackle on sentimental grounds. I can tell Manchester United that Fulham will pull no punches. I am sure Sheffield Wednesday and West Bromwich Albion didn't either.'

All of the semi-final action came inside a pulsating first half as Bobby Charlton scored twice – first to give United an early lead, and then to equalise just before half-time.

The Football Association scheduled the replay for the following Wednesday, and, to United's surprise, at Highbury. United protested immediately on the grounds it gave their opponents more of a home advantage but the FA dismissed the complaint. 'United's problems are whether to drop off-form centre-forward Alex Dawson and left winger Mark Pearson, whose tackling and 'needling' tactics are often an embarrassment to his club,' reported Pennington ahead of the rematch. 'United chief Jimmy Murphy must also decide whether Munich-crash survivor Ken Morgans, the Welsh right winger, is fit to come back after his second game in the reserves on Saturday. This would allow Colin Webster to switch to centre-forward.'

Jimmy Jr recalls: "Dad not only had an eye for a player, but he had a nous for their capability," he says. "He saw Alex Dawson playing as a right winger and brought him in as a centre-forward. Before the replay against Fulham, he changed Alex's position to put him on the wing; he thought he'd get a bit more space and maybe score a couple of goals. Of course, he got a hat-trick."

"The Gods were on our side," Jimmy said. "We won 5-3 and the boys were magnificent."

Pennington was at Highbury, reporting on United's remarkable triumph. 'They fought their way from the ashes of Munich to football immortality. And there were as many tears as cheers as Highbury erupted from 90 minutes of tremendous tension into a near-hysterical salute. Jimmy Murphy, their deputy chief, stood on the touchline, his grey hair dishevelled, waiting to embrace the boys who in disaster had rushed to maturity in just over six weeks. There were tears in his eyes as he thought of the United players who might have known the sweetness of this return triumph. Everybody said they would be back after last year's final. But after Munich only Murphy still believed in it.'

The game wasn't without its own controversy. At 4-3, that celebrated figure Haynes put the ball in the net, but was adjudged to have been offside. United promptly went up the other end and wrapped up the result with a Charlton thunderbolt into the top corner. But the talking point of the match was Dawson's hat-trick and the player revealed: "Strangely, before the game, Jimmy Murphy took me to one side and said, 'I think you will score three today', something I just laughed off." Quite a revelation, considering Murphy's hatred of giving predictions.

The press were just as quick to praise the acting manager as they were the players, heralding a number of tactical changes which proved influential. "I had already decided to bring back Shay Brennan to outside-left," Murphy explained to journalists after. "But that wasn't enough. Then just before kick-off, something clicked. Centre-forward Alex Dawson and Colin Webster, the outside-right had stripped and I called them aside. I told them I wanted them to switch positions. I had to find a way to take the attention of the Fulham defence from Dawson. It worked magnificently for it gave him more room in which to work and the boy took his chances like the good player he is."

In his next column for the *Evening News*, Jimmy wrote: 'Against all expectations – including my own, I must confess – Manchester United are in the Wembley final. The odds against us were terrific. I knew that the lads would respond, but I never guessed that they could rise to these heights.

'To say I'm glad we pulled it off really is the understatement of my life. I'm thrilled. We all are. For one thing the FA Cup final is the highlight of any footballer's life. But more than that,

JIMMY MURPHY

I think we have paid the best possible tribute to the players and staff who lost their lives at Munich. Munich is never far from our minds and the terrible blow it inflicted on the club, their dear ones and friends. It is difficult, in fact well-nigh impossible, to pay adequate tribute when such a calamity strikes so suddenly out of the blue...perhaps we shall be able to go one better than last year and bring back the cup to Manchester.

'No-one can say now that United are being carried on a wave of hysteria. The boys at London were on their own – the great Old Trafford roar was at work in Manchester or at home around television sets. We had many loyal supporters but I'm afraid the Londoners were there in force. But it made no difference to the lads. They played good soccer. Matt Busby would have been especially proud! I only hope it will be possible for the Boss himself to be at Wembley to see the climax for the second year running of many years' careful planning – years in which Matt, with the help of Bert Whalley, Tom Curry and many other workers, laid the foundations of United's policy of encouraging youngsters. Matt's policy paid off on Wednesday. The young reserves did him proud and I am sure he appreciated their efforts to make United great again.

'The final should be a tremendous Lancashire battle. I remember playing for West Brom in 1935 against Bolton in the semi-final. That was a tough game. We drew at Leeds and then won the replay 2-0 at Stoke. George Taylor, who is a staff official with Bolton now, will also remember that match – he was playing at left-half, and I was at right-half. So here's to another great game.'

The Cup replays, as well as the postponement of the Wolves game, had left Manchester United with a fixture pile-up that they would have struggled to cope with even if they had a fully fit squad in usual circumstances.

UNITED SPIRIT

From March 29th to April 26th, United had to play eleven league games; or, put another way, more than a quarter of their league campaign in little over a month. Their game against Sheffield Wednesday on Saturday, March 29th was the start of a run of games which would see them play on Monday March 31st, Friday April 4th, Saturday April 5th and Monday April 7th.

Just at that time, United were boosted by the return of Viollet and Scanlon to light training. The physical demand was beginning to take its toll on the squad. 'Wilf McGuinness, United's ferocious-tackling wing-half, has made a remarkable recovery from a cartilage operation in time to make his Wembley challenge by playing for the reserves today,' reported the *Express* on Saturday, March 29th. 'The slender margin on which United chief Jimmy Murphy is now operating after the Munich disaster is spotlighted by the injury to left-back Ian Greaves. Centre-half Ron Cope is forced to switch to replace Greaves against Sheffield Wednesday today. Taking over the number five jersey is Bob Harrop, normally a reserve inside forward or wing half.'

McGuinness suffered a knock in that Central League game against Stoke City. At least he had a win to celebrate; even though the senior side lost 1-0 at Hillsborough in the first game of their intensive run. Murphy felt cause to be positive in his column for the *Evening News* that day. 'Compare Manchester United's position six weeks ago with today and the transformation is unbelievable,' he wrote. 'The way ahead for United is clearing and our troubles, although still considerable, are lifting.

'It was great to talk to Matt Busby this week. The Boss has always given tremendous personal encouragement to everyone who worked at Old Trafford, and although he is still a sick man I found contact with him once more a big tonic and inspiration for me to help see United through the rest of the season. Matt and I are such a perfect team that soon, please God, he will be with us. By next season, let us hope, Matt will be able to take over command at Old Trafford again.

'While I was in Munich much has happened at home. With the uncertainty of our league programme finally fixed, the club was able to go ahead with arrangements for the European Cup. I think all of us are glad that United are staying in the competition.

'The European Cup Organising Committee have tried to smooth out difficulties for us and it would have been rather ungracious if we had backed out after all their kind help. Let's not forget that Milano, our opponents, are also doing their best to agree to our suggested dates. It is only through the co-operation of the English Football Association, the European Cup Committee, and Milano that we are able to play both legs of the semi-final at the end of our season. Originally they were fixed for a date in April and May 1 – two days before the cup final!

'Even more satisfying is to find that since I went to Munich a week ago three more crash survivors have started training again. A few weeks ago who would have thought that Albert Scanlon, who suffered a fractured skull in the crash, and came home with his leg in a plaster cast, would be running around Old Trafford like a two-year-old! Ray Wood is back in light training and so is Dennis Viollet. That leaves just Johnny Berry and Jackie Blanchflower. To them I say, don't give up heart boys and get well quickly. You'll also note that Tom Heron, the Scottish boy we signed from Portadown, is fit again. Wilf McGuinness had the bad luck to hurt his ankle in the first game after his cartilage operation, but that won't put him out of action for long. Young Kenny Morgans is putting on weight fast after lying in bed in that Munich hospital. Soon I shall have to decide who to leave out of the first team – not who I can put in.

'I think we can say that as far as the club is concerned we have weathered the storm. I tried not to be stampeded into panic buying of new players. You need time to go start playing the transfer market, and that was something we didn't have much of.

'With Matt soon with us he and I should soon be able to get our heads together on this point. So we bought just three players and relied for the rest on our reserves. They responded magnificently and have carried us through. So far we have been fairly lucky and free from injuries. But even if we run into a bad spell now our playing staff is getting stronger every day and we should be able to finish the season on a strong note.

'As I say…our troubles are lifting.'

CHAPTER | TEN

A PROUD MAN

"The players may smile at Jimmy's jokes and mannerisms, but they know that these mask one of the shrewdest soccer brains of all time. When you really know Jimmy Murphy, you know a man of deep feelings and sympathy"

Prior to Munich, Jimmy Murphy already worked so many hours in the day that it seemed impossible to figure where he could fit more in. It was an impossible task, but somehow, he was doing it. So too were the players in similarly testing conditions. Few, if any, believed that they could have got to Wembley. The league form was understandably stuttering. After defeat at Aston Villa, though, United actually started April quite well – drawing with Sunderland and Preston, before playing up at Sunderland in the return and achieving their first and only league win between Munich and the end of the season.

The win had not been expected, and neither had anything remarkable been expected of the players, much less those who had been involved in the crash. And yet Bobby Charlton was called up to the England squad for the the first time.

For Murphy, this news was just what Manchester United needed. He wrote in his *Evening News* column: 'What a proud week for Manchester United…two of our players have been honoured with international caps. Harry Gregg was a fairly obvious choice for Ireland to play against Wales at Cardiff on Wednesday. Bobby Charlton six months ago had a very outside chance, but today, of course, he is a different proposition – price of the youngsters who have risen to the occasion for United so magnificently. He is playing brilliantly at present – and he will be even better.

'We shall miss Bobby's services when he is playing for England against Scotland at Hampden Park on April 19th. But the club is pleased to see him get international honours. Of course, when England wants a player, the Football Association name their man and whether the club likes it or not, he plays for his country. Not so, however, with Scottish, Irish and Welsh players who are playing with English League clubs. In their case permission has to be given by the parent club.

'I know this only too well. For, in my day as a player, clubs used to hang on to their men and if they were at all involved in the championship race, promotion hopes or relegation worries, they were most reluctant to release the Scotsmen, Welshmen and Irishmen they had playing for them. With all modesty, I reckon this cost me half a dozen international caps. West Bromwich Albion, my old club, always seemed to be facing a critical match when an international game came along. Let me hasten to add that Albion were not being particularly hard-hearted. Most clubs were the same in those days. Fortunately now, times have changed for the better. United had no hesitation releasing Harry Gregg.

A PROUD MAN

In any case, think how unfair if Charlton had automatically got his cap while the club refused to release Gregg to play for his country. As an exiled Welshman, I'm delighted clubs are taking an enlightened view these days. All in all, I think the English selectors have done a good job…I wish the new England attack the best of luck. I shall not be able to look at this England side without seeing the shadows of Tommy Taylor, Roger Byrne and Duncan Edwards. But I'm sure the newcomers won't let them down.'

On the day Charlton was making his England debut, a future Manchester United manager was witnessing a future Manchester United legend learn his trade. "I was a seventeen year old playing for Aston Villa against Manchester United in a reserve game at Villa Park on the same day that Bobby Charlton was making his debut for England against Scotland," remembers Ron Atkinson.

"I remember the scoreboard lighting up when England won, and to tell us Bobby had scored. But my most vivid memory was of our skipper Johnny Dixon – captain of the senior side in the FA Cup final against United the previous year – being chased around the pitch and being kicked to pieces by a little midfielder who was being egged on by his coach from the sidelines. 'You'll be a great player son, but you've got to watch it,' said Johnny to this short player who went by the name of Nobby Stiles. Nobby was no doubt being encouraged by Jimmy to get stuck in."

Murphy first saw Nobby playing in a game at Mansfield. "Everywhere the ball went there was a tiny boy drawn to it, as though by a magnet, and when he tackled he did so as if his very life depended on winning possession of the ball," Murphy said. He consulted his programme to discover the young boy was called *N. Stiles* from Collyhurst. He wasted no time in recommending him to Busby, describing him as the 'ghost with a hammer in his

JIMMY MURPHY

feet' – a playful reference to the Welsh boxer Jimmy Wilde. "I have seen a golden nugget," Jimmy told Matt. "I don't know why I feel so certain, but he'll get there. He isn't the size of two pennyworth of copper." Soon afterwards, a conversation between Busby and his best friend Paddy McGrath revealed that McGrath knew the Stiles family and that young Norbert was a red.

Jimmy said that Norbert – 'Nobby' – arrived at Old Trafford no taller than 5ft or heavier than 6 stone; anything but the shape of a player who would become known as the 'Toy Bulldog', or as one writer would put it in 1957, 'Duncan Edwards in miniature.' The way Stiles overcame those hurdles and handicaps – he was also later to have profound sight problems dating back to a car accident he'd suffered as a child – and not only compensated for them with heart and effort, but was able to flourish, made him a wholehearted and unashamed favourite of Jimmy's. He adored him so much he'd often joke with him. After one game at Burnley, Murphy went into the changing room to address the players' performances and thought he would rile Stiles by suggesting he hadn't played in his usual dedicated fashion.

"Well done lads…good game," Jimmy said. "But half way through the second half I saw you stop playing Nobby…what was wrong son?"

"I think you must need these more than I do," Nobby said, passing his infamous thick spectacles to Jimmy.

As a lifelong United supporter, Stiles idolised Eddie Colman, but Colman would enjoy his peak for so many years that it would surely have a negative impact on Stiles' own professional ambitions. Early on, Stiles must have felt overawed being at Old Trafford. He later said how the dressing room appeared to exude the confidence of the Busby Babes which gave him a simultaneous fear and curiosity, such was his admiration for the players who

A PROUD MAN

used it. He told a story of how he was forced by young Mark Pearson to go in with an autograph book and collect signatures; and how Duncan Edwards was the one who took it and passed it around the players. 'Best wishes and good luck in your career,' Edwards wrote to Stiles, even though it wasn't his book.

Back to 1958 and after a 1-0 defeat at Tottenham, United were scheduled to play at Portsmouth on the evening of April 16th.

A schedule conflict saw that Fratton Park game played on the same day Wales and Northern Ireland would face off in the decider for the Home Championships. Ireland were going into the game knowing a win would win them the tournament for the first time since 1914, but Murphy showed split loyalties. He couldn't leave his boys.

'(Harry) Gregg has been released by Manchester United although they play a League game against Portsmouth on the same day,' reported the *Daily Mirror*. 'But Jimmy Murphy, United's acting manager, who is also boss of the Welsh team will NOT be helping Wales. He asked to be released from international duty to be with United at Pompey.'

The goalkeeper for United that day due to Gregg's international commitments, was David Gaskell. He remembers that even weeks on from the disaster, the tension was palpable. "The team talks after the disaster were particularly emotionally charged," he says. "Jimmy was a very emotional man anyway; he was never very tactical, and in those months it really was the emotion and grief that he poured into those team talks to get us all motivated and charged for the game. He'd come around to you individually and give a few personal words of encouragement in his Welsh lilt before the game."

Gregg was an advocate for Murphy's ability to inspire. "I don't think it's out of turn to say Matt was a bad speaker," he said.

"A very poor speaker, he wasn't the most confident. Before the accident, it would be the boss and the trainer Tom Curry who would take training, with Jimmy Murphy looking after the reserves. On a Friday evening we'd have the team meeting – the boss would walk in and pin the team-sheet up on the board. 'If you aren't good enough lads, you wouldn't be here.' Week after week. The simplicity of it. And then he'd walk out.

"After the accident, when he was well enough to play a small part again, Jimmy Murphy would be in the dressing room. 'Up together, back together. Up together, back together. God bless.' They were saying different words, but the same thing, really. It was the most straightforward, common sense idea. When we have the ball, attack, when they have the ball, defend. You hear all the shit about 4-4-2, 4-3-3, catenaccio and so on. It's been taken over by people who've never played the game."

United drew 3-3 at Fratton Park; hardly the worst result, though it didn't mask the fact that despite the romance of their cup exploits, the Red Devils had enjoyed just one league win since Munich. The truth was that the adrenalin which had carried them to Wembley could not, for whatever understandable reason, be replicated for the league form. Try as heroically as they might, the emotional toll of the disaster was still as difficult to comprehend as it had been at its rawest, no doubt compounded by the gradual return of the wounded, as welcome as that obviously was.

United's draw at Fratton Park was not, however, the major news of the day: Busby was finally on his way home after ten weeks in hospital. He was scheduled to be part of a live BBC interview at 9pm, whilst the game was concluding, but instead, he faced the press on the morning of April 16th, just before he boarded the train for home. There he was asked when he would be back in charge.

A PROUD MAN

"At the moment I say next season," he admitted. "This season lasts only three more weeks and it's impossible for me to take over in this short period of time. Beside, Jimmy Murphy's doing a wonderful job. He'll keep it at least until the cup final and I will not attempt to take any part in management until after that. Jimmy had to take over when things looked extremely black, and the boys have responded wonderfully well to him. The development of Manchester United had a great influence on my recuperation and helped me quite a bit."

The little boosts were becoming more frequent, and now, it was less often that good news was followed by bad. United were slowly able to get on. Busby's return to Manchester was followed by Dennis Viollet's first game of football since the crash.

Viollet, who had missed the 1957 final through injury, was desperate to somehow play against Bolton. On April 19th, he scored for the reserves against Bury, prompting Murphy to recall him to play against Wolves for the first team two days later, in the hope it may provide inspiration. "I felt tired," Viollet admitted after playing Bury. "But I feel confident that with a couple of games, I can be fully match fit for Wembley…But, if Mr Murphy thinks I am not ready, then I shall have no complaints. I realise the lads have done well enough without me, and that the cup final team will be picked entirely on merit and current form. If the club think someone else can do a better job, than I shall sit another Wembley out, knowing that it is in the best interests of Manchester United."

Prior to their final league game, reporter Keith Dewhurst paid a special tribute to Jimmy in the *Evening Chronicle*. In a cup final special edition on Wednesday, April 23rd, his column was headlined 'This is the miracle man called… MURPHY!' and read: 'Manchester United's Jimmy Murphy is a short, explosive

JIMMY MURPHY

character who hates crowds and publicity, and people who do not know him well think that he is hard and difficult to approach.

'When they know him a little better they think that he is a kind of spectacular joker. His team talks are epics of colourful language and wild gestures, far removed from the calm analysis of Matt Busby.

'His stock greeting of "Hello, my old pal"– equally effective for handling pressmen, players, genuine old pals, barmen, waiters and the people who pretend to be genuine old pals in the hope of scrounging tickets – has in fact become a joke among the team.

'The players may smile at Jimmy's jokes and mannerisms, but they know that these mask one of the shrewdest soccer brains of all time. When you really know Jimmy Murphy, you know a man of deep feelings and sympathy which he does not choose to expose all the time for the world to knock around. You know a masterly talker and storyteller. You know perhaps the best football coach Britain has ever seen.

'Murphy has the managerial flair, too. His handling of the Manchester United team since Munich has been superb. He has had only a handful of players, and some of those are not really up to first team standard. Yet look at the way he has used them… Look at the dropping of Mark Pearson and the restoration of Brennan in the Highbury replay – another match-winning move. Look at the switching of Ken Morgans to the left wing, a move which has at least solved a desperate problem, and may yet win the cup.

'Look at Murphy, buffooning to keep the players' morale up, and yet all the time thinking, thinking. Staying up all night in London before the semi-final. Deciding on the Morgans switch when everyone thought he was asleep in the corner of the train compartment. I know what he will say to skipper Billy Foulkes

A PROUD MAN

before the Cup Final. I can only say the same to Jimmy. BEST OF LUCK, MY OLD PAL.'

United concluded their league programme with a home draw against Newcastle and an away defeat to Chelsea. As if to emphasise the point about selection difficulties, Dawson scored in the Old Trafford game, to round off what had been an absolutely remarkable contribution. His five goals in ten appearances would have been a wonderful return for a young striker in any season, so to do it in these circumstances, with all of the associated pressure, is – just as in the case of the acting manager – a contribution that is not appreciated as often as it perhaps should be.

But it wasn't just at centre-forward, or at Manchester United, where Murphy had difficulty. 'Ken Morgans, 18-year-old Welsh winger of Manchester United, is the double problem boy on the master-mind of Jimmy Murphy today,' wrote Bob Pennington for the *Daily Express* on April 28th. 'Welsh team manager Murphy goes into conference with the World Cup selectors of Wales at Shrewsbury this afternoon to decide if Morgans should be included in their tour party of 22 for Sweden in June. Murphy, stand-in chief of Manchester United, will also be worrying whether to include Morgans in his cup final side at Wembley next Saturday. While Morgans was rested on Saturday, Murphy played Alex Dawson on the right wing at Chelsea. Dawson slightly injured his right knee, but Murphy announced yesterday: "Everybody will be fit for Saturday."'

In something of an indication about the various headaches associated with being a manager which made Murphy unsuited to the role, he took to his *Evening News* column to write to supporters about the difficulty in getting tickets for the final.

For most managers, the fact that this is out of their hands anyway would mean it was an area they would not necessarily feel the need to become involved with. They might sympathise, but as they were ultimately powerless, it made no sense to make their own views known, unless of course they had a particular need to curry favour. Jimmy had no such need; his comments seemed genuine and transparent. He was frustrated on behalf of all of those supporters who had been on this emotionally exhausting journey with them.

'Fellers…you have my sympathy,' he began. 'Can there be anything more heartbreaking than following a football team through thick and thin, home and away, all over the country, and then be unable to see your favourites in action on that greatest day of all days – a Wembley FA Cup final? One in three Manchester United supporters will be at Wembley. The other 30,000 will be unlucky. I'm afraid that is the hard truth.'

Murphy's last column for the newspaper was, fittingly, dedicated to the game itself, and his message was effectively a summary of thanks to all of the hard work from everyone who had contributed.

'IF SPIRIT COUNTS…IT'S AS GOOD AS OURS' read the headline. Jimmy wrote: 'If enthusiasm can bring success at Wembley then I'm sure the cup is as good as at Old Trafford. In all my years in football, I never dreamed that a team could rally round so magnificently in a time of crisis and disaster. The youngsters who have tried so determinedly that our problem now is who to leave out at Wembley. The old hands have also played with a spirit and co-operation that has been inspiring to those of us who were left at Old Trafford to rebuild after the Munich devastation.

'Unfortunately, enthusiasm is not the only essentials to win the FA Cup. But without making any rash forecasts I think I can safely say that our boys have quickly blended keenest with skill and teamwork. We have a feel that Bolton will find us a much-improved side from those early days when we took what was left of our playing staff to Blackpool and we could just raise enough players to field an 11-a-side practice game.

'May 3rd will be a great day for United. The lads have done a wonderful job in the face of almost overwhelming difficulties. Whatever the result at Wembley – and I still don't make forecasts! – even to have reached there is an achievement in itself. It is a memory which will live with me for ever and far outweighs even my own appearance as a player at Wembley for West Bromwich Albion. I'm proud of the boys, and pleased they were able to win through for the sake of Matt Busby and also a tribute to the memory of the players who lost their lives.

'I think I can safely say that the lads' efforts have been a tremendous help to Matt in his battle for health. It was grand to see him down at the ground again on Wednesday. He made a bee-line for the dressing-room to meet the players. The Boss just couldn't resist turning up that night to see the game against Newcastle.

'But still Matt came – and as things turned out, the game proved a tonic for him. He said himself that he felt it was doing him so much good that instead of going at half-time he stayed until much nearer the end.

'We are delighted with his progress. In fact, only the other day I chatted to him that it wouldn't be long before he and I were turning out together again.

'As for the prospects, Bobby Charlton has just hit his top form at the right time. He merited his international cap and is playing superbly for United. Ernie Taylor has been to Wembley before of course and twice returned with a medal. Third time lucky again, I hope, Ernie! His experience will be invaluable. He

JIMMY MURPHY

has a big-match temperament and we are fortunate to have him with us. Bill Foulkes's fine steadying influence as captain will also stand us in good stead.

'I don't particularly want to pick out individuals because the secret of United's success always has been and, I hope, always will be, teamwork. But I must make mention of Harry Gregg. I rate Harry as an all-time great. It doesn't matter whether it is a cup game or just another league match, he always plays as if his life depended on it. He combines skill with a daring fearlessness. I wish all the lads the best of luck and I have no hesitation assuring our fans they will see a great, whole-hearted game.'

*****

United were stationed in the Norbreck Hydro, though by now, these makeshift headquarters were so well-known that the only real respite they offered was a break from the emotionally tense atmosphere in Manchester.

After one training session, Jimmy was spotted giving a forty five minute intensive tactical instruction to Charlton, Crowther, Goodwin, Taylor and Viollet. The selections of Gregg, Foulkes and Greaves were just about the only choices that the press felt were nailed on. This conversation suggested for the first time that Jimmy had come to a decision on who would play.

Hidden inside Murphy's previous declaration of a clean bill of health was that consequential problem of selection. Desmond Hackett went so far as to headline his piece for the Express 'THE NIGHTMARE OF JIMMY MURPHY', with the sub-head reading 'I WANT TO PICK EVERY MAN…'

'Manchester United caretaker manager Jimmy Murphy bust wide open the secret he had planned for Friday night when this

A PROUD MAN

morning he named the team to play Bolton Wanderers in the cup final,' Hackett wrote on April 30th. 'Murphy confessed to me at United's Wembley training HQ: "I was hoping to hold back the team until Friday, just to keep Bolton guessing. But I couldn't hold out any longer. Every night since the semi-final I was going to bed and seeing a new team lining up at Wembley. I reckon I would have gone on picking and repicking until I had 18 players trotting out at Wembley," he said. "It was the toughest thing I ever had to do, and I hope I never have to do this job again.

"'Listen, pal, so many of these lads have played their hearts out, but you can't pick them all, and you can't leave one out without having a twinge of conscience. But seriously, Des, this is the best permutation I could produce. These were the boys who looked so good against Chelsea. I am really thankful this tough job is over. Maybe the hardest is yet to come. You know me. Watching on Saturday will be 90 minutes of real torture."

'Warm-hearted Jimmy Murphy told the players in a private conference early this morning what the team was going to be. The boys who will miss the Wembley show, Mark Pearson, Ken Morgan, Wilf McGuinness, Bobby Harrop, and Seamus Brennan just murmured: "That's all right by us, boss. Just give us a place at Wembley and we'll work as hard as the other chaps, shouting our heads off."

'The babe of the Babes, 18-year-old Alex Dawson, gets promotion from the 10s. 6d. seats to the outside-right spot. Before last year's final, Dawson was mooching around the ground when big-hearted boss Matt Busby asked: "What's worrying you, son?" Dawson replied: "I haven't got a ticket." Right away, manager Busby said: "Here's your ticket. You just go ahead and we'll look after your expenses."

JIMMY MURPHY

'A big thank-you from Dawson was a top-rating show and a goal against Sheffield Wednesday in the first match after Munich, and three goals against Fulham in the semi-final replay. So Dawson, who set out as a cup player as a centre-forward, gets the outside-right spot on Saturday in a forward line which Jimmy Murphy weighs up like this: "Every player in this line can score goals. They switch and re-switch so easily that the best defence in the world must be wondering who is coming through next." Of the Munich survivors, four who will play at Wembley are Gregg, Foulkes, Charlton, Viollet.'

The story of Kenny Morgans' selection presents an alternative view to the idea that the team was decided on Wednesday. "Kenny maintains that Jimmy Murphy came to him on the Friday and told him he was in the starting line-up," said Gregg. "Then, as the team was walking around Wembley the following morning, Jimmy went over and told him Matt had decided to go with Dennis Viollet instead. It broke Kenny. He seemed to lose a couple of yards of pace after that and by 1961 had moved on to Swansea. Kenny claims Matt and Jimmy promised they would look after him if he made the move to his native Wales but in reality it was out of sight, out of mind."

Jimmy Jr does not speak about this specific incident but confesses that it sounds like the kind of thing that may have happened. "He would sometimes tell players they were playing when he perhaps shouldn't have done," he says. "Matt would know his team and get it ready to put up on a Friday but Dad would go up to the player beforehand and just give them a knowing nudge. He knew which players would respond to it better if they knew in advance. It's the art of management, you either know how to lead or you don't, and Dad knew where his strengths and weaknesses were."

Bill Holden, reporting for the *Daily Mirror*, was wondering if

A PROUD MAN

Busby would be making a big appearance at Wembley. 'Manager Matt Busby, who came home a fortnight ago from Munich Hospital, has not yet decided whether he will lead the team out at Wembley. But Murphy, his stand-in, said: "To complete a grand day it would be just right to have my friend and boss Matt with me at Wembley."'

For Busby, it was a case of waiting until the day of the final. He told Derek Wallis of the *Mirror*: "I'd love to do it with Jimmy Murphy beside me. But it's a long walk. If the doctors say 'no', I can walk from the stand and meet the team on the pitch."

'Matt will travel to London with the team tomorrow. But he will NOT be giving the players a talk on tactics before the match. He's leaving that to acting manager Murphy,' Wallis wrote.

There was word that two Bolton officials had invoked the spirit of Bob Lord when they said: "We want football at Wembley and not an emotional occasion." Busby's response to that? "They are entitled to say what they think is right." Murphy was – perhaps predictably – much less diplomatic. "This is more nonsense. Every Wembley occasion is an emotion. The bands, the singing, and the big issues at stake make it an emotional occasion. We certainly don't want any hysterical scenes, and knowing my Manchester fans I know they will not create any. This is going to be another grand Wembley," he said to Hackett of the *Express*.

April 24th, 1958 was a notable day in United history for another reason. After six years, the club finally relinquished their hold on the FA Youth Cup. After drawing the first leg 1-1, Wolverhampton Wanderers (worthy opponents to eliminate them, considering the history) won the second leg 3-1.

Jimmy Jr is certain that the disaster was the significant factor. "Dad won five FA Youth Cups on the run and in 1958 they got to the semi-final – he couldn't play Alex Dawson and Mark

Pearson, his two best players, because they were with the first team," he says. "Alex was the best goalscorer and Mark was a tough little nut. I saw him punch goalkeepers! With those two they would have gone on to win another."

The United team featured Nobby Stiles and Johnny Giles, with Gaskell in goal possibly the most familiar name after those players.

Another point of interest in the build-up revolved around the future of Murphy. Busby's return and the talk that he would imminently take charge of United affairs following the game against Bolton led to some informal speculation about what may have lay in wait for Murphy. Perhaps it had just been assumed that his time as acting manager and his forthcoming task with Wales had whet his appetite to be the number one at a club.

Two clubs were apparently showing an interest: Liverpool and Aston Villa. The Midlands club would make their intentions quite public, though the Liverpool stories never manifested themselves as more than speculation. Liverpool chairman Tom Williams was a known fan of Jimmy and when then-Anfield boss Phil Taylor was on the verge of losing his job in November 1959, Williams made his interest known. He was indiscreetly knocked back and dissuaded from making a formal enquiry. "There is talk that Liverpool wanted Dad to take over but I'll be honest and say I've never heard anything substantial to back that up," says Jimmy Jr. "I think it's just an old rumour. What I am aware of is a story that when Bob Paisley was taking charge of Liverpool's reserves, he tried to imitate the model Dad had implemented with the reserve and youth teams at United. Dad was a big pal of Bob's, and Bob came to his funeral."

As it turned out, Busby was well enough to give a short speech to the team before the final. He thanked them for everything

A PROUD MAN

they had given to the club. For players like Charlton, Foulkes, Viollet and Gregg, these well-intentioned words, coming from their actual manager, were simply reminders of the human journey they had taken and not the professional one.

Busby gave Jimmy the final word. "Lads, the fact you have got this far is a miracle," he said. "All I want to tell you is thank you from the bottom of my heart for all you have done. This is the last hurdle, and win, lose or draw I am very proud of you."

*****

On the big day, Bolton caught United cold with an early Nat Lofthouse goal – United were only jolted into action by a half-time regrouping and Charlton hit a post as they attempted to level.

Then, Lofthouse struck again; though struck is the operative word – it is perhaps more appropriate to note that what he struck was Gregg, more than the ball, and even though it appeared to be a foul (Gregg said later that even in those days, nine times out of ten a foul would have been given), the ball went into the net and a goal was awarded. Lofthouse himself conceded that it shouldn't have. He declared after the game: "I would sooner throw my cup medal away than think I had not won it fairly and squarely."

'There were certainly no accusations from Manchester stand-in chief Jimmy Murphy when he and Nat met in a London pub yesterday morning for a livener,' reported Desmond Hackett for the *Express* two days after the final. 'Jimmy Murphy told Lofthouse: "Nat, if we had to lose, and it was a bit of heartbreak, pal, I could not wish for a better winner than yourself." The price Lofthouse paid was severe roughhousing from Gregg and Bill Foulkes whenever he came up against them again.'

After the loss Murphy said: "It was a pity we had to come to Wembley to let the lads end their great fight so sadly."

Reflecting later, Jimmy accepted Bolton were the better team and he felt that on the day, United's players were not able to do themselves justice because of the toll the journey there had taken. He insisted that in some ways, the defeat didn't matter, and it has to be said there is a point. Maybe the jolt of human realisation provoked by the pre-match talks added an awareness of the nerves and sense of occasion.

Murphy also wanted to pay due respect to his own team, after it had been said that only a wave of emotion had carried them to Wembley. "I am still very proud of the way these United boys got to Wembley and the way they performed today," he said. "A lot of people said it was emotion that got us to the cup final. That's rubbish. A crowd helps, but we played most of those games away from Old Trafford. You can't win five matches with bloody emotion. You have to play a bit as well, and they certainly did that, magnificently. But there is no question that the better team won."

It is not patronising whatsoever to say that getting to the final at all was a major accomplishment. Manchester United were not supposed to continue. The club should have closed following Munich; there was no reasonable way they could have carried on. And yet not only did they play on, they prospered, and battled their way to the FA Cup final, the grandest day in British football. In this journey a valuable lesson had been taught; a lesson for all who chose to take heed of it, but a lesson which the future players of Manchester United would never forget. Even if it feels like you have nothing, if you keep the faith and push yourself to the limit, then anything is possible. And, so long as you have given of everything then even failure is forgivable.

A PROUD MAN

It is a principle that will be returned to later in this book but in the space of less than three months which existed between Munich and Wembley, Jimmy Murphy's drive and determination had created a culture and personality which the club had adopted. As well as a reputation for fine, attacking football and a dedication to developing players from within, the message had been sent out loud and clear that *Manchester United would never give in*. This would become ingrained in the club's psyche and a key ingredient for the club's future successes.

A comment from Charlton alludes to that. "Jimmy kept our minds on football. He just said we've got to keep the club going and that's really what the cup run meant. We were almost proving to ourselves that Manchester United was alive."

Leading the team out for the final was still, despite the result, one of the proudest moments of Jimmy's life. "He was a very proud man on the day of the 1958 FA Cup final," says Jimmy Jr. "He would have loved it if they could have won but I don't think it diminished his pride any. People say the achievement was getting there; the achievement was putting together a side which somehow defeated Sheffield Wednesday just a few days after the disaster."

Wembley is seen as the crescendo of this difficult season but the truth is that United still had to play against AC Milan in the European Cup. They had been left in no doubt about the difficulty of the task by the reality of their run of form, which, apart from the three remarkable cup wins, had been poor, though still much better than could have been expected.

In an attempt to try and get some of that magic flowing on an Old Trafford occasion which was inevitably going to be difficult, Murphy turned to one of the players who had been more disappointed than most on the Saturday.

JIMMY MURPHY

Young Kenny Morgans was called into Jimmy's office, where the coach apologised and admitted he was wrong not to play him at Wembley. He now needed Morgans to play against AC Milan. In 2008, Morgans said: "On the morning of the final when I was walking around Wembley, Jimmy came up to me and put his arm around me and said, 'You are not playing today.' He felt the atmosphere of the occasion would be too much for me. It upset me because I wanted to win the cup for the boys… The following Tuesday we played Milan in the European Cup semi-final and I was the best player on the park. Jimmy said he was sorry and that if I had played at Wembley he thought I would have won the game for United." Despite that obvious difficulty, Kenny still spoke positively about Jimmy's contribution. "You didn't see Matt for a year," he said. "Jimmy was in charge. He was fantastic but different from Matt."

Ahead of the AC Milan clash, the FA had selected Charlton to play for England and, after flexibility from them and the league earlier in the season, they now refused to allow him to play in one of the biggest games of all. "The FA were reverting to type," complained Harry Gregg. "The suits refused to allow Bobby Charlton to play against the Italians because he was needed for a meaningless international friendly with Portugal."

Milan trainer Gyppo Viani said before the game that United were tired, and the Italians were much smarter. It was the proverbial red rag to a bull which really did not need any excuse and United's display could be described as full-blooded if one was to be kind.

Milan took the lead after 24 minutes but United were level before half-time when Viollet scored. Viollet was then the architect of the first leg winning goal; he was brought down in the box, and little Ernie Taylor, the player who had answered

A PROUD MAN

Jimmy Murphy's call-to-arms back in February, scored the 80th minute penalty to send Old Trafford into delirium and make them dream that anything could be possible in Milan.

Those dreams didn't take into account the reality of the arduous journey which awaited the team. On Saturday, May 10th, they would meet at Old Trafford in the early afternoon before travelling to London. The next day, they would get the boat from Dover to Calais. From Calais, they would travel by road to Milan, a journey which would start at 2.42pm on Sunday afternoon and conclude at 8.20am on Monday morning.

When it came to the actual game, the United players found it equally draining. Milan were unexpectedly aggressive – perhaps remembering the previous week's encounter – and scored an early goal. The visitors fought valiantly but the quality told on the day and Milan won 3-0. The defeat did nothing to dampen the praise Murphy received or deserved for his incredible work and there were plenty who thought the work should be recognised. In the May 16th 'Punchbag' column in the *Daily Mirror* – where readers sent questions and comments into journalist Peter Wilson – Mr J.D. Dickerson wrote in to reply to a comment from the previous week's column.

"I heartily agree with Mr. F. Richardson of Reading that Busby deserves the title (of Manager of the Year) – but surely Jimmy Murphy should get a little of the credit. After all, it was Murphy who rallied Manchester United after the Munich air disaster. Credit where it's due, please." Wilson added an editorial note. "Yes, Matt wasn't alone in building a great team – he had a wonderful assistant."

That was that for the 1957/58 season as far as Manchester United were concerned; but, for Jimmy Murphy, his adventures on the continent had only just begun.

CHAPTER | ELEVEN
WORLD CLASS

"I'm disappointed in these Brazilian players. They're over-rated and if we get stuck in we can get a result. Even their so-called great players have grave weaknesses...Pele? He's got nothing but speed and a shot!" – Jimmy Murphy

Without question, the achievement of getting Wales into the World Cup was seen as a huge accomplishment, even if it was via an unconventional qualification, and even in the context that it was just the fifth edition of the international tournament. In modern context, considering Wales' history in the competition, it becomes an even greater accomplishment.

Wales' reward for eliminating Israel was a group which contained Hungary – a match Jimmy Murphy could not wait for – Mexico, and host nation Sweden. As distressing as 1958 had been for him, the year also provided him with two of the highlights of his life. Jimmy said it was a tremendous relief to leave behind the dark memories of Old Trafford to lead Wales into the World Cup.

Stories of the desire Murphy had to qualify for Sweden and the incentives he was putting forward for his team were surfacing as early as late 1956, before they'd played a single qualifier. 'WALES HAVE HUSH-HUSH VICTORY PLAN' said the headline in the *Express* on October 20th, 1956, ahead of a Home Championships game against Scotland. Bob Pennington wrote: 'Cardiff is crazy with curiosity and confidence tonight and a stocky Welsh wizard, with the Irish name of Jimmy Murphy, is largely responsible. Curiosity over the secret Welsh plan to beat Scotland here tomorrow – a plan finalised this morning by new team boss Murphy, No.2 at Manchester United, and one of the shrewdest brains in the business.

'Confidence that Murphy had worked a two-day training miracle by not only making his boys believe they can be world beaters, but giving them the necessary know-how. Midway through a tough but intelligent work-out, Murphy summoned his inside right John Charles into the centre of the pitch for a long talk. Then he spoke alone to centre-forward Trevor Ford and inside left Ivor Allchurch. Scotland will know what menace Mr. Murphy has in mind tomorrow afternoon. But there was a hint when inside right Charles became the spearhead in the goalmouth, heading balls back for Ford and Allchurch to make the kill. There appears to be no official secrecy about Wales using Charles and Ford in a double centre-forward act.

'Mr. Murphy, of course, has other soccer subtleties in mind to break the lean post-war run without a Welsh win over Scotland… What a dazzling cash prize there is for these Welshmen. Two more home internationals plus three World Cup games before the end of May at £50 a time. Add that financial incentive to the customary Welsh fervour, and with Murphy in command this should be the start of the most wonderful era in Welsh soccer history.'

The following month, Wales were at Wembley. The result – 3-1 to England – does nothing to explain the incredible events of the game. Wales were one nil up with a John Charles goal in the eighth minute and retained the lead despite losing their goalkeeper Jack Kelsey on 12 minutes. Then Mel Charles had to come off in the 41st minute, leaving Wales with nine men for more than an entire half. Both Charles and Kelsey played the second half but their participation was minimal. Kelsey played out on the left wing, out of the way of the game. 'Then England left winger Colin Grainger was carried off after 61 minutes after twisting his ankle turning on the loose, rain-soaked turf,' reported Pennington for the *Express*. 'As Grainger was being treated for a suspected torn ligament and a cracked ankle bone, Kelsey was ordered to the dressing room by team manager Jimmy Murphy. Add to these the second half injuries to Welsh centre-forward John Charles (bruised ankle and ribs), centre-half Ray Daniel (bruised right foot), and England's inside left Johnny Haynes (kicked on right knee) and this reads more like a battlefield communique than a critical analysis of match play.'

Frank McGhee of the *Mirror* called the game 'THE GREAT WEMBLEY ROBBERY', saying supporters were robbed of what looked like being the match of the year, and robbed by 'that ridiculous rule' which bans the use of substitutes in home internationals.

'Welsh team manager Jimmy Murphy told me after the match: "Substitutes for international matches must come. I was pinning a lot of hopes on plans for inter-changing my three inside forwards. That was completely killed by Kelsey's injury."'

In October, 1957, it was reported by Bill Holden of the *Daily Mirror* that Murphy had made Arsenal wing-half Dave Bowen his captain for Wales ahead of their Home Championships game with England. Murphy said: "He is certainly the best captain the side has had since the war. I have complete faith in his ability. He has the knack of pulling the best out of a team and I have given him strict instructions to shout louder tomorrow than ever before. I've told him I want to hear him shouting above the roar of the 60,000 crowd. I want to hear him calling to his players, instructing them and encouraging them. I know he can do it."

Despite having his captain in place well in advance, the Wales squad which assembled at their World Cup base in the Grand Hotel in Saltsjöbaden, Stockholm, was almost as inexperienced as the United team he'd been leading.

The initial forty man squad had been trimmed to twenty-two. Six players were uncapped and another six had fewer than ten international caps to their name. That twenty-two man squad was trimmed to eighteen in a cost-cutting exercise from the Welsh FA. The selectors couldn't agree on the last player to be in that eighteen and it came down to a choice between Ron Hewitt, the experienced Cardiff forward, or Kenny Morgans. Murphy had wanted Morgans to go, but the selectors took a dim view of the player not being selected for the FA Cup final; the United coach had unwittingly put his young protege out of selection. Jimmy was devastated on Morgans' behalf.

For various political reasons within the association, the selectors also denied Jimmy the opportunity to select Ray Daniel, Trevor Ford, and Derek Tapscott, three players who would most definitely have been selected if the assessment were on quality alone. Murphy exercised his influence to ensure Colin Webster was included. Webster had been a regular in the post-Munich

United side and personified the type of person, if not player, Murphy wanted at his club – he absolutely loved the idea of playing for United and would usually be found wearing his club blazer away from official duties.

Things were complicated further still by the fact Italy hadn't qualified for the tournament. The Italian FA decided to hold the Coppa Italia over the summer, which led to Juventus insisting that John Charles must remain with them in Turin to play. By the time he had convinced his club to allow him to go to Sweden, the Italian FA then stepped in, saying it was too late to file the necessary paperwork. "I was beginning to feel very downhearted," Charles said. "It was a relief when I was told I could go. After all, how many times does a player get to play in the World Cup?" He was finally given permission to join up with the Wales squad four days before their opening game against Hungary.

Before that drama, however, on May 31st, Desmond Hackett reported on a behind-closed-doors friendly international between England and Wales in London. England won 1-0 in a forty-minute game which Hackett described as being as competitive as a full international. 'Wales had their vehemently voluble manager Jimmy Murphy talking at the pace of a word a kick,' Hackett wrote.

Murphy had been taking training in Hyde Park; the players complained that this was hardly the ideal way to get prepared for a World Cup. Their camp at a local sports club had been cancelled as the pitch was being seeded. Jimmy walked the players to the nearby park and started an impromptu training session, with tops and tracksuits for goal posts. A warden pointed out "No Ball Games Allowed" but Jimmy persuaded him to give them an hour or so and they would be on their way. There is the suggestion that a few coins may have changed hands! It was unthinkable to consider the great John Charles and top players from the likes of Arsenal and Wolverhampton Wanderers walking through the streets of London to do some World Cup preparation in a park training session; in a way, that summed up Jimmy, his persuasiveness, his charisma and his ability as a true leader – not to speak of his insatiable appetite to just play football!

After the practice game, Jimmy had lunch with Walter Winterbottom, the England manager. Winterbottom said he felt Jimmy had it lucky, having so few players to pick from. Jimmy bit back at him: "Give me two of your headaches, Tom Finney and Bobby Charlton, and I will win the World Cup." This may have been somewhat of a flippant comment – though over the years the merit of it has been debated – considering Jimmy went on record to later express empathy with his English counterpart. "England could have won the World Cup with Roger Byrne, Duncan Edwards and Tommy Taylor," he said. "Their deaths meant new players had to be tried. Whoever comes into a team has to be part of a pattern and it takes a long time for a pattern to develop. It is unfair to expect new players to immediately slip into a rhythm or create a new one of their own."

The Welsh team travelled to Stockholm by plane on June 2nd. Jimmy, of course, had gone to Munich the day after the disaster but had travelled by other means since. A number of officials representing the Welsh Football Association were on board; Jimmy said nothing, but felt uneasy about such a large number travelling by plane. Perhaps it had been a natural consequence of Jimmy's occasional absence from the Welsh party in the recent months, but there appeared to be a lack of unity in the group.

That lack of time also meant a lack of preparation on Jimmy's part; another understandable consequence. Regardless of how reasonable these difficulties were, game plans still needed to be designed, and the Welsh supporters back at home and in Sweden were still going to be watching their boys with some degree of hope, if not expectation.

Realising the limitations, Jimmy considered that a defensive strategy was the best way to set up his Welsh side, with the idea that if he could get through the group with three draws, this may give them a good chance of qualification against all odds. Wales would play a deep defensive game, with the team retreating when the opposition had the ball. In possession, this game plan would rely a lot on the quality of the wing-half. It was a calculated gamble and would require his players to believe in the idea. But it didn't matter if this was a gamble, or if it had been an approach he had planned for months. Murphy's reputation spoke for itself, so when he laid out the plan, his players listened.

Hungary were the opponents in the first game. After five minutes, the approach needed modifying, after József Bozsik scored. Wales' response was good, and they grabbed an equaliser midway through the first half through their star man Charles. Though this was far from the great Hungarian side of the pre-revolution years of 1956, it was nonetheless an encouraging result.

The three point target from the group stage was almost reached in the second game; an encounter that features one of the most infamous Murphy anecdotes. "Bloody Mexicans," he barked, "they're cowboys, they're only good for riding horses!" It was a politically incorrect rant in much the same way as he had attempted to gee up United before their game against Borussia Dortmund in 1956; telling them that they were playing against people whose families had bombed England during the War. Jimmy was a man who not only accepted different cultures but he embraced them in the perennial quest for footballing perfection; these crude speeches were simply a last minute way of getting under the skin of any players yet to require an extra incentive.

Indeed, he wasn't above compromising his own loyalties, as Charlton recalled. "When he was in charge of the youth team, Jimmy was a brilliant brain-washer," Bobby said. "He could make you feel that the game you were about to play was the most important in your life…far more important, even, than any first team game. If you were playing a London team he would insist Cockney footballers were useless. If a Yorkshire side, he would brand Yorkshireman as footballing nobodies. Once, when we were about to play a North Eastern side, he said that Geordies were no good. And I rose to the bait and took him up on that point. When we were about to play Cardiff the great motivator gave the game away. He tried to tell us that Welshmen had no idea about soccer. When a Welshman is prepared to trade his birthright for the good of his team that must be a splendid brand of loyalty!"

Jimmy Jr believes that his father's committed approach was what endeared him to Matt Busby. "I think it was a tremendous compliment to my Dad that Matt saw something in him out in Italy and offered him a job," he says. "They'd only played against each other a few times and football has always been a very insular kind of sport, where managers will arrange their coaching staff mainly from people they were previously close with.

"Matt saw my Dad speaking and by all accounts Dad was something of an evangelist out there in Bari, preaching as he did so passionately about football. But that was Dad, he knew the buttons to press to get players fired up."

Wales were favourites going into the game and took the lead through Ivor Allchurch. An incident following an aggressive challenge from Colin Webster infuriated the Mexicans; it set the tone for a nasty atmosphere for the rest of the game as the

Mexican supporters took umbrage, whistling and jeering at all opportunities. With a minute to go, Jaime Belmonte scored an equaliser. Jimmy said afterwards that in a way he was glad that his team had drawn, because of the learning experience they would get further down the line. However, this was with the benefit of hindsight, and he cut anything but the figure of a contented man as he laid into Webster afterwards and told him he would be dropped for the final, and crucial, group game.

On June 16th, Wales played against hosts Sweden, requiring a victory to ensure guaranteed qualification for the next round, but knowing a draw might be enough. With Sweden having already qualified, it meant for a below-par match. "I know it was a bad match, but to be unbeaten is still an achievement for a small country like ours with so few players to choose from," Jimmy said afterwards.

That match finished 0-0 and so Wales and Hungary had to meet up again for a play-off. Jimmy was relieved by this. He had noted in the first game that this new Hungarian side did not play in the continental style he had prepared for. They played long balls, and Jimmy felt that he could win the game if his team adopted an approach they were familiar with. At first, it didn't appear as if it would work. Lajos Tichy, one of the mainstays in the Hungarian team, scored to give them a half-time lead.

Their approach then turned physical, as they targeted John Charles in an attempt to stop Wales' source of getting back into the game. "They kicked the hell out of me," Charles said. "My legs were black rather than blue from the pummelling they had taken." The other Welsh players stepped up – Allchurch equalised, and Spurs winger Terry Medwin netted with just under a quarter of an hour to go to send the Welsh bench into raptures. "When we went a goal in front, Jimmy and Jack Jones, our trainer, were dancing a jig on the touchline – it was so funny," said Charles.

Jimmy took exception to the over-the-top aggression towards Charles and several times was given cause to jump from the bench and angrily race to the touchline to scream at the officials. With Wales on the cusp of qualification, Jimmy was almost beside himself, only taking breaks from gesticulating to take sips from his flask of whiskey. "Jimmy was running up and down the line beseeching the referee to blow his whistle and end the game," remembered Charles. "In the dressing room after the game, Jimmy was unusually quiet, going around shaking hands with all the players and thanking them. It should have been us thanking him."

Murphy said few words afterwards to the press. "For us Welshmen to take our little country to the last eight of the world's soccer powers is a great, great moment," he said.

Most of the Welsh officials had made their way home after the group stages as the flights were already booked; they had to hastily schedule return flights to Sweden. For many of the fans who had been there to support the side, they would be out of luck; Wales and Hungary played out their knock-out tie in front of only 2,823 supporters.

The suits were so happy that their trip hadn't been wasted that they threw a party at the hotel to celebrate. A few of the players said they would go out into Stockholm for a couple of beers before the party began; Jimmy said that was fine, but to only have a couple and to behave responsibly. In a joyous mood, Jimmy – a few sheets to the wind – rose to his feet and sung 'Land of Hope and Glory' at the top of his voice; he received a great applause, and then apparently decided to call it a night. The Welsh players, however, did not. Webster had returned to the party and allegedly chatted up the girlfriend of a waiter; upon being confronted by the waiter, Webster head-butted him. He was marched out and the management of the Copacabana Club (where the party had been held, underneath the Grand Hotel) demanded that Webster be charged. Welsh officials decided they would try and keep the story under wraps by paying off the management.

Still, Jimmy was incensed by this and was determined to send Webster home. He did not face disagreement from the Welsh officials, but Secretary Herbert Powell advised that sending home the player may do more harm than good with the speculation it would provoke from the press. To complicate matters further, it was clear that following his roughhousing from the Hungarians, Charles was very unlikely to play in the quarter-final. As the game drew closer it was apparent that Webster would be required.

So, as Wales prepared for the biggest night in their history, the quarter-final against Brazil in Gothenburg on June 19th, their injury-hit squad underlined their position as outsiders.

Murphy had been so engrossed in his position as manager that for once he wasn't overly familiar with the opposition, despite their celebrated status – nobody had done the scouting job he undertook so regularly in his club work. "All we know about them (Brazil) is what we have read," Murphy told the *Daily Mirror*. "But after the way our boys have been playing, I have terrific confidence in them and we must stand a chance."

The team talk followed a similar theme. "I'm disappointed in these Brazilian players," he said. "They're over-rated and if we get stuck in we can get a result. Even their so-called great players have grave weaknesses. Nilton Santos is supposed to be the best left back in the world…that's rubbish! Terry (Medwin), you'll pulverise him. Pele? He's got nothing but speed and a shot!"

It may have seemed improbable, yet Jimmy had sold his Wales players on the dream. It was a repeat of the same way he had galvanised his Manchester United players in times of hardship. In many ways, little else mattered. Absolutely nothing had been expected of United as the true horror of the news of Munich unfolded. Murphy was not a manager, but he had done enough to get those players to Wembley. Now he had taken Wales to a World Cup quarter-final against Brazil. Players for club and country between February and June 1958 had found themselves galvanised by Murphy to give more than could ever have been reasonably expected. Success, on these days, was not to be found in the result. It was to be found in the hope and the dream.

And yet. And still. On another day. Wales had chances. Medwin played like he believed what Jimmy had told him, and he had the better of Santos, delivering cross after cross. Charles, sitting beside Jimmy on the bench, was arguably more agitated than his manager, visualising himself getting on the end of these crosses. Reality hit with just a quarter of the game remaining. Pele hit a deflected goal, his first ever in the competition. Brazil won 1-0.

Regardless, Jimmy enthusiastically praised the performances of his players, saying that goalkeeper Kelsey, inside-forward Allchurch and centre-half Mel Charles could justifiably claim to have been the outstanding players in their positions in the tournament. If he had one criticism it was, surprisingly, of Charles, whose game, he felt, had been negatively influenced by his time in Italy. Jimmy felt it had took away the burst of acceleration which had been so crucial in Charles' game in fashioning space before getting a shot away. "The plain fact was that John was a disappointment for me and to himself," Murphy said. "I have had several chats with John about it and given him my advice for what it is worth. I think we shall soon see the return of the great John Charles."

Wales had most certainly over-achieved. "Most of our own

WORLD CLASS

players thought we would be on our way back home within a week," Jimmy admitted. Despite the defeat, it was elation rather than deflation that dominated the mood within the Welsh squad as they prepared to return home. "The performance of the Wales team in Sweden put us all in good spirit," Jimmy later said.

England and Scotland had been eliminated in the group stage and Wales' defeat was accompanied by Northern Ireland's 4-0 defeat to France on the same evening. There was a damning verdict by the press, although Wales' performance gained them the kinder reviews.

Frank McGhee held a 'World Cup Inquest' for the *Daily Mirror* on June 21st, rather crudely, and at least insensitively, reporting in the manner of judge and jury. On 'gallant' Wales, McGhee said they 'proved everyone wrong'. His 'verdict' on them? 'Accidental death – the cruel accident that cost them John Charles in the vital game. Yet even without him they managed to hold Brazil, rated best team there, to one goal…Only the Charles brothers, inside left Ivor Allchurch and perhaps left winger Cliff Jones would stand a chance of getting into the England team. Yet, just like Ireland, they went further than England. Why? They had in charge of them a man in the Peter Doherty (manager of Northern Ireland) mould – Jimmy Murphy, a craggy, uncompromising man who injects every man in his team with enthusiasm, makes them better than they really are.'

In the glow of the glorious failure, Murphy found himself addressing unwanted speculation to Bob Pennington of the *Daily Express*. Murphy was taking a few days to remain in Sweden and was found 'in hiding' taking a stroll on a beach in Saltsjöbaden with forward Charles. Pennington put two and two together and asked Murphy outright about speculation linking Charles with a £75,000 from Juventus to Old Trafford. "I know nothing

JIMMY MURPHY

about these rumours regarding John and Manchester United," Jimmy said, in front of both Pennington and Charles. "I have never made any type of approach to John. He is under contract to Juventus and that's that. It makes me furiously angry to hear suggestions of this type. The whole idea is nonsense." Pennington quizzed the Welsh boss on his own future, asking if he'd had any offers to leave United. "There is always this talk when you get a little success," Murphy told Pennington with a 'chuckle'. "I do not know of any offers – let's leave it at that."

Shortly after this conversation, though, Jimmy did find himself facing a fourth offer of a manager's role in the space of a year. A Brazil official called to congratulate Jimmy on his efforts but made it clear very quickly that the point of him getting in touch wasn't to offer salutations. Would Jimmy be interested in coaching the Brazilian national team? If he would be, there would be an eye-watering salary of £30,000 a year in it for him.

"The salary offered made me whistle," Jimmy said. He described the offer as tempting. However, by now, he'd already made up his mind to remain at United. That decision had been given a stronger solidity because at the start of the World Cup, he had already received and turned down another offer.

Arsenal had waited until there was confirmation of Busby's intention to return to full-time duties and as soon as reports of that nature surfaced, they sent a club official out to the Grand Hotel to sound out the United assistant coach.

In the *Daily Herald* on Thursday, July 3rd, Steve Richards reported: 'Jimmy Murphy, the most wanted soccer boss in Britain, could be seated at Arsenal's most important desk before the start of the new season. The challenge and the chance of personal glory that go with the plum job of football are within the reach of the tenacious Manchester United acting chief. It was Murphy who re-stabilised the Old Trafford structure after Munich and who nearly inspired Wales to World Cup glory. My exclusive information is that approaches have recently been made by Arsenal to Murphy. I gather the move is still a top secret in the Highbury records. Speculation that London's great club want to appoint Sweden's World Cup coach George Raynor or Harry Johnston has been just…speculation. I can tell you that the figure who tops the wanted list is the talented Welshman who is similarly honoured by several other clubs…Jimmy Murphy.'

"Sir Bracewell Smith, who was chairman of Arsenal, sent an intermediary to find out if I would be interested in joining them as manager," Jimmy said in his book *Matt…United…And Me.* "Of all the English clubs who sought my services – and there have been more than a dozen First Division clubs alone – this offer from Arsenal was the only one that caused me to think twice.

"I reckon a lot of the clubs wanted me in the hope some of Matt's genius had rubbed off on me, that I could do a 'Busby' for them. Arsenal was different. I hesitated because after all, when I was a player, they had built up a tradition and glamour and they thought in big terms. There was an aura about them, which made one feel that here was a set-up which could have become world renowned like it was in the '30s. After hesitating momentarily, I turned them down. I am happiest with players as a sort of soccer technocrat, and that is why I have received some fantastic offers."

It was subsequently rumoured that Jimmy had been sufficiently interested in the role to talk it over with John Doherty; Doherty had been one of the young players brought through at the club by Murphy, but had transferred to Leicester City in 1957 before suffering an injury. Around the time of the Munich disaster, Doherty was being told he would never play football again. He later alleged that Jimmy had informally discussed the Arsenal offer with him and had even asked if John would be his assistant if he made the move. It certainly gives the impression, if not that Jimmy would have ever left United, he at least did give the Arsenal proposal some due diligence.

Alan Wardle was one of John's closest friends and confirms the story. "John Doherty had a good eye and Jimmy knew that about him," Alan said. "John told me that he'd agreed to join Jimmy, but Jimmy went home that evening to talk to Winnie. They still lived in a club house at Whalley Range. They talked it over; Winnie was reluctant to move and reminded Jimmy that he couldn't drive. She made him realise that he didn't really want to leave United. And that was that, he turned Arsenal down. For the next year, Jimmy was still doing most of the work of manager as Matt came back to full health."

So far, Juventus, Brazil and Arsenal had all made offers which Jimmy was more than happy to discuss. However, there was one club who made an approach in the closer, more immediate aftermath of Munich. Far from being flattered, Jimmy was in fact offended. He said: "While I was wrestling with the problems at Old Trafford after Munich, and while Matt was still desperately ill in hospital I had a phone call from one of our biggest rivals. 'Join us and do the same job you are doing for Matt and we will double your salary.' That offer shattered me, to think anyone would be so cruel as to try and tempt me away when United needed my presence to keep the club going until Matt recovered sickened me. I put the phone down.

"Even now I don't want to stir up trouble revealing the name of the man who made me the offer, but when I look back it seems to me it was a deliberate attempt to wreck Manchester United's hopes of staying a force in the game."

The speculation as to who that club was will remain. There is no solid evidence that associates that with the rumoured Liverpool offer and so it must be presumed these were two separate approaches.

Later, Jimmy remarked in a *Magic Moments* section of the *United Review* that the proposals put to him over the years reached double figures.

"Judging by all the feelers that were being put out I could have had my choice of about ten top clubs," he admitted. "But some of those direct offers were naughty…very naughty, and terribly thoughtless as well. There was Matt, still gravely ill, and the club deep in mourning, and people had the nerve to approach me. Even if I had ever contemplated leaving Old Trafford I would not have done so in such circumstances. However, as I told people many times, it would have been unthinkable for me to leave United. Like Matt, I had become wrapped up in the club and in the players on whom we looked as if they had been sons. The greatest joy I had at any time in my career was seeing the kids make good…or, as I used to put it, watching the little apples grow."

Jimmy Jr feels that no offer could have tempted his father away from United. "He wouldn't have left Manchester," he says. "He couldn't drive, for one. He had a wife and six kids who were all settled. But he loved his job. He couldn't wait to go and work with the kids every day. There are plenty of interviews with the likes of Denis Law who speak about how driven and motivated he was but I think that was a side of his character which became more prominent after Munich. Fundamentally, Dad was a fanatic about football, he was absolutely bonkers, head over heels in love with the game of football. He loved his job, the task of developing young players."

JIMMY MURPHY

Even as a labour of love, though, and even with the prospect of Matt Busby back at the helm, returning to Manchester United to resume the incredibly draining challenge he had taken on was not one Jimmy Murphy would enjoy looking forward to.

CHAPTER | TWELVE

NOTHING WILL TEAR US APART

"If it had been my father in the crash and Matt had been the one running the club without his players, the club would have collapsed. He didn't know the players left behind. That wasn't his fault, it was just how it was" – Jimmy Murphy Jr

Matt Busby and Manchester United confronted their demons head on. Their first task in preparation for the 1958/59 season was a return to Munich, albeit by boat and train, to commence their warm-up for the campaign. United lost 4-3 against a combined Munich XI and gave a performance that left Matt Busby far from happy. "Something will have to be done," he said.

Survivor Albert Scanlon played in his first game since the crash but said he felt terrible. An injury to Colin Webster in the following game, a 2-0 defeat to Hamburg, depleted United's resources further still.

In truth, Webster was on borrowed time anyway. Jimmy Murphy had reported to Busby the events of Sweden and it wouldn't be long before the player was on his way. However, Webster bore no ill will towards Murphy, later saying: "Jimmy did a job that no other manager or coach could possibly have done with the players at his disposal. I'm not saying this out of favouritism either, because it was me who Jimmy rollicked more than anyone. I know he was instrumental in me leaving Old Trafford, but I have nothing but good to say about the man." Webster played in seven games and scored five times before being transferred to Swansea in October for £7,500; a further sign that United's attitude and principles would not be compromised, even in such testing circumstances.

Whilst Jimmy had been in Sweden, Manchester United had received an invitation to play in the European Cup for the forthcoming season. It was a benevolent offer, considering the financial windfall a club might expect to receive. A figure of £20,000 for participating in the first round alone was an attractive proposition for a club whose total accounts held something like £112,000. United accepted the invitation and were drawn against Berne Young Boys in the first draw on July 2nd.

On July 8th, the club received a letter from the Football League which refused to give the club permission. United appealed, and won the appeal, but a committee made up of representatives from the Football League and Football Association decided the matter should be referred to the FA Consultative Committee.

In late August, a letter was received by the club from the committee; it stated that as the European Cup was a competition of clubs who had won their domestic championship, Manchester

United did not qualify, and consent was therefore refused. United were, however, granted permission to play their tie against Young Boys as two friendly games.

The club started the season improbably well; beating Chelsea by five goals to two at Old Trafford and then winning 3-0 at Nottingham Forest. Bobby Charlton was the star both times, scoring a hat-trick in the first game and two goals in the latter. Despite a defeat at Blackpool, a 6-1 thumping win over Blackburn Rovers gave the impression that United may have enough in them to put up a challenge.

This was commendable indeed considering the fact that the club had not made any new signings. In fact, the playing staff was not only depleted by the departure of Webster, but the sad news that Jackie Blanchflower had been forced to retire as a result of the injuries he suffered in Munich. Blanchflower had been part of that difficult pre-FA Youth Cup period but nonetheless was one of the first kids who had come through the 'system' and Jimmy was suitably sad. "He was a lovely, quiet lad," he said. "He was a cultured pivot and eventually played for Northern Ireland. He battled with Mark Jones for the centre-half position in our first team…two wonderful players, so sad."

The club announced Johnny Aston, the former player, was going to join to help out with the youngsters; Murphy's skills now being needed more with the first team. Aston would effectively fill the role that Bert Whalley had performed so wonderfully while Jack Crompton led first-team training. Both Busby and Murphy were acclimatising to the new dynamics of their old relationship.

"If it had been my father in the crash, and Matt Busby had been the one running the club without his players, the club would have collapsed," Jimmy Jr says. "He didn't know the players that were left behind. That wasn't his fault, it was just how it was. It's often said that Matt would say 'go out and play your football' as if it was as simple as that; but they play football all week. You see managers on the sidelines making all these hand gestures and it makes you wonder what they've been doing on the training pitch all week. They're professional footballers.

"When Noel Cantwell came to United, he'd been playing at West Ham and he said 'Where's all the tactics and the team talks?' He was told: 'We wouldn't have bought you if you couldn't play football!' At the time of the disaster, Matt had said something like, 'There's so much talent coming through, I can sit in my office for ten years and that gives some indication as to what his duties and responsibilities as manager were.

"Bert and Jimmy were the ones moulding the talent. Bert would take a player like Bobby Charlton and say, 'You're the best player in the North East, but you're just one player, an individual, and football is a team game.' Dad would work with the players on the practical side. He'd spend Sunday mornings with the players refining the parts of their game that needed help. He'd get them running again to build up their lungs, because when it came to senior football matches, they'd notice the difference. He'd never been on a coaching course in his life but he somehow was able to be such an effective coach and, more impressively, a developer of young players. Two European Player of the Years. Nine European Cup winners. More than twenty five international players. Six international captains."

This success was eventual. However, in those early weeks in the 1958/59 season, Jimmy made a promise to Matt. "It may have been too big a task but the intention was to keep Manchester United as successful as they had been and to do it with the same ideals as before," Jimmy Jr says. "They did that by winning the FA Youth Cup in 1964 with players who formed the basis of the team that won the European Cup in 1968. They finished runners up the following season and Dad was in charge for most of that season. After Munich, he promised Matt that he'd deliver another FA Youth Cup winning team, and he did."

In Eamon Dunphy's *A Strange Kind Of Glory*, Dunphy suggests the prospect of rebuilding their dynasty was what drove Murphy and Busby on: 'A lesser man left to save another football club could have been excused for inculging the sorrow Murphy experienced in the weeks after Munich. There is no more remarkable testimony to the work Matt Busby had all but completed before the Munich tragedy than Jimmy Murphy's unflinchingly courageous commitment to the task he now faced.

'Matt and Jimmy were never personally close, but they understood each other. What they shared was a love of the game and pride in what they had achieved at Old Trafford. That also shared values which, although ostensibly irrelevant to professional soccer, had formed the club they'd built together. Both were family men and United was a family club. Both of them were decent, paternal, each placing great store on loyalty. United's success had encouraged other clubs to covet Jimmy, yet he'd never seriously considered any of the offers. He was happy to serve Busby's cause because it was his too.'

Dunphy gets as close to the articulation of the point than many have. There is nothing different, there is nothing to separate or distinguish the ideals of the Manchester United philosophy to be belonging to Murphy any more than they are belonging to Busby. It is, of course, incontrovertible that as the manager Busby deserves all of the credit that he gets. But perhaps what is missing – or barely referenced – in the summarising of the events is Murphy's toil and labour in the practical application of these values, the thousands of hours spent with the youngsters as a group and individuals. The matter of whether or not he is more responsible for the success is a subjective argument but it is absolutely reasonable that he felt everything so keenly and personally because of the extent to which he was involved in the development of the strategy he and Busby put in place. And, it is not even a matter for debate that Jimmy adored the set-up as it had been.

"He was never bitter or even bothered about the 'Busby Babes' tag," says Jimmy Jr. "In a way, I think he would probably have preferred it like that at the time. It took the spotlight away from him, after all. It's more for someone like me – I meet plenty of United fans, and some of them might think that Matt Busby was the youth team coach, that he did all of it, and that he rebuilt the club after Munich by himself. People think that he led the team out in 1958.

"[My wife] Pam and I were holidaying in Austria, and we befriended a couple of Scottish ladies who would sit on the next table to us for breakfast. Over one conversation one of them mentioned she had worked in West Bromwich so I brought up the fact my father had played football in the area. They noticed that our name tag was displayed on our table and a few minutes later she asked if my father was Jimmy Murphy; when I confirmed it was, she said she knew all about him. Apparently she'd worked with a big West Bromwich Albion fan who was fond of saying that his club was responsible for supplying the man who made Manchester United what they are today."

As Jimmy's reputation was on the rise, it was natural that some wondered just how fundamentally crucial he had been to the work at United. Certainly, there had been the perception – and one, it should be said, the man himself was happy to fuel – that Matt had done the majority of the work. "There are misconceptions about the work that was done by the people at United," Jimmy Jr says. "In a piece about Duncan Edwards you might hear about how his manager was Matt Busby and in the next sentence it might say that Duncan was signed in the early hours of the morning on his doorstep. The implication is obvious – that Matt made the signing – but that was Bert Whalley and my father. It's a similar thing with George Best, and the perception people have about he and Matt having a father and son relationship. George himself has said that if he wanted advice, he'd go and speak to Jimmy Murphy."

Despite this, and the natural frustration that Matt may have felt about this speculation even undermining the incredible work he had done, the pair never fell out, even on the occasions where they disagreed.

"Jimmy and Matt's relationship was great, particularly at first, as Matt was Godfather to one of my sisters," says Nick. "Jimmy idolised Matt and even though he could have named his terms anywhere else as manager he was immensely loyal to him. I think he was just so grateful for having been given this opportunity by Matt at the club he grew to adore that he could never imagine not being a part of it, and that's why he was so hurt later on when it seemed as if other people wouldn't listen to him."

Nick's brother agrees. "Matt and Dad would have disagreements all the time, but Matt was strong enough to make his own decision, even if he disagreed, and Dad was loyal enough to keep his own counsel and not fall out with him," says Jimmy Jr.

"I think Johnny Giles is a classic example. He went to Leeds United for around £24,000. Matt had bought Albert Quixall and favoured him in the same position; on the other hand, Dad had nurtured Johnny.

"They each had their own preference and it's not difficult to see why. But Dad would be deferential to Matt, even if he was right, as I think he was in that case."

The case of Giles would be prominent a little later but Quixall is a name who, in September 1958, was very prominent. Manchester United made a British record offer of £45,000 to Sheffield Wednesday and it was accepted; a player long admired by Murphy and Busby was on his way to Old Trafford.

It was Quixall who scored the third goal of the 'second leg' in that friendly tie against Young Boys. United had lost the first game 2-0 and looked set to 'lose' the overall aggregate scoreline as the second leg reached its climax. It had been a tumultuous game at Old Trafford, treated by both the players and supporters as if there was actually qualification riding on the result. The second half was chaotic and Webster effectively signalled the end of his career at the club by getting sent off; however, United recovered, to get a second from Viollet before Quixall scored late on. So, despite everything, the club would have qualified for the second round. It ultimately meant nothing, but United had at least proved a point; they were no whipping boys.

In the October international break, Matt and Jimmy were pitted against each other as Busby led Scotland in their home game against Wales on the eighteenth of the month.

Scotland won 3-0 in Cardiff, leading Murphy to express how disappointed he was at his team's 'lack of fire and enthusiasm', but despite this, it seemed as if the reminder that he was still manager of Wales provoked more column inches and speculation linking him to club jobs. Who could succeed where Arsenal, Juventus and Brazil had failed? Well, it seemed that Leeds United thought they had a chance, and although no formal approach was made, Jimmy was forced to answer questions about the interest. "I have heard nothing at all from the Leeds chairman or anyone connected with Leeds United," he said emphatically, adding, "my family and I love it here in Manchester. We are settled and I still have a huge job to complete here at Old Trafford."

However, one club was sufficiently encouraged to make their interest public. Perhaps the perception of directors at football clubs was that Jimmy, having had a taste of football management, may be intoxicated by the praise which had been deservedly bestowed upon him for his achievements which, even in relative terms, were nothing less than miraculous. Maybe his refusal of the offers he had received was simply down to the fact he hadn't received the right one.

Reporting for the *Express* on November 20th, 1958, Alan Williams told the story of Aston Villa sacking their manager of five years, Eric Houghton. 'Jimmy Murphy, Matt Busby's No.1 man at Old Trafford, will be asked to take over at one of soccer's highest salaries, which means more than £60 a week,' Williams wrote.

"He turned down several lucrative offers to take control of other clubs because Manchester United were his heart and soul," Harry Gregg later said. "Everyone needs money to put food on the table, but Jimmy Murphy's life was not about pounds and pence. Football meant everything to him – in fact, he was anti-anything which got in the way."

With speculation intensifying over the weekend, Murphy repeated his intentions to stay put: "I am not leaving Manchester United. That is definite. These words should end all the speculation regarding my future," he said. "I made a pledge to my manager, Matt Busby, the day following Munich. That pledge will not be broken. At the time Matt was dangerously ill. None of us knew whether he would pull through. I told Matt then that I would stand by him no matter what happened."

And he went further, addressing the rumours circulating about his relationship with Busby. "There have never been any secrets between Matt and myself. All this talk about a rift between us, about jealousy, is just utter nonsense. Certainly, we have had our differences of opinion, maybe we'll have more, but Matt and I are good friends as well as business colleagues. Surely, it is when two people can differ and pool their ideas for a common cause that real friendship exists?

"My association with Matt Busby has lasted for 13 years and they have been very happy years. I hope we will share many more and see the club rise to its former greatness. That is the tremendous task that lies before us at Old Trafford – to rebuild a side as great as that which perished at Munich. It means much hard work. It may be some time before we can see more than the glimmer of light for the future. But the job will be done. Matt and I have dedicated ourselves to that task. This is the greatest club in the world, we mean to put it back on the top."

It gives an indication of how much Murphy was wanted that it took more than a month for Villa to find and decide upon an alternative – that man eventually being Joe Mercer.

Part Three

13. Resurrection

14. The New Crop

15. Destiny

16. The Fall

17. Legacy

CHAPTER | THIRTEEN
RESURRECTION

"My father said, 'In my career there are only two players I have never coached. Duncan Edwards was one because he could do it all, and the other was George Best because it would have taken away from his genius'" – Jimmy Murphy Jr

Certainly, despite the professional reputation, Jimmy's own children found him to be a warm man, when he could tear himself away from Old Trafford. And, even in an era when a smack on the bottom was common, Jimmy was cut from a different cloth.

"He wasn't a strict dad, not really…if he ever said anything that was a bit too much Mum would always tell him," Nick Murphy remembers. "He once hit me, nothing serious, just a clip, and sent me to bed. When I was upstairs I shouted down to him, 'Fatty!' and I could hear him laughing downstairs."

The most serious thing Nick can remember is an accident. "There was no central heating so he would take a kettle of hot

JIMMY MURPHY

water upstairs to shave and I ran down the stairs past him; I knocked into him and the water went down my shoulder," he says. "I still have the burn. It wasn't his fault, but I can remember Mum screaming at him." This quiet home-life persona is corroborated by Nick's older brother, Jimmy Jr. "He didn't bring his work home with him," he says. "He might have been a ranter and a raver on the training pitch but when he was watching from the stands he'd be very quiet, observing the game. If anything happened of interest he'd kick you or nudge you with his leg."

Jimmy also found time to go on holiday with the children, though they would sometimes remain with their aunts and uncles in Wales as their father returned to Manchester to work. "We always used to get the train back to Wales," Nick remembers. "Dad would often get off the train at a station where they'd have a buffet cart or a small shop where he could get a drink. The train would set off and we'd be wondering where he was; what he would do is get back on in another carriage, and then come down to where we were sitting and laugh at us. 'Ha ha, fooled you all!' He was very much a joker. Our holidays might be in Rhyl or up in Blackpool at the Norbreck because he knew the staff. We'd go to Nan's in Rhondda Valley for weeks sometimes. He loved Mary, his step-sister, and Arthur, his brother."

As a younger child, Nick's recollection is a little different to Jimmy Jr's. "Dad was such a workaholic that we only ever had two holidays as kids," Jimmy Jr says. "We had a week in Rhyl when I was thirteen and about six years after that, we had a week in Newquay."

Jimmy would also accompany young players on trips to other countries; ostensibly to help spread the word of Manchester United, and also do the odd scouting mission, but also to try and establish a greater bond with those players he took away. "He was

RESURRECTION

very fatherly and protective of the players," Nick says. "He took Duncan and Wilf on their first trips out of the country when they went to Ireland. He was doing some scouting out there in Bray."

In those months after Munich, Murphy and Busby had pledged to rebuild the club using the same philosophies as they used to establish such an incredible system in the first place. The truth, though, was that would be nigh on impossible.

For a start, the coaches they had were different. It didn't matter how fantastic John Aston and Jack Crompton were (and in the late 1950s there was enough reason to believe they could be just as good as Bert Whalley and Tom Curry). The simple fact is that over the decade, the groove had become so consistent and second-nature that Manchester United represented a body, a body able to depend on the various people within it constantly fulfilling their obligations and reaching expectations. One may have reported to the other but within the confines of their work, the trust was implicit.

Jimmy was immensely grateful for the help provided in those tough post-February 1958 months, and when Matt returned, he too made his changes to the staff. But it was different. The championship-winning team of 1956 had been crafted through eight years of hard work and the reason that Busby had felt confident of a decade of success was because more players were coming through the same system and would therefore be subject to the same procedure of first team introduction – gradual, and conducive to the development of the player.

Now everything had changed and a new strategy was required. United had to find a quicker way of establishing themselves as the premier force in the country. This would involve scouring the country for the best players that they might have otherwise

JIMMY MURPHY

missed. The best men for this job were Joe Armstrong and Murphy. Thus, Jimmy's role was transformed and with it, the structure within Manchester United changed.

After the adrenalin fuelled by the disaster had worn off, and after Murphy no longer had to work every waking hour to run the club, the toll taken by the grief became all too apparent. It wasn't, after all, just the shock of losing friends he had to deal with. Jimmy had been out to Munich, he had witnessed the devastation of the wreckage, he had seen the hospital wards.

What is relayed as an emotional and heartbreaking anecdote as Jimmy held Duncan Edwards' hand must unquestionably have been a traumatic experience. "Dad thought the world of Duncan," Jimmy Jr recalls. "Dad's words are inscribed on the statue of Duncan in Dudley; I know he would have been honoured by that. He could speak about almost any of the lads who died, eventually. You could ask him about Eddie Colman and he'd be able to tell you what a lovely lad he was. Just the mere mention of Duncan was enough to have him in floods of tears."

Wilf McGuinness wasn't too proud to admit that Jimmy's fondness for him was probably rooted in memories of Duncan. "I would say Duncan was United's best ever player," Wilf admits. "I played in Duncan's position, nowhere near as good as him of course, but I think that part of the reason which endeared me to Jimmy was I reminded Jimmy of how he played. With Duncan having the kind of ability he had, you can make your own mind up about how he would have felt watching him."

Nick Murphy says their father would become just as emotional when speaking about any of the players who died in later life. "In the '70s and '80s he would quite openly talk about the boys who had died in Munich, it wasn't ever a subject he would shy away from," he says. "He'd talk about how brilliant they were but the tears would always follow whenever he did speak of them. It never, ever left him. He never got over it."

In those early weeks and months of the 1958/59 season, though Busby was back, he was still recuperating, and so Jimmy was the man still assuming most of the managerial duties. Bill Foulkes explained: "With Matt Busby on the mend but still far from fully functional at the start of the campaign, it was the heroic Jimmy Murphy who set the tone once more, preaching a non-stop sermon of togetherness. 'Defend in strength, attack in strength' was Jimmy's motto, and we followed it to the letter."

United's defence had been fairly leaky; Foulkes admitted he was playing within himself, that he felt a different person after Munich. He was moved to the reserve team in the late winter – not to prepare for a departure, but instead, to retrain to play at centre-half. A successful run of games meant that a return to the first team beckoned, but Foulkes was then sent off in a Central League game at Chesterfield in March 1959; given the player had never even been booked before, this was most certainly the most remarkable thing to come out of the goalless encounter. Foulkes was livid, feeling that neither bookable offence was warranted.

"I was absolutely dumbfounded and so was Jimmy, who was turning the air blue on the touchline," recalled the defender. "I announced that I was not going to let the official get away with such a diabolical decision and that I wanted a personal hearing. Jimmy supported me to the hilt and we enlisted the help of the Professional Footballers Association." It was discovered that the referee had sent off seven Manchester United players at Central League level, at a time when red cards were extremely rare, as ironically evidenced by Foulkes' previously blemish-free record. The referee was suspended and the case against the defender was thrown out.

United rallied following an inconsistent start to the season and put together a run of eight wins on the bounce. They in fact lost just three games from mid-November until the end of the season (one of those was on the final day), and in late-March, even went top of the table on two occasions. One of the major surprise success stories in this period was that of Warren Bradley, the Bishop Auckland player Jimmy had signed; Bradley had impressed Busby enough to be given a part-time professional contract and a chance in the Football League, and by the end of the season he was not only playing and scoring goals, he was selected for England.

Murphy's ostensibly lighter workload (still the regular eighty hours, even if the tasks appeared to be less labour intensive) meant that instead of watching Central League fixtures, he was instead usually found at Football League fixtures looking at forthcoming opponents; if neither team were scheduled to play Manchester United, then there would generally be much cause for speculation about just who he was there to see.

'Look at Aldershot! They continued their plucky points-taking at Walsall – and had Manchester United No.2 Jimmy Murphy weighing up 19-year-old left-winger Dennis Parnell,' reported the *Express*. This was small news on a day when a Football League revolution was announced with the following changes proposed for the 1959/60 season – the implementation of substitute players; the suggestion of a transfer deadline for December 31st so that 'cash-salvaged clubs would no longer be able to bribe their way out of trouble' and the removal of Christmas Day fixtures.

At the end of February, it was reported that Mel Charles – brother of Welsh legend John, and already an experienced international like his sibling – was set to leave Swansea City. 'He is a close friend of Jimmy Murphy, United's assistant manager who is also the Welsh international team manager. It is no secret Jimmy would like him at Old Trafford,' Tom Lyons reported. Had this been a year earlier, without question Charles would have been in Manchester. However, the manager was not Murphy, it was now Busby, and the time had been and gone.

In addition to scouting future opponents and assessing potential recruits, Busby would call Jimmy back to Old Trafford if they were suffering a poor run of form. He would be asked to watch United play on a Saturday and report where he thought they were going wrong. Jimmy would sit in the stands and try and get a bigger picture.

Jimmy may not have moved elsewhere but that did not stop others trying to emulate his ideas at their own football clubs. There was an interesting 'Junior Soccer' report by Willie Evans in the October 30th, 1959 edition of the *Daily Mirror*. 'The Youth team with the Manchester United look – that's Ford United, the Dagenham works side,' Evans wrote. 'All because manager-coach Harry Johnson spent two years as an amateur with United. Harry learnt a lot from Jimmy Murphy. And now he is putting the Old Trafford ideas into practice. I saw his Ford lads when they beat St. Joseph's (Greenwich) 5-0 in a London Minor cup tie. And Johnson's insistence that they should play FOOTBALL all the time is very apparent. Keep it up, Harry!'

*****

The 1960s appeared as if they would be very tough days for Manchester United. The second-placed finish in 1959 was a false dawn; two consecutive seventh placed finishes were followed by a 15th place in 1962 and at the end of the 1962/63 season United were fighting off relegation; only a 3-1 win over Leyton Orient in the penultimate game of the season secured their place in the First Division.

During this time, Murphy completed his return into relative obscurity, his name only garnering press attention should he be spotted on one of his scouting missions. Despite these regular deployments, the greatest source of Jimmy's passion remained the work that Manchester United did with young players, and even though some big name players started to arrive for big transfer fees, these would generally be players who fitted the bill in terms of character and personality (such as Pat Crerand) or even be players who the club had previously wanted but failed to buy, such as Denis Law.

Of course, this transitional period saw many outgoings, too. Alex Dawson left in 1961, despite an incredible goalscoring record of 45 in 80 league games. For him, according to Busby, his peak had already been and gone. In the same year, Kenny Morgans left for Swansea City. Wilf McGuinness had already retired after suffering a terrible injury and was relieved to have been offered a position coaching alongside Jimmy.

In fact, Wilf and Johnny Aston were, in effect, the new Bert and Jimmy. Jimmy ceased his Tuesday and Thursday night sessions at the Cliff, as well as his infamous afternoon coaching, which were generally replaced by similar but infrequent drills with senior players (and, in the case of the younger players, replaced with general, well-meaning conversations about their wellbeing). With their absence went the fear experienced by the likes of Bobby Charlton and McGuinness, who would be forced to work through hours of monotonous practice to prove a point. It made the youth team dressing room, and that of the reserve team, a much more laid-back environment.

Other young players looked like breaking through but just

RESURRECTION

failed to make the grade. Ian Moir was one such example of a youngster who Jimmy would dedicate his time to as much as he could in the same way as he did before. "Ian was a bit of a character and often found himself in trouble because he couldn't keep away from girls, so Dad would often be round at his parents' house talking to them and giving them advice," Jimmy Jr remembers. "Dad would be like that with all of the players, that was his job. 'There's nothing good that happens after eleven o'clock at night!' Dad would say."

By the time the players came to Jimmy, they were – usually – at least seventeen, and their first steps into professional football had been taken under the tutelage of others. Johnny Aston was Manchester United through and through and had seen the process at work so he knew what was expected and demanded. However, he wasn't Murphy; few people could rival that natural tenacity and few, if any, had the dedication that Jimmy had to his job. This was not a failing on Aston's part, and indeed, many excellent footballers came through during this period.

Tony Dunne was nineteen when he was scouted by Joe Armstrong. Armstrong, like Aston, knew only too well of the attributes desired in prospective Manchester United players and so his eye was crucial in the rebuilding years. Dunne had already informally agreed to join United but had remained at Shelbourne as they had qualified for the Irish Cup final and Busby felt he should play it. By the time Armstrong returned to see him again, the player had developed so significantly that he instructed the club that the move should be accelerated.

Jimmy, alongside Aston, met him at Manchester Airport. Dunne couldn't believe it. "I was in awe of everything to do with Manchester United," he said. "Then to be met at the airport by Jimmy Murphy, the man who single-handedly kept them afloat after their darkest hour, well, I couldn't believe it." Jimmy took to Dunne immediately, singing his praises to both staff and players, acknowledging the player's great attributes and his willingness to listen.

"Jack Crompton was in charge of first team training and it was mostly fitness work," said Dunne. "Matt Busby selected the team. It would be Jimmy who corrected any mistakes the players made. He was great to me. I'd heard that before the crash, he was always in a tracksuit working the players out on the training ground. I don't know, because I wasn't at the club then, but he always used to be out with me on the pitch, wearing his tracksuit…he would break down my game in detail. It was comical really watching him demonstrate the point he was making, the way he sort of did a little hopping and dancing. He made me believe I was the greatest full-back in the universe…after listening to him, I would go out on the field and practise what he had told me, to work on the faults he had pointed out in my play. He was always right!"

John Aston Jnr's recollection is similar. "I wouldn't exactly say Jimmy took a back seat in training but he and Matt were not hands on," he says. "They were great delegators, and you'd often find them watching from their office."

Dunne's recollections highlight the modification in Jimmy's approach. He may well have been getting the players a little later than he was used to but he still believed that in getting through to them at a young enough age, he could drum home the value of practice and repetition. This would make these potentially great individuals even better and equip them to be part of a Manchester United team drilled in the same principles, even if the significant difference was that the majority of the Babes had gone through it simultaneously so as to make their own patterns of play appear to be telepathic.

Murphy's team talks had changed, now, too. When he followed Busby he rarely spewed the same sort of vitriol as before, though he still set out to inspire and motivate. "You are playing for Manchester United, the greatest club in the world, and you are all great players," he would say, and the players would feel elevated because of it.

"He was so passionate, he spoke with authority and every player respected him like they did Sir Matt, but in a different way," Dunne recalls in Brian Hughes' *Starmaker*.

"Jimmy would have a drink with us after the game and a laugh and joke. When we lost a game, Sir Matt wouldn't rant and rave, but if we lost and played badly he wouldn't be happy and we would feel guilty we had let him down. On the other hand, Jimmy would be agitated and go round explaining to the players where the team went wrong and offering advice. He was so sincere and honest in his analysis of how and why we had lost. He would organise the play and point out to individual players what they should have done. And he was right!"

If there was one player who was well placed to give an appraisal of Murphy before and after Munich, aside from Bobby Charlton, then it is surely Nobby Stiles. Jimmy had taken heed of Nobby's Collyhurst upbringing and vowed to make him the footballing equivalent of the area's great boxers. In training, he would run the touchline alongside Nobby, encouraging him into tackles, telling him the right moment to go for the ball. Jimmy would often take to the pitch himself, and would aggressively tackle Nobby to toughen him up.

The principles about the simple things being the most effective; efficiency of ball recovery and then intelligence in moving it on. These were not only the two uppermost staples of the Jimmy Murphy footballing rule-book, they were the two areas Stiles learned to excel in. Nobby also had excellent positioning awareness. Stiles was a much better player than most gave him credit for, however, Murphy never once understated his importance, even when the likes of Charlton, Denis Law and George Best were receiving all of the praise.

The relationship between Jimmy and George was a strange one. In those pre-Munich years Jimmy would affectionately speak about his promising players as 'golden apples'; after the disaster, there was a touch of melancholy, if not separation, in all of his mannerisms. The boys were never far from his thoughts. And so when Best, the most sensationally gifted youngster since Duncan Edwards arrived at the Cliff, unearthed by Bob Bishop, Jimmy was keen to see for himself what all the fuss was about.

Jimmy loved him immediately. The first time he watched him, George was a fifteen year old playing in a training game against the first-teamers. He picked up the ball on the half-way line and beat no fewer than five players before scoring past Harry Gregg from the edge of the area. "When I saw that, I knew Bob Bishop was right, we had a genius," Jimmy purred.

Nick Murphy tells a great story about George. "I ran a local church team and every year I'd try and get a celebrity down to present an award down at our local hall, St. Herbert's," he said. "I booked the hall and we got [legendary boxing trainer] Brian Hughes to come down and do a speech. There was a bit of a mix-up as about half of the lads who were playing for the team were going to a wedding on the same day, but were going to attend the award ceremony in the time left between the wedding and the evening do.

"It transpired that Brian was going to the same wedding, so he borrowed the mini-van he used for the boxing club to bring over the lads and we ended up having a very successful awards ceremony with a couple of hundred people there. Brian gave a speech which he begun by saying he didn't want to embarrass me but it would be about my dad. He said he'd written to Jimmy when his brother was about fifteen and he asked if he could have a trial; Jimmy wrote back to him inviting them down to the Cliff one Tuesday night.

"They went down and the trialists took on a team comprised of other trialists and apprentices. The apprentices won something like 12-2 and after the game Dad put his socks inside his trousers and went on to the pitch, grabbing hold of one of the apprentices and walking him around the pitch, pointing and gesticulating. Brian couldn't understand why this lad seemed to be getting criticised when he'd just scored six or seven goals. Dad let the lad go and walked over to Brian. 'Hello Mr Murphy, you alright?' 'Aye,' he said. 'So what do you think of that player?' 'He'll make it, but your brother won't,' came the response. The player he had frogmarched around the pitch? George Best.

"The strangest thing about that story is that the DJ at the do would always have a fella helping him with the gear. It was usually his dad, but this time, his dad had a cold, so it was one of his mates over from Ireland, and he must have been pushing 80 at that point. Unbelievably, he came up to me afterwards and said, 'I was at that game.' Dad had been telling George everything he'd done wrong, despite him having scored so many goals.

"I was later told a story by John Doherty about the very same game. John had scored three goals himself that evening and he was told to report to Dad the following morning at Old Trafford. He was told to get changed, get some balls and meet him out on the pitch. Dad walked him out to the centre circle and had him kicking balls to empty spaces and then retrieving the ball, doing the same dozens of times. After a while Dad pulled him over and said, 'On Saturday, you hit a great long pass that went to nobody, instead of hitting a simple one.' He'd punished him by making him take the pass he should have made over and over again. John said it was a lesson that remained with him for all of his career."

Jimmy Jr can remember how much his father loved watching George. "George rekindled some of the twinkle in Dad's eye," he says. "He was a genius. My father said, 'In my career there are only two players I have never coached. Duncan Edwards was one because he could do it all, and the other was George Best, because it would have taken away from his genius.'

"They were instructed to leave George alone. I have a long-standing running bet with my pals that they can never find anything negative that has been said about my father and the closest they tend to get is a quote from George who said, 'I couldn't understand the fuss about how good Jimmy was as a coach, because he never seemed to coach me!'

"He would call players like George, or Denis Law, deckchair players. He said it once in reference to an incident that happened in the 1970s when Martin Buchan gave Gordon Hill a clip around the ear for not coming back to defend. Gordon was a deckchair player. What he meant was, a player that good at attacking can sit on a deckchair and wait for the ball to be played to him so he can go and do his magic. The others can do the work."

"To me, a penny worth of practical skill is worth a pound of theory," he said of George, who he felt was sure to become the greatest player of all time (though he would always add the caveat that he felt the best complete player ever was Duncan Edwards).

"George was like Edwards," Jimmy said. "Best didn't need coaching at all, he was an individualist; a pure and out individualist, was George Best, and if you'd have taken that from him George Best would have ceased to have become a player."

RESURRECTION

Even so, Jimmy was impressed by how dedicated George was to the game and self-improvement. When speaking about such a special talent maybe it is a fool's errand to consider if and where he could have improved his game. Perhaps he could not. But there are many 'what if's' surrounding Best and one of those is what if Busby had been harder on him – something Best himself pondered in his autobiography. Alternatively, just how disciplined might George have been had he been given the same sort of dedicated, personal attention in the fashion of an Edwards or a Charlton?

Certainly when George spoke of Jimmy there is a tremendous affection, and yet, there is a slight discrepancy in the way George talked about him as opposed to say, a Charlton or a Stiles. "If I had poured my heart out to anyone at Old Trafford it would have been Matt's number two, Jimmy Murphy," George said in his autobiography *Blessed*.

"He was a dour Welshman but with a heart as a big as a house. He and Matt were of similar ilk, they had been brought up rough and ready and seen it all, been through everything together. And of course, Jimmy did a magnificent job as stand-in manager when Matt was recovering after Munich. Matt and Jimmy played the good cop, bad cop routine. They were both good cops really, but someone had to play the hard man and that was Matt, while Jimmy would soften the blow after you'd been punished.

"Sometimes, after Matt had given me a dressing-down, Jimmy would call me into his room and say, 'You don't want to listen to that old bugger.' That was how they worked it and I don't know whether it was deliberate or not, it made for a perfect partnership.

"You rarely saw Jimmy on the training ground, though, which was strange. You would have thought it would have been the other way round, but the Boss always took training and Jimmy

JIMMY MURPHY

would sit back a little, spending time in the office making phone calls to sort out young players from other clubs. He probably did more than Joe Armstrong when it came to the youngsters.

"Jimmy's bark was definitely worse than his bite and I found him easy to talk to. Sometimes, after I'd done one of my disappearing acts, he would have a quiet word and if I had a problem I wanted to talk about, I would have gone to Jimmy and not to Matt. But I never did because I just wasn't the sort to open up to people."

Jimmy had just one criticism of George the player and that itself came with a caveat. Best would over-deliberate on the ball and perhaps take it all upon himself when, Jimmy felt, he might even score goals if he played the ball and went to receive the return. But still he left Best to his own devices. "Better to hold it and play as he does, than just be another run of the mill player," Jimmy reasoned.

Best had yet to make his debut as United flirted with relegation in 1963 and it is difficult to comprehend how a team including Tony Dunne, Pat Crerand, Bill Foulkes, Denis Law and Bobby Charlton could have finished 19th in the league.

However, Jimmy felt that the 1963 FA Cup final would prove to be a turning point. Busby said: "During that bad league season of 1962/3, when we won the cup and finished fourth from the bottom, Jimmy Murphy and I had discussed the situation, point by point, player by player, result by result. What must we alter if anything? What was going wrong? We decided that what we were doing was right, on the right lines anyway, and that results were bound to come if we maintained even slight progress. The play was good enough except for the finish, and we were not by nature a couple of fellows who take bad luck as an excuse...Jimmy and I had decided that we could see we were about to climb the staircase."

RESURRECTION

One element from that cup final which stuck out for Jimmy was, in particular, the performance of Denis Law and his attitude even in victory.

Jimmy praised Law for his goal and man-of-the-match performance in the 3-1 win – United's first trophy since 1957 – but the Scot said he felt he should have scored more than one goal. "One of those he 'missed' was that fantastic leaping header which beat Gordon Banks and hit the bar, an effort that brought the 100,000 crowd roaring to their feet…Denis could not understand that only Denis Law could have got to it in the first place!" said Jimmy. "That May day in '63 when we won the cup paid for all the anguish and anxieties of the previous weeks as we fought for survival in the First Division. Somehow, that day, everything clicked for Manchester United."

Jimmy was just as enthusiastic about Law as he had been when he first watched him play for the Huddersfield Town youth team. He insisted the £115,000 Matt Busby had paid Torino was a bargain. "Denis scored a few goals that I firmly believe even the great Brazilian Pele wouldn't have been able to score," he said.

Law said that Jimmy was a great motivator and that he admired his enthusiasm and aggression. "Because Busby was not really fully fit after Munich, our training was mostly in the hands of Jimmy Murphy," Law said, in an account that differs somewhat from the recollections of Best. "He wanted plenty of grit, and he didn't like cheats…everybody was to help everybody else in the team. He instilled that into the youth and reserve teams, which over the years brought many great players into the side. We sometimes played better for Jimmy than we did for Matt. He was very popular. I always felt that while Matt Busby gave United their subtlety and sophistication, it was Jimmy Murphy who put a little bite into our play."

Law's 29-goal haul not only saved United, but it helped them on the road to prosperity again. The club's run to Wembley was not dissimilar to that in 1958 in the respect that where the league form was inconsistent (to be kind), the best performances were saved for the cup. Having qualified to play against Leicester City at Wembley, Jimmy was determined that this would be third time lucky, following the defeats in 1957 and 1958. "You just watch us click at Wembley," he said to the press. They did.

Rather than that FA Cup win representing the end of an emotional journey, Murphy believed it could signal another beginning, and so dedicated himself to assisting in building another great team. That meant one of the toughest decisions he ever had to make; the eighty hours he was putting in a week at United meant something had to give, and unfortunately, that something was his position as Wales manager.

After the excitement of 1958, Wales did make it to South America in 1962, but only to Brazil by request to play two friendlies against the Seleção as part of their own World Cup preparations.

Jimmy's final game in charge of Wales came in the Home Championships, a 3-2 home defeat to Northern Ireland at Swansea's Vetch Field on April 15th, 1964. Wales finished bottom of the group, a sad end which was in no way reflective of the work he had done.

He took some time before he finally called it a day, resigning in the summer of 1964. It was plainly obvious that Jimmy's intentions to create a Manchester United-like family atmosphere amongst the Wales players had worked to an extent. The players adored him, and, as Alf Ramsey had astutely observed, he had made them feel as if they could beat anyone when they pulled on the red shirt.

RESURRECTION

"All the players thought the world of him," said John Charles. "He was the best manager I ever came across." This was some praise from the legendary figure and it was most certainly reciprocated by Jimmy, who said that just as he had felt privileged to work with Duncan Edwards, England's greatest player, so too did he feel that privilege working alongside Charles, who he deemed to be Wales' greatest ever. He admired the way John would use his skill instead of the power and physicality he had which, like Edwards, would dominate almost every other opponent.

One of Jimmy's favourite stories about John was recalling the March 1957 fixture between Leeds United and Manchester United at Elland Road. Charles took a free-kick and hit it with such ferocity it nearly ripped the net off as it went in. Jimmy said it was the hardest shot he'd ever seen. Busby turned to Jimmy on the bench and complained that he felt someone in the wall had moved. Jimmy said: "My Welsh pride won the battle of conflicting emotions… 'Then he was a damn good judge Matt.' I replied, 'Anyone who got in the way of that shot would have ended up in the net with the ball.'" Charles admitted that the day Jimmy died in 1989, he cried.

It becomes a common theme that Murphy, the patriot that he was, could have worked with some of the great Welsh players at club level, because he recommended so many of them. That said, the ones he did recommend were always certs to make it.

Murphy pleaded with Busby to sign a young centre-half from Blackburn Rovers, Mike England, and long after his recommendation, the tall Welshman enjoyed many successful years with Tottenham Hotspur. Charlton recalled that Busby actually made an offer for England; Spurs eventually signed him for just £7,000 more than United had been willing to pay, a fact that had Jimmy complaining for years (though at the board and not Matt).

One player Jimmy had tried to sign in February 1958 was Cliff Jones. Jones became a world-class player who lit up the international stage but said: "The highlight of playing for Wales was listening to a Jimmy Murphy pep talk. Those players who have never listened to Jimmy have missed one of soccer's great experiences."

The plaudits ran thick and fast. Stuart Williams, then of Southampton but formerly of West Brom, said: "We all thought the world of Jimmy. He was a very passionate man and would transfer that passion to us. He would spit fire and sawdust in his team talks."

Murphy left the Wales position having instilled something precious which had previously been missing: a pride and desire to wear the shirt.

CHAPTER | FOURTEEN

THE NEW CROP

"Eusebio was given the golden football award for the best European player of the year just before the game. Halfway through he offered it to me if I would only let him have a few kicks at a real football" – Nobby Stiles

If Jimmy Murphy was committed to one thing, it was delivering on a promise he had made to Matt Busby: To create another FA Youth Cup winning team. But that was easier said than done. The dynamic had changed. Jimmy himself had changed. He had mellowed; not through complacency of achievement but simply due to the terrible reminder he had experienced about the fragility of life. He was surrounded every day by the memories of everybody he'd lost and the consequence of that was that he could no longer bring himself to be as aggressive as he once had been.

In some ways, his role was no longer defined; Jack Crompton, Johnny Aston Snr and Wilf McGuinness were doing much of the work he once did. Jimmy was there, sure, but he was not the omnipresent slave-driving task-master he had been. So, as the hierarchy changed, Jimmy's new mellowed persona transformed. Somewhat, anyway. "I'm not sure Jimmy was ever 'good cop'!" former player Jimmy Elms said. "He definitely mellowed after Munich, he definitely changed, he was much less aggressive."

Busby, as explained by George Best, became the bad cop, the man who players could fear. Busby was going through similar turmoil to Murphy; living with the grief and guilt (however misplaced) had made him more distant and withdrawn. In a strange way that became conducive to his power as the figurehead, the one players ought to fear.

The club had changed, too. They had been forced to sign a bunch of players and that led to a greater turnover than United had ever been used to. Dawson, Pearson, Morgans – all of these players who had come into the team in trying circumstances and given it such personality were now all moved on by the end of 1963. Of course, some young players remained; Charlton and Foulkes were mainstays of the side and Nobby Stiles was well on his way to becoming a regular, to name just three, but a cursory glance at the 1963 FA Cup final side shows no fewer than seven players bought in at a combined cost of over £300,000.

These were not players brought up in the Jimmy Murphy school of hard knocks or even the post-1958 school of slightly gentler knocks; in some ways, it was similar to the early 1950s Central League, with senior players who, when faced with this supposedly revolutionary coach, were met with instructions such as 'keep it simple' and 'play it to a red shirt'. Jimmy's reputation was strong enough for the new players to know his knowledge ran much deeper, so they weren't as dismissive as some older heads in those days.

THE NEW CROP

Those shifting plates at the club – as much to do with the evolution of the game itself as Munich – were evidenced in the handling of Johnny Giles' departure at the start of the 1963/64 season.

Giles disagreed that he performed better as a left-winger and would not accept the experienced opinion of Busby or Murphy. United, and Giles, put in a poor showing in the 1963 Charity Shield, and Busby had a meeting with Giles where he put the player on the spot about his display. Giles didn't back down, and requested a move. Busby, not wishing to keep a troublesome player, accepted that request and Giles moved to Leeds. Murphy must have despaired when he heard that the player wanted out but Busby had been backed into a corner; Jimmy may well have preferred Giles to Quixall, but the manager had no option.

Whilst harbouring the disappointment that things did not feel the same, Murphy tried to re-create the atmosphere in the youth team which had been so successful a decade prior. The players United had were not quite registering victories with twenty-three goals but Murphy had quietly assembled a tremendous young cast of talent. Best was the star name but the 1963/64 FA Youth Cup team was not only about the Northern Irishman.

Jimmy received a tip-off about a young player living in Maidstone, so he and Joe Armstrong made the long trip south one weekend and tried, as hard as they could, to remain incognito. They based themselves at the pub closest to the ground where the young player would be performing the following day, and Jimmy tinkled the ivories of the pub piano while he and Joe kept an ear out. "A prophet is without honour in his own country," was a Bible verse Jimmy was fond of and he used that reference for young David Sadler, whose name was mentioned plenty of times amongst the regulars who were excited for the game.

JIMMY MURPHY

It was obvious to Jimmy that Sadler was a talent, and not just because other scouts from Arsenal, Chelsea, Tottenham and West Ham were interested. Jimmy and Joe watched the player again and told Busby he should sign him; Busby watched him and agreed. Sadler was playing as an amateur and had a promising career ahead of him in the bank.

Ahead of Sadler's international debut some years later, Frank Taylor recounted the story in the *Daily Mirror*. 'If Jimmy Murphy hadn't been a pretty good piano player, it is doubtful whether David Sadler would have been playing centre-half for England against East Germany last night…Murphy had no doubt Sadler was a must for Manchester United. "But," said Mr. Sadler senior, "my boy has security. He is a bank clerk." Quipped Murphy: "He is also a natural footballer. If he listens and learns he can play for England and make enough to own his own bank."'

Jimmy went back to Maidstone, after discovering the Sadler family owned a pub in the area, to talk to David's father. Mr Sadler was unconvinced, saying professional sports were a risky business; his son could break his leg. "I might fall and break my leg in your bar Mr Sadler, but it wouldn't stop me using it," Jimmy said. Mr Sadler insisted, still, that his son had security in banking.

It took a visit from Busby to persuade the Sadlers to allow their boy to look around Manchester. The family was also uneasy about allowing him to be so far away from home. Jimmy mentioned to them that Old Trafford had its own railway station and it was basically on the premises of the ground. After arriving in Manchester, and seeing that Jimmy wasn't exaggerating, the Sadler family knew they could trust the club and took a chance.

When Sadler was spotted he was playing as a forward and Jimmy had been impressed by his footballing ability, as well as his strength in the air. He was a good enough forward at Central

League level but Jimmy felt that he would be better served, long term, as a centre-half. Naturally, Sadler took some convincing. "Get to the ball first son," Jimmy told him. "Come in hard for it. And always be first for that ball. As a defender, always remember the rough handling you yourself received as a forward. Come in hard and fair for that ball."

It was at centre-half where Sadler made his name during an absolutely outstanding career; though, in retrospect, Sadler himself feels that if he had trusted in Jimmy's instinct more wholeheartedly, he could have been even better. "From the word go, Jimmy felt I lacked a certain amount of aggression," he said. "He would cite Denis Law's approach as ideal. Jimmy was right. If I had had that, I would have been a far better player. Jimmy always believed in me and helped me to switch positions to play at the back and my career expanded." Sadler also says that Jimmy was more prominent in training than the manager. "We didn't see a lot of Matt Busby during training. Jimmy Murphy was the one we saw…he brought through players like me," he said.

As well as Sadler there was John Fitzpatrick, a Scottish wing-half in the aggressive mould Jimmy enjoyed so much. "He loved developing talented players, of course, but I think it was equally rewarding for him to bring through a Nobby Stiles for every Duncan Edwards, a Billy Foulkes for a Bobby Charlton," Jimmy's son Nick says. "He did love a dirty player, he loved John Fitzpatrick who was from that mentality."

A few years later, Fitzpatrick would be in and around the first team when they were on the hunt for the European Cup in 1968. Ahead of the second leg of the quarter-final against Polish side Gornik Zabrze, Foulkes failed a fitness test, and after a reshuffle, John was told he would have to play full-back against the opposition's best player on a frozen and snow covered pitch in

JIMMY MURPHY

Poland. Jimmy faced Fitzpatrick, put his hands on his shoulders and rasped: "John, you know what you have to do? Get stuck in and give the winger no space and time." Fitzpatrick stuck to his task and gave a great performance; Jimmy was proud of the sacrifice and application.

Jimmy was also a big fan of Bobby Noble, who was in the same youth team as Fitzpatrick and had all the potential to become a legend for club and country. Again, Jimmy enjoyed Noble's aggressive tackling approach ("Remember, Bobby, they can't play without their ankles!" Jimmy used to tell him) but Noble was much more than that; this left-sided defender had an assurance and composure beyond his years. His passing accuracy was outstanding; Noble warmed to Jimmy just as much as Jimmy warmed to him. "I never bought into the Busby myth that he was a gentle, paternal figure looking after his family of young men; encouraging them and protecting them," Noble said. "Busby was an emotionally distant man. It was John Aston Snr and Jimmy Murphy who made me the player I was, not Matt Busby." Noble was the captain of the United Youth Cup team and also won England youth caps. The world seemed his before a terrible car crash in April 1967 effectively ended his top-flight career.

Another left-sided player in that side – one who may arguably have benefitted from Noble's cursed luck – was John Aston Jnr, the son, obviously, of the former player and now coach at the club.

John Jnr would often find himself in the car with Jimmy on the way to training. "When I was younger I would get a lift in with Dad and he would pick Jimmy up from Whalley Range," he says. "On the way they'd stop somewhere so Jimmy could buy cigarettes – always 60, always *Players* – and immediately start smoking them back in the car. Inside the car the air was blue with

THE NEW CROP

smoke; he would turn around in that gruff voice of his and say 'John, it's a filthy habit, don't you ever start!'"

One of the interesting things to observe from talking to people who met Jimmy and worked with him is their tendency to do an impersonation of the way he spoke. His family don't, not really, but that's not to say that others do it out of humour. It's more to do with the impression Jimmy left; he was obviously a very distinctive character, a complete individual, and the impersonations are done with affection and reverence, almost in the way one tries to repeat a joke in the style of the comedian they heard it from.

"He was a bit special, Jimmy," Alan Wardle, former reserve player, and now a prominent figure in the association of former Manchester United players says. "He was intimidating, mainly because of that scary gruff voice, but he was also a real character. The great thing about him was that even though he mellowed there was the old flicker which occasionally came in. He'd come into the dressing room and say, 'Good luck lads, go out there and enjoy yourselves.' If we were playing City, and it was always City, he'd always add, 'but beat these bastards today!'

"We'd come in at half-time and we'd walk past the referees' room and there used to be a little telephone booth which had a sliding door. Jimmy would go in there and for years I believed he was making telephone calls at half-time enquiring about other players. Then one day I saw behind the door a glass of whiskey and a bottle!"

The team that started the FA Youth Cup for United in the 1963/64 season included Best and it would normally have included Sadler. Best had already made his first team debut as a 17-year-old a couple of months previous while Sadler had played twelve consecutive games in the senior side; considering the opponents were Barrow, and a comfortable victory was expected, he was given the night off. United racked up a 14-1 win and after disposing of Blackpool, Sheffield United, and Wolves (their great rivals at this level), they faced neighbours City in the semi-final.

The importance of the tie meant that Best was called back in. With the Northern Irishman, the Scot Fitzpatrick, and the Londoner Sadler to name just three, United's team was positively cosmopolitan compared to City, who had just one player born away from the Manchester district in their side.

As it was, it turned out to be Liverpool-born Albert Kinsey who was the main man again, getting a hat-trick, with Sadler scoring the other. United won 4-1; their route to the final almost secured. The second leg, at City, was a predictably closer affair and a more entertaining match.

City started on the front foot but Murphy had clearly instructed his players to protect against any early bombardment and try and hit their opponents on the counter. The game plan worked a treat, with Best getting a goal on 15 minutes to put this tie well and truly in the hands of the red half of Manchester. City levelled before the break, leading to a thrilling encounter as United confidently attacked while their hosts committed themselves forward. United eventually claimed a 4-3 win, with Best getting most of the plaudits, though the local press were keen to point out that the second leg had been such a feast of football that the future of the game locally looked very bright indeed.

United had qualified for their first final since 1957 and so were close to fulfilling the promise Jimmy had made to Matt at the start of the 1958/59 season. As they prepared for their trip to Swindon Town's County Ground, the youngsters were only too aware that the '63/64 season as a whole was starting to feel like it was 'so near yet so far'.

THE NEW CROP

United had tasted defeat in the FA Cup semi-final and also failed at the quarter-final stages of the European Cup Winners' Cup; their second leg to Sporting Lisbon was a catastrophe, as they surrendered a 4-1 first leg lead to lose 5-0. In the league, United had finished second, four points behind Liverpool; a startling turnaround from the previous season that was enough to herald Busby and Murphy's patience as a success – particularly after the Charity Shield result – and yet, close enough to glory to make it disappointing. A 3-0 defeat at Anfield in early April had been the crucial result.

The squad that season included eleven players from the youth system, though admittedly, a few of those were long established names such as Charlton. Gaskell was not quite of the standard Busby had hoped to be first choice but Harry Gregg had suffered a few injuries over the years and had only played 25 league games. Stiles had played 17 times but was now breaking through into a permanent position.

Bill Foulkes had adapted from full-back into one of the top centre-backs in the country. "When we had a problem at centre-half, Bill Foulkes quietly and competently took over that job and, for reliability alone, you couldn't name many better centre-halves throughout the 1960s," said Jimmy. "He developed into a true dreadnought stopper, just what we needed…you could never begin to put a price on Bill Foulkes because you just could not buy the type of loyalty he gave to Manchester United."

However, this should not dilute the success of the youth team in the mid-'60s. Foulkes ended the 1963/64 season celebrating his 491st appearance for the club. In the same game, Charlton celebrated his 299th, and Shay Brennan – the one youngster introduced into the team after Munich who had managed to keep his place – played his 198th game for the club.

In many respects, the situation paralleled the one United faced in the early 2000s when receiving criticism for their apparently underperforming first team. At that time, Ryan Giggs, Paul Scholes and Gary Neville were still amongst the best players in the country, and in the former two there is a case to be argued for the best players in the history of their countries. How, therefore, can it be a fair argument that the youth system was underperforming when there were three now senior players with almost a thousand appearances accumulated between them?

In the 1964 FA Youth Cup final it was pretty clear to all that Best, luck permitting, would be a certainty to make many first team appearances. There was none of the outcry which had surrounded some of Duncan Edwards' performances at youth team level but Best still proved to be a crucial player, scoring United's goal in the 1-1 first leg draw.

Earlier that month, he had made his international debut. Just 24 hours before the second leg, Best had played against Uruguay in Belfast, but flew back to Manchester joking that he would request a transfer if he wasn't selected to play in the game against Swindon. Best was in fine form, but it was David Sadler's hat-trick which ensured the FA Youth Cup would be returning to Old Trafford. John Aston Jnr scored the other in United's 4-1 win. It was just another great moment in a fantastic year for Aston Jnr, which would be followed by the offer of a professional contract.

John was yet another success story from the conveyor belt which was being jolted back into action. Perhaps helped by the family connection and the close bond Jimmy had developed with his father, John Jnr had an affection of his own for the Welshman, citing his honesty as one of his favourite traits. John was another to observe the simplicity of Jimmy's methods and his effective strategy articulation, and also, the personal touch which set him apart; though his recollections are of the later Jimmy, the more kind, less aggressive version. "He would tell me what great pace I had, he'd tell me I crossed the ball better than anyone in the country, and pat me on the back," John said. "I'd go out on to the pitch feeling like a million dollars…he was very honest, and I think that's why he and Dad got on so well."

Jimmy had come good on his promise to deliver another FA Youth Cup winning team, though only Best from that team would be a significant influence on the following season's success. Instead, Busby signed Pat Dunne to solve the goalkeeping issue, and after starting the season in the Central League, Dunne quickly established himself as number one, leaving Gaskell and Gregg to fight over a Central League spot. John Connelly was also signed to give some experience on the wing, having previously won a title medal at Burnley. They were experienced signings with a winning mentality – something which would prove crucial. It suggested that Busby anticipated a tightly-fought league and he couldn't have been more right; United eventually triumphed on goal difference.

This meant a renewed assault on the European Cup and an evening in Lisbon which would make everyone believe United could actually go the whole way. On March 9th, 1966, Best starred as United won 5-1 against the great Benfica side. "It's the match which, I suppose is the the greatest I ever saw Best play," Jimmy later said. "He scored three goals, taking the ball from the halfway line for one of them, and beating several opponents before hammering it in from 20 yards. The touch of a master. Yet on that night of triumph, I don't think George Best was even aware there was a fellow named Eusebio playing for the other team."

United's following game was at Chelsea; the result in Portugal had given the press the same kind of belief in Busby's team as they had felt after watching them destroy Anderlecht by ten goals. Desmond Hackett, reporting from Lisbon for the *Express* on March 11th, said: 'That wonderful bunch of lads came to London to play Chelsea on Saturday with bruises they bear as pride. I doubt if Nobby Stiles or Tony Dunne will be fit. Both have badly bruised legs. But Busby's assistant, Jimmy Murphy, told me: "Can you imagine that tough little so-and-so Stiles complaining that Eusebio kicked him?" Cock-a-hoop Stiles chipped in: "Eusebio was given the golden football award for the best European player of the year just before the game. Halfway through he offered it to me if I would only let him have a few kicks at a real football." The peak European Eusebio may have been before the game. But I could name 11 better and they all played for Manchester United.'

Frustratingly, the season shared other parallels with United's 1956/57 campaign. They suffered cup heartache at the semi-final stage for the second year in succession, whilst their European exploits were ended in the next round.

Partizan Belgrade won the first leg 2-0 and even though United won the return, their 1-0 victory wasn't enough to see them through over both legs. Jimmy observed how disciplined the Yugoslav team had been in defence. The busy schedule took its toll on United's relatively small squad – Best was missing from the second leg with injury. Foulkes later said that had it not been for that injury, he was certain United would have won the European Cup that year. By that time, United had lost three league games out of their last five, a run which put them out of contention to win Division One.

However, Foulkes was probably right to have such a view. United had three of the players who had a justification to describe themselves as the best in the world. In 1964 that accolade had

THE NEW CROP

been awarded to Denis Law, and in 1966, following England's World Cup triumph, Bobby Charlton was named the best player on the planet.

Charlton had been key to England's success and nobody was more convinced of that, or proud, than Murphy. "It was his mastery in midfield, his consummate artistry, and the way he slowed the game down and directed attacks, which was the key to England's World Cup triumph," Jimmy said of his golden apple.

Bobby scored both goals in England's 2-1 semi-final win over Portugal but his most famous goal was arguably the long range thunderbolt over Mexico in the group stage.

The player revealed that Jimmy's words had echoed in his mind as he picked up the ball on the halfway line. He said: "I moved forward and followed Jimmy's advice and just hit it towards the rectangle. [I heard] Jimmy's voice, *Don't place it, let the keeper wonder where it's going...if you don't know, then how can he?!'* The ball flew in so sweetly!"

United were also represented in the World Cup-winning side by Stiles, whose toothless smile and dancing was one of the most iconic sights of the celebration photographs. Stiles' aggressive nature made him a favourite to United fans but something of a mixed bag for rival fans. However, following the World Cup, he had won the nation's hearts.

Murphy described Stiles as "the player who began the World Cup series in 1966 as though he was to be the heavyweight villain, and ended it the hero who won millions of friends by his bulldog tenacity. Nobby Stiles epitomised the spirit of Sir Alf Ramsey's men."

Stiles and Charlton would star the following season as United recovered from an early season stumble to storm into the second half of the season. They were helped by early exits in both cup competitions (the 1966/67 season being the first time that United had played in the League Cup, a competition that was initially created as a consolation prize for those teams who were knocked out of the FA Cup), but more to the point, a blossoming of talent from that 1964 FA Youth Cup team.

Best continued his rise to prominence following that night at the Stadium of Light, while Aston Jnr, Sadler and Noble all became regulars to complement an outstanding cast (though, as previously mentioned, Noble's career would tragically be cut short as United celebrated their triumph). Goalkeeper Alex Stepney had been signed at the start of the season to finally provide a consistent pair of hands between the sticks. Following the turn of the year, United were unstoppable, not losing a league game from December 26th on their way to their fifth league title under Matt Busby.

Another go at the European Cup awaited Busby and Murphy. Jimmy felt that victory in the competition was fated.

CHAPTER | FIFTEEN
DESTINY

"Duncan Edwards' parents approached Jimmy to say how much their son would have enjoyed the night. Duncan had always told them Manchester United would win the European Cup. Jimmy nodded, tight-lipped, tears in his eyes"

Manchester United's aims at the start of the 1967/68 season were to try and accomplish what the Babes should have done in 1958. That was, to win a treble of League Championship, FA Cup and European Cup.

As usual, Jimmy took issue with newspaper predictions of such a windfall of trophies; though the ambition was there, knee surgery for the player Jimmy dubbed 'the human dynamo', Nobby Stiles, as well as an injury to the same part of his body for Denis Law, would severely restrict United's ability to seriously challenge on all of these fronts. Yet challenge they did.

Jimmy did not blame bad luck for United's failure to win the league. He graciously congratulated neighbours Manchester

JIMMY MURPHY

City as worthy champions, though was keen to point out how frustrated he had been with United's form in the second half of the season. From February 17th, 1968, they somehow contrived to lose five of their next eight league matches – and still, they were given a chance to get back into the title race, leading the league with three games to go. They promptly lost two out of those three and surrendered the title to City after losing at home to Sunderland on the final day. Had they won that game, they would have won the league on goal difference. Jimmy said United's form was that bad it was enough to give him and Busby ulcers! "Nothing would go right; and when a team loses as many silly points as we did in the final months of the season, it is true to say they don't deserve to be champions," he said.

Europe was entirely different. They went on quite a remarkable adventure which began in September 1967, against Maltese side Hibernians. Law and David Sadler scored a brace apiece to send United into the second leg, in Malta, with a 4-0 scoreline which was enough to see them qualify. The press reckoned United might run up a hefty score in the return.

Father Hilary Tagliaferro, manager of Hibernians, said: "The English press was very harsh with the Maltese players, calling them waiters, saying United would thrash us 10-0. Contrary to the press, Jimmy and Matt were very respectful to me and the players...maybe it is because we were Catholic."

Jimmy Jnr says that his dad and Father Hilary struck up a fine friendship. "Father Hilary was also a sports reporter. Dad grew close to him and was impressed with his capability as a coach; he was also grateful because he gave him advice on the Portuguese players later on.

"I went to Malta years after Dad died, the year of the ash cloud. We were looked after by Joe Glanville of the Maltese Supporters

DESTINY

Association. While we were there I went to see Father Hilary and I asked him how he got on with my father. "He treated me as if I was the coach of Juventus, or one of the world's top clubs. He was Jimmy Murphy, coach of the famous Manchester United and talking to me as if I was the same," he told me. He showed me a picture of them together. It was incredible. Father Hilary was holding a tape recorder, clearly interviewing Dad, and I've never seen my father so relaxed. Undoubtedly, just out of shot of the camera, there must have been a couple of drinks!"

United drew 0-0 in front of a home crowd who mainly supported Manchester United as their second team – and a fair few as their first! Jimmy praised Father Hilary's tactics. "They held us to a goalless draw, thanks to the magnificent tactics and coaching of a priest, Father Hilary," Jimmy said. "I was enchanted by Father Hilary's great love of the game. We became firm friends." Father Hilary turned out to be an expert on Benfica and later provided Jimmy with a 'dossier' which he described as 'inestimable' in its value – though it has to be said United had already shown their capabilities against the same opponents. As Jimmy Jnr says, his father and Father Hilary remained close. "He'd write to him every other week," says Nick.

Their second round opponents were FK Sarajevo and Jimmy said that United's intention in that game was to do what Partizan had done to them previously and put up a disciplined defensive show. They unapologetically returned to Old Trafford with a 0-0 draw; a suitable base from which to approach the second leg, which they duly won 2-1.

Jimmy took numerous trips to scout United's next opponents, the Polish team Gornik Zabrze. United won the first leg 2-0 but they knew the second leg, away from home, would be a difficult proposition. "There was certainly no false optimism when we flew out for the return on March 13th, 1968," Jimmy said. "I had already made the nightmare journey before with Matt in the heart of winter where we seemed to spend most of the time either shivering, watching the football, shivering in airports, or flying!

"Every now and then I think about that game and still shiver, for the ground was dusted with snow and icy blasts of wind cut like a knife through clothing so that conditions were aptly described as borrowed from a Siberian horror film. It was tough enough keeping your feet, yet so brilliantly did Nobby Stiles, David Sadler, Francis Burns, Tony Dunne and John Fitzpatrick cover one another and tackle, that the Poles, despite the presence of the amazing Mr Lubanski, had few direct shots at goal."

Zabrze won 1-0 on the night; United qualified to play Real Madrid in the semi-final. Jimmy was as consumed as Matt was with the idea of qualifying for the final, which was to be held at Wembley; but the Welshman had something more than desire. He had belief; he was sure it was meant to be.

"During our European Cup run, Jimmy honestly believed it was our destiny to win it," John Aston Jnr recalls. "He'd say 'This is our year, John!' to me all the time. He was always optimistic and that rubbed off on us…we were a bit nervous ahead of playing Real Madrid but Jimmy said, 'We'll beat these buggers John, they're nothing.' It made us believe we could. Jimmy believed Manchester United were the best club in the world, the greatest club in the world, and we believed it too."

Stiles says that during the season, Jimmy had urged, more than ever, the need for concentration, and was redoubled in his determination to ensure that every legal and fair advantage was taken. "Jimmy knew the game, the detail that could make the difference," he said. "Shay and Tony Dunne were neat and clever round the ball. They'd track the winger down and instead of knocking him onto the track or hoofing the ball into the stands, Shay and Tony would just poke it out of play. Jimmy would have a go at them: 'Put it into the stand, give yourself an extra ten or 15 seconds to get organised for a throw-in. If you just touch it out of play they've got it back straight away and before you know where you are they're in your goalmouth and you're under pressure.' It seems nothing, but football is all about that kind of professionalism, if you like, at one level."

Aston wasn't the only player who was nervous ahead of the semi-final. Shay Brennan understandably had a lot to live up to. He had been involved in the 1958 game against Sheffield Wednesday. He was part of that group of players who were on the periphery; would he ever have made his breakthrough if not for the disaster? The game against Real Madrid was the opportunity to prove that he had made a name in his own right.

"Shay told me a story about something that happened before the semi-final against Real Madrid," says Nick. "When he told me, it was at the unveiling of Dad's bust in the museum; it always tends to be that way, doesn't it, that you hear story after story about someone once they've passed on? Shay was up against Francisco Gento, probably the best winger in the world at the time. He was dead nervous about facing him in the Bernabeu in such a big game. He said that Dad approached him personally before the game and sat beside him, slapping him on his legs. 'Alright Shay, don't worry about anything tonight you know, I found a lovely little bar you know, and we can have a drink after the game.' Didn't say anything about the game, didn't suggest any tactics. He was calming him down, telling him he had nothing to worry about."

This was classic Murphy. He had a track record for this kind of thing. John Doherty recalled: "An example of Jimmy's clever psychology was his treatment of Albert Scanlon after our left winger had endured a nightmare first half at Preston. At half-time Jimmy said: 'Well played, Albert,' and when I caught him on his own I asked him what the hell he was talking about. But in the second half, Albert was a different player, suddenly full of confidence, and it came home to me that Jimmy had handled him perfectly. People have got different temperaments and all play a different way, so you can't treat them all the same. Jimmy Murphy was ahead of his time in so many ways."

United had taken a 1-0 lead to the Bernabeu, courtesy of a George Best goal scored from an Aston cross. Jimmy likened the return game to playing in a Turkish bath, and expressed his sympathy for the players who had to play in such a raucous and deafening partisan crowd. "Only those who have played in these conditions know just how hard it is to keep composed, when it seems that thousands of yelling supporters will spill onto the pitch," he said.

However, Jimmy felt these were the nights you played for, the occasions where you can prove yourself to be among the greats. United's game plan was just as it had been in Poland; hold tight and try and break.

It went well for half an hour before Madrid scored through Pirri; Gento made it 2-0 to the Spaniards in the 41st minute. Then, a stroke of luck – Ignacio Zoco sliced his clearance and the ball flew into his own goal. Amancio Amaro scored to make it 3-1 to Madrid; Jimmy described it as a quarter of an hour spell of football he never wished to experience again, though admitted that it was part of the thrill and the rush of the sport to be on the precipice of such a great achievement – that intense slug between two great teams, where victory is on a knife-edge.

DESTINY

Jimmy said that Matt gave one of his best team talks at half-time. He told the players not to panic, not to be too urgent in their chasing of the play. He calmly explained that the score was not 3-1, it was 3-2, by virtue of the first leg score. United did not need to throw away this game by chasing it. They were more than capable of scoring a goal. Whilst Matt spoke slowly and deliberately, Jimmy was giving the players some encouragement. As they rose to leave the dressing room, Murphy cajoled: "Come on boys, one final effort, get stuck in for the ball and make them chase you!"

Jimmy described it as one of the most incredible transformations he'd ever seen on a football pitch. The players had clearly listened to every word and played the second half cool, much to Madrid's surprise. They played patient, patterned, responsible football in the hope an opportunity would present itself. Pat Crerand hit a long free-kick which Best headed on; there was Sadler at the back post to bundle it home.

United had their goal, and suddenly, with 15 minutes to play, Madrid were the anxious ones. The visitors were finding their groove and Bill Foulkes felt confident enough to join the attack. Call it instinct, call it fate – Foulkes timed his run perfectly to receive a Best pass and slide the ball in across the goal. United were in the European Cup final, ten years after the great team before them had perished on the Munich runway. Afterwards, Jimmy asked Bobby Charlton why he hadn't been the one making the run to get the equaliser. "Jimmy," Bobby quipped, "I was covering for Bill at centre-half!"

And so to Wembley, where there was little point pretending that it wasn't the emotional event that it was; that this didn't represent ten years of heartache and effort. Busby would remind the players before the game to play the game and not the occasion.

JIMMY MURPHY

To remember what they did in Madrid. Jimmy felt United should have been a couple of goals up at half-time but, after a reminder at the interval to keep playing their game, the reward came early in the second period, when Charlton scored. Against the run of play, Benfica scored to level it up, and in the dying moments it seemed as if they would snatch the win when Eusebio stormed through and unleashed a blockbuster of a shot. Alex Stepney not only saved it, but kept hold of it. Murphy despaired and caught his breath at the same time; the pre-match talk had been a relentless emphasis on stopping the supply to the great forward.

The full time score after 90 minutes was 1-1; the players immediately collapsed to the pitch, exhausted, trying to build up energy for the forthcoming 30 minutes.

Busby was straight on the pitch telling them to stand up as their muscles may cramp up. Jimmy, meanwhile, was in the ear of Paddy Crerand and Nobby Stiles. "Their legs are gone – they're knackered!" Murphy stressed, feeling that United could seize the initiative if they went in for the kill. Jimmy had been particularly impressed by Johnny Aston Jnr and reserved special praise for him after the game. "This was young Aston's finest game in a red shirt," he said of the man-of-the-match. "He was a revelation as he tore the experienced Benfica full-back to shreds."

It was appropriate that the scorers were all 'apples' from Jimmy's 'orchard', and it was equally fitting that the goals were registered in that quick-fire fashion which had devastated and decimated many a team under his tutelage.

Two minutes into extra time and Best rounded the goalkeeper to score one of Wembley's great goals; two minutes after that, and Brian Kidd – celebrating his 19th birthday – scored to make it three. Benfica were on the ropes when Charlton landed a knockout blow in the 99th minute.

DESTINY

By this time, Murphy admitted that he and Matt were already celebrating; he was already crying tears of joy, for he was sure that United were on the verge of glory.

The second half of extra time was a 15 minute period of arduous anxiety. "Now it was like a dream as we waited and willed the seconds away, until the final whistle brought merciful relief, and the great red and white cliff of United fans rose to hail their heroes," Jimmy said.

The final whistle went. Manchester United were European champions. Jimmy must have felt overwhelmed as he finally allowed the gravity of the last decade to sink in alongside the realisation that he and Matt had achieved the Holy Grail.

Jimmy did not go to the United players first. Instead he went to Benfica's distraught stars. Jimmy had been there; he had experienced Wembley defeat. He knew what it was like to watch the winners celebrate. He first approached José Augusto and told him hard luck – he knew how he felt.

"When you see the aftermath of the European Cup final, you barely see any footage of Dad on the pitch," Jimmy Jr says. "António Simões and José Augusto of Benfica were upset after the defeat and Dad took them back to the dressing room and gave them a drink. He was kind-hearted and sportsman-like like that – though, truth be told, he probably wanted a drink himself anyway! He had tremendous empathy."

At the victory party afterwards, families of the players who had died in Munich were present, making it a very difficult evening for Jimmy.

Duncan Edwards' parents, first of all, approached Jimmy to say how much their son would have enjoyed the night. Duncan had always told them Manchester United would win the European Cup. Jimmy nodded, tight-lipped, tears in his eyes.

Then the parents of David Pegg came over to offer congratulations; so too did the Colman family. It was all too much for Jimmy, who did not even try to hide his tears.

This victory was as much for them as it was the current team, as it was for Matt Busby and Jimmy Murphy.

CHAPTER | SIXTEEN

THE FALL

*"I think he needed someone to talk to more than I did He pointed to the ground. 'Look at this... all of it, I built this f*****g place, we built it: Bert, Tom, with our bare hands...and now...'"*
– Shay Brennan

Shortly after winning the European Cup, Matt Busby became Sir Matt, and rightly so. What he had achieved was nothing short of incredible. Nobody was prouder of him than his right-hand man Jimmy Murphy, who described the honour as a fitting climax to a wonderful career.

Matt and Jimmy were both of mining stock, with no airs or graces, brought up in cramped and overcrowded housing. Family was king. And yet, no matter how many times you read Jimmy's account of events, and hear his glowing praise for Busby, there are numerous opinions in print and conversation which suggest that the relationship between the pair was either not as close as it would seem, or not as close as Jimmy would like to have believed.

JIMMY MURPHY

In his book, Eamon Dunphy spoke about the 1960s as a time when Jimmy felt slightly unnerved by the change at Old Trafford. 'Jimmy and Matt, never close, grew further apart as time went on,' Dunphy wrote. 'Matt was in another kind of business, necessary but different. Jimmy had only been in the Cromford Club once, for Roger Byrne's wedding. He took his leisure in the Throstles Nest in Whalley Range, in the bar rather than the lounge. He drank too much. To kill the pain of disappointment. Often after games he'd talk with the old boys Bobby, Wilf, Shay, Harry Gregg and the best of the new men, Denis, Paddy, long into the night… after a game Jimmy would reflect on what had made United great…His eyes would fill with tears: "What's happening?" He meant to the club. The old lads loved him in a very special way. They respected Matt, were in awe of him; they loved Jimmy.'

It has to be said that Busby never once suggested that Jimmy was not deserving of the praise he received, nor did he shy away from giving him it. "As partners, we worked together to bring greatness to Manchester United," he once said. "Jimmy was the best friend, helper, companion and right-hand man any football manager could wish to assist him. No one outside the club will ever know how important Jimmy was to the huge success and fame of Manchester United."

In a report by Norman Giller of the *Express* on November 15th, 1968, Busby gave advice on what Giller described as the 'most hazardous job in sport'.

'The first five years are the worst, they say,' wrote Giller. 'That's the danger period for the men in soccer's hotseat.' Busby listed a number of important factors – a supportive board and chairman, dedicated players, and supporters, before closing with, "one more thing – a manager must be very careful about picking his staff. These are the men who can make or break him. Anybody who knows my right-hand man Jimmy Murphy and the United training staff will appreciate just what I mean. A manager cannot survive alone."

In November 1973, Sir Matt Busby wrote a series of columns in a week-long feature for the *Express* entitled 'Soccer At The Top'. He wrote about the disaster and the aftermath. 'In Walter Crickmer, Tom Curry and Bert Whalley we had lost backroom men of inestimable value and experience. Jimmy Murphy was not with the Munich party. He was doing his job with the Welsh international team. That is why poor Bert Whalley was there. The bond between Jimmy Murphy and myself had been forged years earlier, mere miles away from the battlefront in Italy....

'In the early days when he was watching the reserves we won the Central League championship. And then he said: "Matt, we have won the championship with our reserves but there isn't one of them who is going to make the first team at our standard." In our relentless search for the best of the boys there are Busby-and-Murphy adventures in the James Bond class (without the ladies, of course). We have travelled tens of thousands of miles together. He has been my protecter against pests, of whom football has its quota, my great aide in triumph and tragedy. Among players, the ones he could not stand were malingerers. He could not put up with deceivers or the chicken-hearted.'

In later years, there was never any suggestion that Jimmy was upset about the fact that Nick, who had played for United as high up as the Central League, wasn't given a chance in the first team. In fact, Jimmy tried to stay as far away from Nick so as to avoid accusations of nepotism. "By the time I was playing there, Dad was coaching the first team and often away scouting players and opposition, so I didn't see much of what he was like as a coach," Nick admits.

JIMMY MURPHY

"Occasionally he'd come in but he'd never say anything to me about my game. The only advice or feedback he ever gave me was that he felt I lacked confidence. He was right, to be honest. My path to United had nothing at all to do with my dad. I was playing locally and was spotted by Jack Crompton who invited me down to play and that's how I got involved, and yet I always had that self-doubt that I may have only been there because of who my dad was, even if it wasn't true. I was a bit embarrassed by it. I think Dad may have been, too, though that's just my own interpretation of it, it wasn't anything that anybody made me or us feel. He was encouraging of me being a footballer but didn't say anything else."

Jimmy Jnr feels that Nick should be proud of how far he did get. "We've got a squad photograph with Nicky alongside the likes of Bobby Charlton and George Best," he says. "That's something to have on your CV! There was no favouritism given to him though. He was a substitute on only two occasions and in one of those games United were 3-0 up. Matt never brought him on. I can't say why and I wouldn't want to speculate but I know John Aston was pushing for Nick to get a chance."

In the numerous interviews conducted in the planning and preparation of this book there is the suggestion in some of the things that aren't said; the silent statements which hang between conversations and float like elephants in the room. One such idea or suggestion – one not made or supported by anyone in the Murphy family, I hasten to make clear – is that in being protective of his legacy, Busby, while not exactly actively diminishing his pal's contribution, perhaps did not make completely good on the promise that the club would always look after Jimmy.

It is suggested that the motivation behind that attitude was a jealousy of the credit Jimmy received; as if he was worried that

THE FALL

his right-hand man's reputation as one of the finest coaches in football was perhaps seen by some as the main reason for United's success.

"I can't say that, but all I can say is Matt and Dad knew the truth," says Jimmy Jr. "Certainly from my dad's side, there was absolutely no jealousy, he loved his job and lived for it. Going out to play and coach football, with the enthusiasm he had for unearthing the next big star and the work he would put in… the foresight and excitement of forecasting just what this player might bring to the first team in a year or two. It's infectious, and something I picked up. I loved watching the way Marcus Rashford moved with the ball in the youth team; it's a rare thing for a British player to be able to dribble past players. I knew that ability would be welcomed into the senior side."

Wembley 1968 had been a momentous occasion but the emotional journey Busby and Murphy had been on meant that the final whistle on that humid May evening was more a moment of relief than celebration. It would be wrong to suggest that the pair had been running simply on adrenalin because they made calculated choices together to create another magnificent football team, but it appeared very clear that May 1968 represented the culmination of a journey rather than the beginning of one.

And so, when Busby announced his retirement in January 1969, the football world should probably not have been quite as stunned as it was. On January 15th – the day after the announcement – Frank McGhee, reporting for the *Mirror*, wrote: 'Sir Matt's right-hand man, Jimmy Murphy, assistant manager throughout the Busby regime, was not considered for the job because he is only a year younger than *the boss*. But his wisdom, experience, and inspiration are still readily available, freely offered.'

"I couldn't say for sure but I'm sure he was a little disappointed

JIMMY MURPHY

when Matt decided to retire," Jimmy Jr says. "They were both relatively young. Dad's job was different from that point but I still don't think he would have wanted the retirement."

After retiring, and moving onto the board of directors, Busby had promised that there would "always be a high and honoured position for Jimmy Murphy at Manchester United." In the immediate aftermath, he was kept on as assistant to Wilf McGuinness, who had been promoted from the reserve team manager role he had inherited from Jimmy in 1964. Following the FA Youth Cup win, Jimmy had been exclusively working as an assistant manager with the first team.

"When I became reserve team manager in 1964 Jimmy's advice to me was to be myself," Wilf says. "Pretty solid advice, considering I was just copying him! Because I had to retire young with injury, I think Matt and Jimmy were quite happy for me to go through the coaching ranks and be taught to do things in the way they wanted. So, when it came to coaching the younger players, I would not be shy in getting stuck in either verbally or physically in the same way Jimmy had when I was a kid. I was delighted that they took me under their wing."

Wilf became part of the Sunday club, who would meet up at Old Trafford to discuss Saturday's game and the plans for the following week. "To be involved in those meetings was a great privilege, a great learning experience," he said. "To listen and absorb all of their wisdom and knowledge was incredible and I would sit there taking it all in over the communal bottle of whiskey – that's where I learned to drink! Matt would never overdo it; he was calm, nice, understated. Jimmy would orchestrate the meetings with his fire and passion."

Initially, Jimmy continued his duties as assistant. In March 1969 it was reported that Jimmy had been up to watch Milan beat Celtic 4-0 in Glasgow; United were scheduled to play the winners. And later that year, Murphy was wheeled out as a 'big gun' to try and secure the signing of Ian Ure from Arsenal. 'Busby, McGuinness, and Jimmy Murphy – United's Big Three – swooped on Highbury yesterday afternoon like a syndicate of high-powered business men,' said a report in the *Mirror*. 'They left in a hired car two hours later with the signature of Ure barely dry on the contract that will be registered with the Football League this morning.'

However, the truth is that by then, Murphy's role at Manchester United had been altered in a way that he would never emotionally recover from. What followed Wilf's appointment was one of the most tragic misunderstandings.

"Theoretically Jimmy became my assistant when I took over as manager of Manchester United but, really, you couldn't call Jimmy Murphy my assistant," Wilf says. "He taught me most things I knew. To have that experience to call upon, you wouldn't want for anything else. Jimmy may have been the assistant but I would often find myself in deference. I would do certain things without telling him or asking him but on most things I valued his opinion. Even when I was manager he maintained his desire to win. Jimmy, and Matt were wonderful advisors. They wouldn't come to me – although perhaps they may have done if necessary – but they made it clear I was always welcome to go and ask for their opinion or advice."

And so, out of a mutual pride – Wilf's fear to ask, Jimmy's reluctance to interfere – an impasse was reached where Jimmy felt as if his opinion was no longer needed, or wanted. Wilf's stance is completely understandable and had he been aware that it had hurt Jimmy, you can't help but feel Wilf would have sought to compensate for that. "I would have thought Wilf would have

JIMMY MURPHY

asked for advice. But Bobby was the same when he went to Preston; no matter how well he spoke of my dad since or the high esteem he held him in before, they never went to him for advice," says Jimmy Jnr. "Maybe it was a pride thing."

Nick has the same opinion. "His working relationship with Wilf, once Wilf became manager, wasn't great and Wilf will admit that," he says. "I think that had Wilf confided in Dad a bit more or called on him more for advice, he would have lasted longer in the job. If he was too proud to be seen to be asking for advice he could have done it privately. Dad would have been happy to give it.

"He loved Wilf. Wilf was trying to do things on his own, but of course he couldn't tell Dad that he wasn't welcome at the club anymore, nor would he ever have said that. So Dad kept his office and I think that's when he just became a scout full-time, because he was no longer required as an assistant. Obviously some of the managers were more grateful for his knowledge than the others. He was down there every single day."

Eamon Dunphy's account goes along with the perception of Jimmy's heartbreak. He wrote: 'Shay Brennan, Bobby and Jimmy Murphy were Wilf's closest friends at Old Trafford. Jimmy was the most difficult to know how to deal with now…Wilf had always been Jimmy's protege. He was Jimmy's type of player, all hearts and guts, desire. Now Wilf blanked his mentor. Jimmy was hurt. Badly. The last thing Jimmy Murphy needed at this time was blanking.'

After Wilf was sacked less than two years into the job, Busby took the reins for six months to stabilise the club while they found a new permanent manager. But this was no return to the dream team of the '50s and '60s; Jimmy's role was more unclear than ever. "I think he felt badly treated by United and he was hurt by

Matt Busby, who'd told him there would always be something or other for Jimmy at the club," Jimmy Jnr says. "Then they stopped paying for his taxis. And the thing was, at the time, everyone knew that Matt *was* the board. Louis Edwards was a figurehead but Matt was in charge. He never spoke about how much it hurt him because my father loved Matt Busby.

"Matt gave him his dream job and Dad always felt that if it weren't for Matt, well, he might have gone on to be a teacher or a pianist. His football career was over when he went to war and he was only 28. They met in Italy and then took over at United which, at the time, had to be the poorest club in the First Division. They had nothing. The ground had been bombed. On the other side of town City were raking it in, getting their own crowd and then United's. They were making a fortune off the back of it. They were the poor neighbours.

"Deep down, I'm sure Dad was very upset about what happened. Dad had all that experience, nobody knew Manchester United better than he did, but more than that, he was obviously a top coach. There was a reason why Brazil, Arsenal and Juventus wanted him. He could have walked into any job in world football. It's incredible to think he wouldn't get a job these days because he wouldn't go away for three years to take coaching badges!"

Jimmy Jnr remembers: "Years later I was given a print of the 1968 European Cup winning team at a reunion, all dressed up in dinner suits, and right there in the centre was Matt Busby. And, as manager, he should be.

"All of the team got copies and then family members of the team, too; but Dad wasn't on it, and he wasn't mentioned. When he'd done 20 years' service, they acknowledged and rewarded him, but he refused to have the service in the boardroom. He was in his office."

JIMMY MURPHY

It could be said that the marginalisation of Jimmy unwittingly exacerbated another of the club's problems. United were in a downward spiral after the McGuinness era with many senior players not taking to the new management style.

George Best's behaviour had become erratic. Over the years there was talk about how Busby could have handled him differently but Best himself admitted that even if he had confided in anyone, it would have been Jimmy.

There is a poignant and important moment that occurred at the end of the 1969/70 season. Shay Brennan was called to see McGuinness and Busby at the Cliff, where Busby told the player he was being placed on the transfer list. "Shay was sick," recalled Eamon Dunphy. "Hurt, scared and confused, Shay went back to Old Trafford. Jimmy was there. 'Come on, come upstairs,' Jimmy said. They went up and sat at the back of the stand. Jimmy was consoling. He'd been blown out himself, and he knew what Shay was feeling. Suddenly Jimmy's anger and hurt burst out; he'd never had a go at the Boss before, but now it poured out."

Shay recalls: "I think he needed someone to talk to more than I did. He pointed to the ground. 'Look at this…all of it, I built this fucking place, we built it: Bert, Tom, with our bare hands… and now…'" Tears flowed. Jimmy's and Shay's. John Aston Jnr recalled that Jimmy had grown very fond of Brennan. "One time we were on tour and between games," he said. "I was rooming with Shay Brennan and after our evening meals, we went out for a walk and went back to the hotel. Our room was facing Jimmy's, and when we got back, he poked his head out asking if Shay had a minute. I didn't see Shay until the next morning and I asked him what Jimmy had wanted. 'A minute…I was there until half three in the morning talking football! Still, we had a bottle of whiskey!' Shay said."

THE FALL

Fast forward twelve months and as Busby stepped aside for a second time, there was much speculation about who would come in to take charge. 'It is not just a question of finding a successor for Sir Matt, it is what happens to the faithful servants such as Jimmy Murphy, John Aston, Jack Crompton and Bill Foulkes. A new manager would probably insist on bringing his own lieutenants with him,' reported the *Mirror* of May 26th, 1971.

Frank O'Farrell, the Leicester manager, was given the job and along with his boss came Malcolm Musgrave.

Harry Gregg recalls the time very well. "It was agreed during Wilf McGuinness' spell as manager, and later implemented during Frank O'Farrell's reign, that Jimmy would accept a job as scout at United," he said in his autobiography *Harry's Game*. "He also received a nominal one-off payment…but it would have been the principle which rankled most with Jimmy. I've seen it written several times that he blamed Matt Busby for not doing more to help. The bitterness which was to sour their friendship festered away as Jimmy watched how others were treated. He travelled by British Rail, and yet others at the club were given their own car.

"To direct his discontent at Matt Busby, though, was not altogether fair. I have never set out to defend the boss, but I have to be even-handed. Jimmy Murphy should never have been edged out of playing affairs at Old Trafford, but surely the responsibility for ensuring a man with so much still to offer remained down to the man in charge of playing matters. He more than anyone else should have realised Jimmy's worth. I know that Matt Busby felt he was in an impossible position, in fact he told me as much… Jimmy and his family felt Matt should have been in his corner but I don't really think he had any other choice than to give the new regime its head."

JIMMY MURPHY

After some time in limbo, Jimmy had finally received the clarification on his future, and he was absolutely despondent. A £20,000 retirement settlement was given to him and a £25 a week scouting sinecure was proposed to him. It wasn't the money that mattered to Jimmy, although his life would now be difficult in that aspect. It was the fact that he had been pushed to the sidelines of the club he had loved, and worse still, that these decisions had been made with the blessing of Sir Matt.

He was further insulted when he received a letter from Les Olive, the club secretary, telling him that the black cab journey he'd made from Whalley Bridge to Old Trafford (a £3 fare each way, paid for by the club) was being discontinued. Additionally, the club would no longer pay his telephone bill.

John Aston Jnr recalls another story from around the time. "John Fitzpatrick saw his career ended with an injury. United paid him off with a lump sum of £25,000, which in those days was a huge amount of money. In the car on the way home Jimmy complained 'That's £25,000 more than I've ever been paid.'"

Frank O'Farrell convinced Busby to give up his office, and, upon their first meeting, Jimmy exclaimed surprise that the new man had got his way. "How'd you get him out of here?" Jimmy asked, jokingly. Previously, Jimmy had been forced to give up his office when Wilf became manager, as Matt kept his. Jimmy moved in to share with Joe Armstrong. "Jimmy was 63 when he eventually stood down as assistant manager," said Gregg. "His connections with the club were not cut completely, but he soon found himself marginalised in a way that lacked understanding of what he had achieved and what he still had to offer. As a coach I used to sit in the chief scout's office (Jimmy's old office) and wonder why Jimmy wasn't there."

For what it's worth, O'Farrell distanced himself from the

decision to marginalise Murphy. "I thought if Matt Busby and Manchester United are the good guys, what are the bad guys like?" he is quoted as saying in Dunphy's *A Strange Kind of Glory*. "In the boardroom after matches you'd see showbiz celebrities, prominent businessmen, priests, lawyers and judges all enjoying lavish hospitality. At the same time they had taken Jimmy Murphy's taxi and telephone off him, and Johnny Aston the chief scout was driving his own car; the contradiction was sickening."

George Best was distressed at the news that Jimmy had effectively been forced into retirement. He said: "I never thought of leaving because I'd had such great times at United and couldn't imagine playing for anyone else. But when Jimmy Murphy was pushed into a scouting role in 1971, it really did seem like the end of an era… Jimmy was 'pensioned off' in 1971. He was given a scouting job but felt let down by Matt, to whom he had been so loyal and he expected more in return. With Jimmy gone, there was nobody to turn to for advice."

Gregg remembers quite clearly that there was a tremendous division revealing itself; a few years later, on March 21st, 1978, the club held a sportsman's dinner in Jimmy's honour in the Executive Suite at Old Trafford.

Bobby Charlton gave a moving tribute where he declared that whatever he achieved in football, there was one man and one man only whom he owed everything to, and that was Jimmy Murphy. Gregg said it came across as an incredible snub to Busby, who was next to speak.

"I can only imagine that he was deeply hurt by the inference that he had no influence on Bobby Charlton's career, that Jimmy was the sole figure who shaped his destiny," said Gregg. "If it comes as a surprise to know that the boss and Bobby didn't see eye to eye for several years, it was nothing compared to the shock

JIMMY MURPHY

I felt at seeing the tattered remnants of the friendship between Matt Busby and Jimmy Murphy.

"From the moment they'd joined the club after the War they were the perfect foil for one another: Matt, the man of few words, the quiet authoritarian; Jimmy, the wonderfully warm Welshman who shouted at you, played with you, laughed with you and drank with you. Together they accomplished so much. Together they built a club.

"The Munich air crash also revealed a friendship that transcended a mere successful working relationship. I stood with Jimmy and Bill Foulkes in a Munich hospital beside Matt Busby's bed, the boss in an oxygen tent and near death's door. I listened as Jimmy, in his husky Welsh tones, talked to his friend. This was the same man whom I found on the staircase of the Stathus Hotel, sitting alone in the darkness sobbing his heart out. There was a bond between men, a bond I could never see broken." According to Eamon Dunphy, Busby and Murphy were 'strangers at the end'.

There is an upturn to this story, however, and it is provided by the oft-maligned figure of Tommy Docherty, who arrived with a controversial and divisive reputation due to his outspoken nature.

Tommy didn't realise just how poorly the situation with Jimmy had been handled. "I knew something was wrong, that Jimmy hadn't been looked after, I just didn't know how bad it had got," he said.

"United were a big club and they should have done things in a big way. Jimmy was a wonderful man. I re-engaged him. After all, he had been Matt's number two, he was a seasoned campaigner with a vast amount of football knowledge. Jimmy was paid £15 per week in 1974. He didn't consider this a wage, it was more 'expenses' to do a job he loved. Jimmy Murphy was a great man in football. He didn't receive half the credit he deserved for his part in the huge success of Manchester United."

To that end, it should be noted that most people who worked with Jimmy are only too keen to stress just how important his work was. "You cannot deny the contribution that Jimmy Murphy made to Manchester United, it was just colossal," David Sadler said.

Gregg concurred. He said: "It should never be underestimated just what Jimmy contributed to the history of United… The Old Trafford faithful enjoy the sweet smell of success, but they also recognise the way in which it's achieved. That is the legacy of the past, of Matt Busby, Jimmy Murphy, and all those who went to Belgrade."

Gregg had mentioned to journalist Max Arthur that if he ever won the pools, he would like to reunite the Munich survivors. During Gregg's spell as Swansea City manager (which spanned 1972 to 1975), he received a phone call from Arthur saying the *Daily Express* had made the arrangements for the reunion and were footing the bill for expenses such as Dennis Viollet flying from North America.

"Eight of us gathered in the Midland Hotel," Gregg recalled. "We laughed and joked, revelling in each other's company. Albert Scanlon confessed to Jimmy Murphy he'd been terrified of him. Jimmy told Scanny he should still be!"

*****

After being brought back into the fold, Jimmy enjoyed a new lease of life. "He scouted Stevie Coppell; the Doc had never seen him kick a ball," says Nick (incidentally, Jimmy sent Coppell a telegram to congratulate him on his England debut, something he did whenever a United player made his international bow – going as far back as April 1948, when he sent a telegram to Stan Pearson before his England debut at Hampden Park saying *Best wishes for personal success from Jimmy Murphy and boys*).

"Dad went to tell Tommy about him and Docherty said, 'Great, I'll go and see him next week.' Dad said it would be too late by that time, so the club signed him on Dad's recommendation. I was sure that Dad had talked a lot about Stuart Pearson as well; I bumped into Stuart years later when he was doing hospitality at Old Trafford and he said that as far as he knew, his signing for United was because of Tommy's previous work at Hull City. But Pearson was a reserve and I'm absolutely certain that Dad went to scout him, even if it was just to make sure, because I remember him talking about him. The same with Jimmy Holton, a player who Dad absolutely loved. He was Dad's type of player."

It's true; Jimmy did go to watch Stuart Pearson. Tommy sent him to get an opinion on whether or not Pearson could play First Division football. After seeing him once, Jimmy returned to Old Trafford, knocked on the door of Tommy's office and popped his head in. "Yes he can!" he said, and shortly after, Pearson was signed.

His reborn enthusiasm was a far cry from the days before or just after Docherty's reign, where Murphy felt his words consistently fell on deaf ears. "There were a few occasions where Dad would speak highly of a player and then perhaps they wouldn't come to United and wouldn't go on to fulfil their potential…He would usually speak wistfully about such players, 'if only I'd had the chance to work with him'… I wonder what a coach like my dad might have done with someone who had the talent and rough edges of Ravel Morrison," says Jimmy Jnr.

"The knowledge he had of football was incredible," says Nick.

THE FALL

"The number of players he tried to recommend to United, but they were having none of it. 'They won't listen to me down there,' he would complain. Gary Lineker was one (under Dave Sexton). Within a couple of years some of these players turned out to be world beaters. It started after Wilf took over, and they just didn't listen to his advice as they should have done. He became more of a scout and less of a coach and while all of the players he was recommending went on to be brilliant, United went down. As soon as they started listening to him again, they were on their way back up."

These aren't just the thoughts of a loyal son. After the club's relegation in 1974, David Miller wrote a column for the *Express* chronicling what he felt was the demise of 'Sir Matt Busby's Manchester United'. Amongst the incidents listed was the three year spell between 1968-71 where Miller suggested there had been a 'decline of Jimmy Murphy's influence as assistant manager.'

Jimmy certainly became disillusioned with the way the team performed at various times. He started getting lifts from his old player Harry McShane, who by now had had a son, Ian, the famous actor. "He went to one game with Harry and they got seated in the stands while Ian went to get the coffees," Nick says. "When he came back, Dad said he'd seen enough. The game hadn't even kicked off!"

Jimmy's relationship with Docherty was fine – and it was a blow when the Scot was sacked in 1977 following the revelation of his affair with Mary Brown. "Tommy loved him from what I remember; whenever they would meet, Tommy would bow and kiss my Dad's wedding ring," says Jimmy Jnr. "Dad scouted and recommended Jim Holton and obviously when someone thinks of the Docherty years, Gordon Hill is one of the first names that stands out. I know Tommy was always appreciative of him. I

JIMMY MURPHY

never heard Dad say a bad word about Tommy; I know his brash attitude rubbed some up the wrong way but Dad admired his outspoken ways."

Nick says that the affection in their relationship was an honest one. "He got on well with Tommy and there was a healthy mutual respect there," he says. "In fact, Tommy wrote him a letter where he was open and honest about the way everything had happened to have got him sacked." Jimmy had been clueless about the affair, but when news broke, he said, "Ooh, aye, I thought they were pally!" over a pint with Jimmy Jnr.

Breaking through at the time was a young defender, Mick Duxbury. He remembers that Jimmy would often attend reserve matches. Mick says: "He'd pop his head into the dressing room with the classic line, 'Come on you Red bastards, let's stuff the opposition!' Years later, Jimmy said one of the most lovely things to me that I kept with me forever.

"I was in the players' lounge and he came up to me and he said, 'You know something…you'd have been in our team as well.' He'd no need to say that but you can imagine how that made me feel. People say things like, 'He's a Manchester United player' like it's an almost ethereal quality and that's what it felt like Jimmy was saying to me. I can still remember his face as he said it to me. It's something I've treasured since. If you were to say that Manchester United belonged to the identity of one or two people then Sir Matt and Jimmy Murphy would be right at the top of anyone's list, and a compliment like that from someone like Jimmy was worth every bit as much as a trophy or a medal."

Docherty's successor was Dave Sexton. "He liked Dave as a person, he said he was a lovely fella, a smashing guy," says Jimmy Jnr. "He hadn't been particularly keen on Frank O'Farrell because he was aloof."

THE FALL

Sexton kept Jimmy on in a scouting role and it was Murphy who was identified keeping an eye over one of the manager's most controversial signings.

After dumping the Murphy find Hill (who had been top scorer from the left wing at the time of his sale to Derby in April 1978), Chris James reported for the *Mirror* on United's £250,000 bid for Mickey Thomas, which Wrexham were to reject and request £300,000.

'United's Jimmy Murphy watched Thomas in Wrexham's 3-1 win over Orient. United, with £1,000,000 to spend on strengthening their squad, have been turned down in their bid for Wolves midfield man Steve Daly,' wrote James. 'They have now made Thomas their prime target in their search for a left-sided midfield player.'

Thomas was signed but was symbolic of United's regression under Sexton; he was hard-working and, to be fair to him, capable of the spectacular. However, he was anxious about his capability to play at Old Trafford and lacked the flair and magnificent goal return of Gordon Hill. Sexton was sacked in 1981, even after winning his last seven games, because it was deemed that the football wasn't entertaining enough. And so Ron Atkinson was hired – the fifth full-time manager to take the reins post-Busby.

"Like Docherty, Atkinson was brash, but I think Ron actually sought Dad out because of his West Brom connection and spoke warmly of their shared past so they got along quite well too," Jimmy Jr says.

Atkinson confirms this was the case. "I was aware of his role in West Brom's history, people talked about his performances in midfield alongside Jimmy 'Iron' Edwards in the side that got to the FA Cup final in 1935. He was a much revered figure at the club," he says.

JIMMY MURPHY

"Jimmy's official capacity at United was to find players for the first team and we would have regular catch-ups about the players he had been to see but, most of all, he remained enthusiastic about the young players coming through and I know he tried to get to see them whenever possible.

"One player he really did take to was Mark Hughes. He was a big fan of him, he said very early on that Mark was a tremendous talent who was one we should have high hopes for. I'm sure Mark's nationality helped him; young Clayton Blackmore was another one who Jimmy was excited about."

Ron took full advantage of having someone of Jimmy's experience around. He says: "In the course of conversation there were plenty of things we discussed where perhaps I asked for his opinion or advice because those were the sort of informal chats we would have.

"I do know that I made it a point to glean as much experience as I could from people who had experience such as Jimmy, I was never afraid to do that; when I first went into management at Cambridge United, I often sought the advice of Bill Nicholson, who would come and watch us. There was a wealth of experience to learn from.

"Jimmy may have been coming towards the end of his career but he remained active and would often pop in to have a cup of tea with me in my office.

"He was a big football man, a very enthusiastic man about the sport and loved to talk about it. I was aware that he was still at the club almost immediately because he was always around the place, and rightly so, as well he should have been, there was always a place for Jimmy.

"You'd always see him with Harry McShane. He was a very enthusiastic and approachable man; for him it wasn't about money, it was the love of the game, although that was in an era when such an attitude wasn't exactly uncommon."

Interestingly, Atkinson felt there was still an element of the old fire within the Welshman.

"He was certainly a strict character," he says. "There was definitely that element of the sergeant major in him, the perfect foil for Matt Busby who was the calmer one of the two. I know Sir Matt would have found him invaluable. I got the impression that the players had a very healthy respect for him. In fact, I can say that for definite because in more recent years, many of the older players who worked with him told me that. He was always somebody they could go to."

CHAPTER | SEVENTEEN
LEGACY

"He helped make Manchester United the club we know today. His love for the club was undeniable. There are certain people in life who make a lasting impression and for me, Jimmy Murphy was such a man" – Sir Alex Ferguson

Jimmy Murphy was involved in football until the day he died. He once said: "How we are in the future will be founded on how we behave today," but it is doubtful that even he could have had any idea of just how influential the work he did would be to the future of Manchester United.

In his later years, as Jimmy's family extended with nieces and nephews and grandchildren, the idea of him being a family man who spent time with his children was no longer the laughable thought it once was. In the '70s, he would often drink with his sons.

"He wouldn't talk about his playing days; we'd go out for a pint and he'd talk football for hours, most often about the Munich team," Nick says. "When it came to the Munich team, he was never far from tears, he would always get upset." Jimmy used to say: "The team we had, if it wasn't for the crash, we'd have won everything, we'd have won the Grand National!"

Nick does remember that Jimmy would often talk enthusiastically about the better players of the day, and how he might approach coaching them. "Wilf became an expert player with his left foot thanks to Dad," he says. "Can you imagine if Dad had coached Ryan Giggs? He would have turned him into Lionel Messi!" On the subject of talented left wingers, Nick says that Jimmy's last notable recommendation for the club was one Lee Sharpe. "When Lee Sharpe was at Torquay, I know he was one of the last players Dad went to see, and he really liked him, so I can imagine he was recommended to the club," he says.

Nick saw Jimmy on Wednesdays; Jimmy Jnr on Saturdays. "He had his football life and his family life," Jimmy Jnr says. "He'd come around for a family dinner and a few beers but would never talk about football around the family table. I used to play football on Saturdays in Didsbury and would meet Dad in the evening for a pint.

"I would meet Dad at 7pm – and it had to be seven; he was a funny old sod and if it was even five past, he would complain and not go out! He retained his enthusiasm for football and would always ask how I got on; he told me to keep playing for as long as I enjoyed it. I didn't ever know this until years and years later, but Dad had come to watch me play once when I was at school. He didn't come and see me again. Maybe that was a message!

"He liked his boxing, he liked his tennis. He was very forthright in his opinion and you couldn't argue with him because he was always right. I had an argument once with him about Ivan Lendl, who I thought was great. 'But he's never won Wimbledon,' Dad would say."

On his own achievements, Jimmy Jnr says his father remained humble. "Dad would never talk about his success," he says. "He wouldn't say it as it is; that he was the most successful youth coach Britain has ever seen. I was at a dinner a few years ago with Eric Harrison and tributes were pouring in – rightfully – about the great work he did bringing through the likes of Ryan Giggs and Nicky Butt. The compere mentioned my Dad and Eric said: 'Don't ever compare me with Jimmy Murphy – my success came over two or three years, he did it for 20.'"

As far as Paul Murphy – Nick's son – was concerned, Jimmy wasn't a Manchester United legend. He was just Grandad. "I didn't realise he had a connection to United when I was a kid, I think it was at his funeral when I began to properly acknowledge it," he says. "John Charles was at his funeral and I shook his hand and had no real knowledge of him, it was only afterwards, and I began to wish that I had asked Grandad more about his time at the club and everything he'd done."

Nick says that Jimmy, far from the impression one might have, was a typical grandfather. "He was never the life and soul; he'd be chatty, and he'd be Father Christmas for the kids every year, but he'd be quite content sitting quietly in his chair," he says. "He had no money. He moved to Poynton to be near his sister and would get the train into Manchester from there. At Christmas he'd always give the fellas at Poynton train station a card.

"MUTV did a documentary in 2016 and 2017 on Dad, and Jim went around with the crew everywhere. They went to the station and Jim spoke to one of the attendants and asked if they wouldn't mind if they filmed there, explaining they were doing a film about somebody famous who used to catch the train there.

They asked who, and when Jim told them, the guy went and pulled one of the cards out that they'd kept. I was close to Dad, I certainly felt a closeness to him. I loved him, he was great, he was my hero."

*****

Jimmy Murphy died on November 14th, 1989.

"He had a friend, Tom Ball, who lived near him in Poynton," remembers Jimmy Jr. "Someone had bumped into him to tell him that my dad was dead and he said, 'He can't be…I saw him this morning!' Dad had been watching a schoolboys match that morning, and was on the path outside the house when his aorta burst and he collapsed.

"His last words were 'Don't make a fuss', as he was being loaded into the ambulance…I was playing table-tennis when I received the news that he was at Macclesfield Hospital so I rushed down there to find him unconscious, completely stone-white. He'd lost so much blood and they had to switch the machine off. It was a big shock, even though he was 79, a good age."

Grandson Paul recalls: "After he died, the Welsh commentator Cliff Morgan called the house to pass on his commiserations and he said this, which really upset Dad at the time, but was something none of us ever forgot. 'Jimmy Murphy's dead, but you don't have to believe it.'"

Jimmy's death was noted in the November 16th, 1989 edition of the *Daily Express*. The report read: 'Jimmy Murphy, Manchester United's former assistant manager, died last night aged 79. Sir Matt Busby, who heard of the sad news after returning from holiday, was devastated to learn of the sudden death of his dear friend. 'It has shattered me. Jimmy and I worked together to

LEGACY

bring greatness to United, and no one outside the club will ever know how important he was to our success."'

Then-United manager Alex Ferguson (pre-knighthood!) made a statement to the press. "I cannot close without paying tribute to Jimmy Murphy who was still scouting for us just a few days before he died last week," he said. "He was 79, but his enthusiasm was undimmed. He used to phone me on a Sunday evening with an excitement about football which must have gripped him when he helped make Manchester United the club we know today. His love for the club was undeniable. There are certain people in life who make a lasting impression and, for me, Jimmy Murphy was such a man."

Jimmy's passing was acknowledged by the *United Review*. 'Jimmy was the man who put the fire in the bellies of the United players,' the tribute read. 'His role with United was clearly defined from day one. He was charged with the responsibility to seek out new talent to be groomed to United's methods and standards.

'The young 15-year-olds who came to Old Trafford as awkward schoolboys, later to stride the world's soccer stages, are too numerous to mention. Let it be said, though, that our young men who first brought world recognition to the Manchester United name in those pre-Munich days were shaped largely by Murphy. They were his boys and he loved them like a father.'

The column went on to express just how crucial the Welshman had been to the club in no uncertain terms:

'One of the mysteries of Jimmy's career was that a man of such a pedigree and enormous ability should be happy to stay in the shadow of Matt Busby when he could have walked into the manager's office at almost any other club. There were, indeed, very many offers and Sir Matt, in fairness to his old pal, always told Jimmy when approaches were made. He did so, it must be said, with bated breath for he, more than anyone, knew Murphy's value to the club. Murphy's response was always an emphatic "no".

'His reason was simply that Manchester United was his club and no-one would entice him away. Having said that, he was prepared to take on the part-time job as Welsh team manager, always ensuring that it did not conflict with his Old Trafford duties. That decision probably saved his life for on the day United were playing that ill-fated game in Belgrade, Jimmy was with the Welsh National side, his seat in the aircraft being taken by Bert Whalley. Had Murphy died in that crash, the chances are that United may never have recovered.'

A short while prior to his death, Jimmy had been rushed to hospital; whilst there, he was visited by Freddie Pye, then chairman of Manchester City. "Dad was in hospital with wires sticking out of him; and there he was, telling Freddie he should sign Paul Stewart. He did," says Jimmy Jr.

Jimmy Jnr says that his father was heartbroken that Matt Busby didn't visit him.

It appeared that it was a sad ending to one of the most wonderful partnerships the sport has ever seen.

*****

Few people are aware of just how influential Jimmy continued to be even after his death. There is the *Jimmy Murphy Young Player of the Year* Award, a fitting tribute which was created the year after he passed away, but this is only the start of it. "The decision to name the Young Player of the Year award in Jimmy's honour was a collective one by us at the club," Sir Alex Ferguson says. "The first player to receive it was Lee Martin, who scored the winner in the FA Cup final replay in 1990. I think it's a terrific award and the club has done really well acknowledging Jimmy's contribution, and how it was mostly focussed on young players coming through."

Sir Alex succeeded Ron Atkinson as the manager. Atkinson was sacked in November 1986 after winning two FA Cups and coming close but failing to win the league title. Most people are aware of how the new man revolutionised the youth system at the club but few know that it began with a trip to see Murphy. It should be established that former Aberdeen manager Ferguson had a great track record of bringing young players through in his previous positions, and so his decision to seek out the legendary United figure was more to supplement his own thinking and to get an inside track into the inner workings at Old Trafford.

"For the first two or three weeks I was at the club I was never away from the training ground, I was trying to come to terms with the size of the work," Sir Alex says. "After a few, maybe three, weeks I went down to Old Trafford to familiarise myself with the staff and the different offices and that's where I met Jimmy the first time.

"By the time I introduced myself to him, my intentions for the future of the club as far as the redevelopment of the youth set-up at the club was concerned – because it wasn't in a good state – were well known. He said, 'You're doing the right thing.' I was a firm believer that was the right thing to do anyway – I'd done it at St. Mirren, done it at Aberdeen."

Still, Ferguson made an effort to discuss his plans with Jimmy personally. "I made a point to have dinner with Jimmy because I thought it was important to get that knowledge of his time at United," he says. "Matt was getting older and was always nothing but helpful – there had been a myth about the managers who had followed him, that they hadn't been able to handle being in the shadows of him and Jimmy. But I never experienced that at all.

"When I took Jimmy for lunch, he took the opportunity to tell me again that he thought I was doing the right thing. 'Stick with the young players and you'll get the rewards,' he said. I knew that, and it was something I believed in, but because they were such giant figures, and Jimmy was such an influential figure, it was important for me to get that form of acceptance and vindication.

"I was grateful for the encouragement because I believed that was important to the history of Manchester United. It was, of course, a great story when they won at Wembley in 1968 but for me, the real story was that they did it with mostly young players – only two on the day, Alex Stepney and Pat Crerand, were bought, and the rest were produced by the club. That is quite amazing.

"We implemented an extensive scouting network; United had around 50 scouts around the nation but in Greater Manchester there was something like four, and the ones we did have, like Jimmy, were getting older. That needed an overhaul and I was glad to have the endorsement from Jimmy that we were doing the right thing – we were doing all the things they were doing back in 1948."

Ferguson was aware of the club's history but hadn't quite realised Jimmy's significance before he arrived. "The whole history of Manchester United under Busby and Murphy was concentrated around young players," he says. "To have won the FA Youth Cup five times in a row tells you that, and the string of players they produced for the first team throughout that period was quite phenomenal.

"I was well aware of the history of Manchester United and I can always remember the day of the Munich air disaster. I'd been in the library studying for an exam and I went to training that night. When I arrived I found players – older players, of 30 years and older – sitting there crying. I wasn't aware that Jimmy had missed the game because he'd taken charge of Wales against Israel in the World Cup game. The story of Jimmy taking charge of United and the level of the work he did was something I only really learned after coming to United," he admits.

Jimmy approved of the decision to bring back Nobby Stiles and Brian Kidd to work with the young players. "Brian Kidd had come in and we'd developed a great scouting network across Manchester including some school teachers who Brian knew were United fans. Joe Brown was in charge of the scouting department, welfare and youth," Sir Alex says. "So, in his later days, Jimmy would be scouting senior players, or looking at players we were interested in and just seeking the rubber stamp of approval for. When I told him I was interested in bringing Mark Hughes back from Barcelona, Jimmy was enthusiastic about it. 'That's the kind of player you want to be going for, he's tough, he's never injured.' The truth was that we didn't have much money in those early days and we didn't buy many senior players."

Sir Alex says Jimmy was one of the most loved figures at the club in the final days of his life, and that he retained all of his infectious enthusiasm in his down-to-earth way. "As Jimmy was getting older we tried to slow him down, and Harry too. Jimmy was in his late 70s and he was still going everywhere. I'd have loved to have had a camera in their car! They were both great with the kids, but still as feisty as anything. When young players came from different parts of the UK and Ireland for trials on holidays, Harry and Jimmy would be there. We'd split the boys up into groups, the Welsh boys on one table, the Scottish on another, and Harry would always lead a sing-song – 'The Inverary Inn'. Eventually I had to have a word with Harry's son Ian to ask him

JIMMY MURPHY

to slow his father down. 'Not on your life – he'll chew the head off me!' he said. I asked Les Kershaw and he declined so it was left to me. I invited Harry in for a meeting but I bottled it! 'Harry, take it easy!' I said. He and Jimmy were cut from exactly the same cloth."

Jimmy Jnr confirms that his father was nearly always at the club in his final days. "He would go down to the club three or four times a week because he had letters to answer," he says.

Eighteen months before he died, the club marked the 30th anniversary of the Munich disaster. It was a tough time for Jimmy. "The love and the passion he had for Manchester United was fantastic," Sir Alex recalls. "On the 30th anniversary of the disaster we were playing Coventry City at Old Trafford, and beforehand I bumped into Jimmy. 'I'm not looking forward to Saturday,' he told me, with tears welling in his eyes. Being such a passionate man, it obviously lived with him for all of his life. I wondered if it was because he wasn't there."

As Cliff Morgan had said – 'Jimmy Murphy's dead, but you don't have to believe it.' And so, the spirit of what he achieved, and perhaps far more importantly, how he achieved it, lived on.

Jimmy's reaction to Munich was absolute. Total commitment. How we are in the future will be founded on how we behave today. Whether he knew it or not, he was creating a philosophy and a personality of commitment and dedication.

This hybrid Irish and Welsh man, with Gaelic blood raging through his veins, had instilled a sense of pride in a club shirt usually reserved for that of a national team player. Make no mistake, this was present before Munich, in the politically incorrect team talks, in that effort to create a siege mentality that it was Manchester United against everyone else. After the disaster, it came became more of a 'do as I do, not as I say', and

LEGACY

the message became all the more profound. Murphy was likened to an evangelist and a 'pied piper' before February 6th, 1958 but the truth is that he was much more of both after, because he inspired by his actions and not by his words.

His actions inspired an ethos and a philosophy that even the greatest football manager of all time is keen to say he took full advantage of. After all, it is present in Ferguson's greatest successes. Manchester United just did not know when they were beaten. So, is he happy to acknowledge that he used Jimmy's reaction to Munich in that literal sense?

"Absolutely," he insists. "On the 50th anniversary, Bobby came in and spoke to the players, because we had a lot of players from foreign countries like Anderson, Nani, Cristiano Ronaldo, and two or three young Brazilian players – some of them had never heard of Denis Law before!

"When Bobby came to speak to them about the Munich air disaster, you could have heard a pin drop. You could feel how riveted the players were. When Bobby did his fantastic book with James Lawton I bought 24 and gave them to Paul McGuinness to hand to the young players. If you don't know your history, you don't know your future, and your future is to be what was happening in those early days of Matt Busby and Jimmy Murphy.

"Telling them what Jimmy did, planting the seed of the work that man did, it's the most important thing you can tell a young player who is representing Manchester United. Telling them what their expectation is and helping them fulfil that. Playing for Manchester United isn't playing for Bury or Rochdale, it's playing for the biggest club in the world. I think that's what's missing in youth development these days. Of course you try to make them into good players but we tried to make them into good human beings."

JIMMY MURPHY

There are few bigger advocates for Jimmy Murphy than Paul McGuinness. The former Manchester United academy coach was raised by his father Wilf on stories of what an incredible coach the Welshman was and though no apology was necessary for what just seems to be a devastating misunderstanding, Wilf made up for it by the way he eulogised about the ways of his mentor to his son.

"I always used to pass it on to the young players – 'United always come back' – and that is something that goes right the way through to when Jimmy literally brought the club back after the disaster," Paul says. "Over time it became part of the fabric of the club to the point where it can be found in its greatest successes and some of its most famous victories.

"We'd show the players games where United score in the last minute and these are subtle reminders of what they can achieve and what is expected. Most have it in their head anyway as 'Fergie Time' or whatever, but I always used to say that went right back to those days after Munich. They carried on and they got to the FA Cup final. The next year they finished second in the league. Ten years later they win the European Cup with a team made up mostly of young players developed through the club. In a way, it's indoctrination. It's an incredible asset for a coach to have and unique to United because of its history and their accomplishments; it's part of the DNA, part of the culture and spiritually I don't think it can be credited to anything other than the recovery after the Munich disaster."

Paul had been a youth player at the club in the early '80s and his personal memories of Jimmy are fleeting. But he understood exactly what the Welshman stood for and in his later academy role, the Murphy message was something he was keen to pass on to future generations.

"I tried to subtly get across the message to the players in a variety of ways, often dressed up in little sayings, like, 'don't show them you're hurt', 'fight until the last minute', 'two passes square, the next one has to be forward', 'up together, back together'… little phrases that have some connection to the club's history to be presented as encouragement for perseverance.

"No matter where you go in football there are certain principles I feel that you have to adhere to or adopt if you want to be successful. You want to build your own reputation, of course, but the main reason I was convinced that trying to replicate Jimmy's teaching – or, if not replicate, convey the message Jimmy was trying to get across via other methods – is simply because it was so successful. Of course I'd been exposed to some scenarios that were reminiscent of my dad's stories and so it was natural that you feel a responsibility to uphold that lineage…

"On a Sunday after a game, Dad would go to Old Trafford and have meetings with Matt, Jimmy, John Aston Sr, and Ted Dalton. They'd talk about the various teams at the club and what the plans for training would be the next week. It was a real tight-knit communication network, they all knew each other's responsibilities. I believe that is something that just went on down the years.

"When I was learning the ropes it would be Sir Alex, Brian Kidd, Eric Harrison, Jim Ryan – just a few people in their meeting room down at the Cliff, and the experience I picked up from listening to them was invaluable. The whole idea of the history of the club, the romance of the local lads coming through and having so much success…it was impossible not to become enamoured with it… I thought that if I couldn't be a player, I'd want to be a coach [like Jimmy]. I'd want to leave that sort of legacy. You've got to dream big. I wanted those five FA Youth Cup wins in a row, I wanted to even go further than that if possible."

Paul recalled one foreign trip where Bobby Charlton went into detail about 'personal' coaching. "We were having a bit of down time and there were seven or eight of the kids and a couple of us coaches sat around a table listening to Bobby tell us stories of the World Cup, 1968, and so on," he remembers. "He asked at one point, 'Do you still do individual coaching?' and I answered that yes, we would work on striking and crossing. He said, 'No, no, I mean, I had a personal coach, Jimmy Murphy, he felt like my personal coach.' He explained that Jimmy would be so intense and work you so hard that it wasn't uncommon for some players to cry. He paid so much interest that it felt like he was only concentrating on one player. He'd have Bobby on the pitch at Old Trafford on Sundays hitting passes all over the place, screaming at him.

"Of course, Bobby was one of the fittest players and had such an elegant running style. Jimmy had identified that this was a strength that could be developed even more. He did the same with Bobby's shooting in the same way that he had my dad working on his left foot, round the back of the stands at Old Trafford, and made them both feel as if they were the one he was concentrating on. If you ask Dad he'd say he was one of Jimmy's favourites, and Bobby would say the same, but that was just the way that Jimmy would make you feel.

"Listening to those kind of stories was an incredible influence on my career and my approach to coaching; yes, I was following in my dad's footsteps, but I was also following in Jimmy's footsteps and felt that if I wanted to emulate the success he had, it was important that I honoured the way he earned it.

"How I would accomplish that, for example, would be to take two or three of the players to games, and talk to them throughout the journey to and from the ground, and during the game, about their family, their general mood, things I might see in the game which might be useful for them to observe. It was a way of building the connection and also establishing that family feel that was so prominent in the days of Matt and Jimmy."

Paul emulated Jimmy as much as he could. "I would get involved simply to kick players' ankles just to see how they reacted, to test their temperament," he laughs. "We'd have phrases like 'following in footsteps', to let them know you're passing on the Manchester United way and you're a guardian of that when you're at the club."

In modern days, there has been the propensity for those who deem themselves to be neutral to suggest that Barcelona's style of football in the mid-to-late 2000s and onwards is the standard which all teams ought to strive for. There is, of course, logic to this but as Paul says, "the real beauty was that those most successful Manchester United teams, the ones that reached the pinnacle of the game, those teams were capable of doing anything. They could beat you in a scrap and they could play you off the park."

To instil such a winning attitude in young players in the 21st century required a strategy all of its own. Here were players who were given a leg up for life with their first professional contract and so their incentive had to be found in different ways.

"I loved it when Jimmy Jr would come to the youth games," says Paul. "It felt like a connection to those older generations. I'd let Jim sit on the bench and I know there were a few people who disagreed with that but to me that was part of helping to cultivate that special feeling, that connection that lets people know just how much these young players meant. The coach's son, from all those years ago, is still coming because he has such an interest. That's what you want in a club.

"It was incredible when Sir Alex would come down and watch

from the bench. When we'd have cup finals, win or lose, the parties were always incredible events and did feel like big family gatherings. All of the different departments would be there, a chance for the younger players to see the senior players, but also, the Busby family, the Murphy family, the Edwards family – it was such a special atmosphere.

"It needs to be the case that the youth team is seen as the most important part of Manchester United, and that's the way that Jimmy Murphy saw it and the way he wanted it. He would make the FA Youth Cup more important than any first team trophy. If you don't give that sense of importance to it you're not giving it the best chance to succeed.

"When I was a young coach and there was the likes of Nobby Stiles and Brian Kidd coaching and involved, I was inspired by the investment of time and effort that had clearly been put in by the manager, which was also present in his own behaviour, the way he'd talk to a fourteen year old player's parents and already know their names.

"I'd show young players and their families around on a match day and at 2pm we'd go up to the manager's office; the mother and father would get very nervous but within two or three minutes they'd be loving it, as Alex would be cracking jokes with them and putting them at ease. He'd be saying how he'd look after their son and how important it was that the boy also understood the sacrifices he would have to make. Half an hour would go by and he'd look at his watch and go, 'Oh, I need to go and give my team talk now!' He'd already given the team talk, but the impression it put across was that he was so interested in their son he had almost forgotten his own duties. He had invested time, and what an impression that left.

"Most clubs have a model of expecting their manager to be

LEGACY

there for two or three years and so it's almost sensible in a strange way that managers don't pay significant attention to the youth teams. A lot of clubs ring fence the academy and let the youth coaches get on with it. It's a dangerous game because a youth system can only truly thrive if a manager believes in it, if they have faith in it and have strong connections to it. If he is only being introduced to players as eighteen or nineteen year olds, how well can he know them, how much can he truly trust them? How much should he, if he knows he won't be there for too long? Sir Alex knew them from the age of fourteen and fifteen and, of course, Jimmy was doing the same sort of thing back when he was at the club.

"You have to believe in it and you have to select a manager for your club who you have faith to be there for a long enough time. Surely the aim is to leave a legacy and create a dynasty? The most celebrated and loved teams in history tend to be those who came through youth systems. It's obviously a special thing that is notable by its rarity.

"The Babes in the Fifties captured the hearts of the entire country. Their last game in England, winning 5-4 at Arsenal, sums up everything about their attitude to playing football. The disaster, while devastating, immortalised those players and also crystallised everything they stood for, for all of the future generations to follow. What Jimmy did in developing those players is therefore one of the most crucial elements of it.

"For Jimmy to do what he did in the club's revival after the disaster, to lead them back into competition again, is one of the most important things in Manchester United's spiritual history. He's at the very heart of their recovery.

"If you were to ask me to describe two characteristics which define Manchester United's history I would say the way they express themselves playing football and the way they never give in, and both of those characteristics were given to the club by Jimmy Murphy. Those are certainly the two characteristics which were the most important traits I tried to instil in players when I was coaching at the club."

Sir Alex agrees that the personality of the club which is associated with his tenure should also be attributed to Murphy. "I think it's absolutely right to say that," he says. "Of course I wasn't aware of that at the time of seeing the likes of Bobby break through with the other players, but from talking to them in later life, I think that's exactly what it was. He was hard, but he never gave in and he liked players to express themselves. I don't think he was the type of person who liked weak people. He liked to toughen people up.

"To play for Manchester United you need certain qualities anyway, because every time they play, it's a cup final for the opponent. You can't have off days. You have to develop a character and a winning mindset…when you come out of that dressing room and you are representing Manchester United, you are taking some of Jimmy Murphy's mindset with you. Jimmy instilled that winning mentality in the players."

Jimmy missed the emergence of United's next great youth team by just three years. "The young players are the spirit of Manchester United," says Sir Alex. "You need a bit of luck, like we got in 1992, that there were so many with the ability. And with the right development and guidance they went on to achieve so much, starting with the Youth Cup win in 1992. Sadly Jimmy wasn't around to see it – he would have been the happiest man of all. He was a terrific influence on the history of Manchester United."

LEGACY

*****

On February 2nd 1999, a bronze bust of Jimmy was unveiled at the museum at Old Trafford. Jimmy Jnr gave a speech on behalf of the family for this overdue recognition; sadly, by this time, Jimmy's wife Winnie had passed away too.

In 2008, United commemorated the 50th anniversary of the Munich disaster. Murphy's name inevitably was frequently mentioned. "On the 50th anniversary commemoration, only John, Nick and myself went. Harry Gregg spoke about Dad, as did Bobby Charlton," says Jimmy Jr. "Bobby said, 'Jimmy used to treat us like his sons. In fact, although his sons are here today, he probably treated us better than his sons!' It made us laugh because we understood what he was saying. Manchester United was his life. That's just being honest.

"When they were setting up the anniversary, there was a meeting which John, Pat and I attended on behalf of the family. The late John Doherty, who was the head of the former players' association, was also there. There were a few younger employees who had never met my father so they were asking questions to find out a little about him. 'What sort of person was he?' they asked – and John said 'He was a right bastard!' and us three just burst out laughing."

Nick remembers a story that sums Jimmy up. "I went to the commemoration ceremony for the 50th anniversary of the disaster at the club and I was approached by the son of one of the journalists, George Follows, who'd died in the tragedy," he says. "He explained that he was the only child and Jimmy was the only one who remembered them – he sent him and his mother tickets for matches. It meant a lot to me. I filled up."

On March 23rd, 2009, a historical marker was put on the Murphy home in Treharne Street, Pentre. "When they unveiled the blue plaque on the house where he lived, I went down with some other club officials, and you got a sense of what made him the man he was," says Paul McGuinness.

"It was a small house on a tiny terraced road on a hill that led down to the pits. You can imagine playing football against some of the miners, who must have been some of the toughest characters. Against that you had the social side of it, the fact that the game was their release. It obviously helped to build and develop his character, and it's amazing to think that those are the roots of something which is so evident in a club the size of Manchester United."

In 2011, the film *United* aired on BBC Two. It focussed on the introduction of Bobby Charlton into the first team and the work done by Jimmy in the aftermath of the disaster. In a scene from the film, there is a Jimmy quote. It is paraphrased from the following:

"I know these lads. I found them. I nurtured them. I was with them every morning, noon and night, mud and rain and gales and snow. They let me mould them from the ground up. They repaid me, they repaid this club with their skill, passion and now their lives. It's not about honouring their memory, it's about showing who we are to the world. Showing we'll not be bowed by tragedy. Because how we are in the future will be founded on how we behave today."

These words are written next to the wooden plaque for the Jimmy Murphy Memorial Award at the club; it does seem, therefore, that he did utter these inspiring words at some stage.

A bust of Jimmy sits in the museum at Old Trafford and in 2013 the club named one of the units in their Carrington training centre after the Welshman. Before it was revealed, a huge banner

LEGACY

concealed the façade of the building, with the image of Jimmy and the words 'Arguably the most influential United first team coach of all time.'

In recent years, there was a greater concerted push for even more recognition for Jimmy. The Association of Former Manchester United Players appealed for a statue. A few years later, a coalition of supporter groups got behind that appeal and the club listened. On May 3rd, 2023 – exactly sixty-five years to the day that Jimmy led out the United team in the FA Cup Final against Bolton – a beautiful statue was unveiled at the back of the Stretford end, depicting Jimmy in training gear, holding a ball and barking an order. It overlooks the area of the grounds where the old training pitch was.

The statue was created by sculptor Alan Heriot, and a special poem was written and performed by the Mancunian poet Tony Walsh on the unveiling. The title of the poem was 'Without Whom', a reference to the dedication made to Jimmy by United youth coach legend Tony Whelan in his book Birth Of The Babes, and Tony also informed the crowd, of which I was a part, that he had read the original edition of this book. He later said he used it as his main research to write the poem, with many lines directly inspired by it. To say it made me feel emotional and connected to the historic moment is an understatement.

It is a wonderful and emotive piece of work that I urge you to find for yourself, but I wanted to share two of my favourite passages which resonated strongly:

> And Busby left his deathbed, reunited with his friend
> "We'll never die, we'll never die" they taught the Stretford End
> We will play on for ourselves, lads, we will play on for the badge
> We will win the European Cup, and show it to *those lads*

JIMMY MURPHY

And it took magic, it took genius, it took Jimmy's way with kids
It took, *it took your breath away.* They *did*, you know. *They did!*
[...]
Men like Jimmy Murphy and the fire that burns inside them
The men who came before them and the ones that stood beside them
Let the ones no longer with us tell the ones lined up today
This is Manchester United built on Sir Matt Busby Way!
There is a bond, there is a code, there is a way that reds should play
And "the future will be founded on the way we behave today"

Now the statue stands proudly in a place fitting for the work Jimmy did. Supporters young and old have a prominent, visual tribute that can serve as the starting point for an important education. Yet perhaps the biggest tribute of all continues to be the open admission that the modern successes of Manchester United have Jimmy at their heart.

The spirit of the club can be traced back to those dark days of February 1958 when one man insisted that the club must continue. It was Murphy's love and passion for Manchester United which led the club through the most emotionally charged period in its history and those qualities which have presented contemporary managers and coaches with a psychological and motivational tool which transcends football.

It is incredible to think that the essence behind some of the club's greatest moments is inspired by the decision of one man who refused to give up. It's a triumph that isn't really about football, it's about the human spirit and what can be achieved.

As far as Sir Alex Ferguson is concerned, telling Jimmy's life story is way overdue. "I'm surprised it's taken this long," he admits. "It's the right time because it's a good story.

"Certain people in football make an incredible sacrifice, to put

LEGACY

football first. Every now and then you find people with that kind of enthusiasm. Archie Knox was similar to Jimmy; an impossible fanatical football man. We lost a game once and on the Monday Archie was in such a bad mood that he didn't want to take the training. Bryan Robson had to plead with him. Jimmy was exactly the same; he loved the game so much and was completely dedicated to it. Passionate, committed, honest – he was 100 per cent honest. He had great integrity."

Years after his death, a couple of stories surfaced about Jimmy. "I received a letter via the museum from a girl in the Midlands who said she had letters from my dad to hers, inviting him for a trial when he was 20," says Jimmy Jr. "That was unusual in itself because 20 is a pretty old age but Dad's words were deeply kind and reassuring. "You come up here for a trial and we'll look after you, if it doesn't work out you can go back to what you're doing." I think the lad never went up for a trial in the end because his mother became poorly; but she had all these handwritten letters from my dad expressing genuine, personal concern. This lad never made it – I think the highest he ever got was semi-professional."

On November 14th, 1997, exactly eight years after Jimmy's death, a similar story made the national press.

'All his working life, Roy Sutcliffe assumed he had not made the grade at Manchester United,' reported the *Daily Express*. 'When the club failed to get in touch after a schoolboy trial in 1950, he became an apprentice electrician. Nearly 50 years later, however, Roy discovered his absent-minded mother scuppered his chances of becoming one of the Busby Babes.

'A letter had been sent inviting the 16-year-old to further trials at Old Trafford but Mabel put the note in a drawer and forgot about it. Father-of-two Roy, now 64, of Higher Blackley, Manchester, finally received the note after he had retired from

JIMMY MURPHY

British Telecom.

"'She just handed me the letter and said: *This is for you*,' Roy explained yesterday. 'I opened the envelope and it was from Jimmy Murphy, Matt Busby's assistant in 1950, asking me back for another trial.' Ken Ramsden, United's assistant secretary, joked: 'The letter appears to be genuine but I think the offer is closed now. At 64 I think he would find it hard work in training!'"

Those two stories perfectly describe Jimmy Murphy's relentless quest to leave no stone unturned to find the best young players for Manchester United. A caring man with a big heart who would give anyone a chance if he felt they could make it.

"It was said in 1964 that my father was the heartbeat of Manchester United and I like that description," says Jimmy Jnr, although maybe it is more fitting, as far as Jimmy is concerned, not to say what he meant to the club, but what the club meant to him. "I don't know how you explain what Manchester United meant to him," says Nick, "other than to say it was his life."

Despite his lifetime of dedication to soccer, Jimmy did truly love his family. As far as Nick is concerned, his father did what he had to do. "Football's a selfish game," he says "the club comes first and those that achieve the most tend to be the ones that understand the sacrifice."

In return for that sacrifice, Jimmy Murphy shaped the personality of the biggest football club in the world.

POSTSCRIPT

A MAN AHEAD OF HIS TIME

The Lost Manchester Evening News columns

In the research of this book, some rare newspaper columns were discovered revealing the innermost thinking of Jimmy Murphy during the season in which he was thrust, in tragic circumstances, firmly into the football spotlight. Murphy's columns for the Manchester Evening News' Saturday football paper started in October 1957 and continued until the end of the 1957/58 campaign.

These supplements are so rare that even the regional and national libraries do not have copies from this era. They provide some of the most incredible insight from a year where his opinion would have been sought more than many. Some have been reproduced within the body of the book and some more are shared here – revealing the remarkable vision of a football coach clearly years ahead of his time.

JIMMY MURPHY

Developing young individuals

When an outstanding schoolboy footballer is signed by a professional club, many people seem to think he has merely to continue his schoolboy prowess to make the top grade and perhaps even senior international ranking. But, believe me, this coaching and grooming of youthful talent is not only an important part of the 'backroom' activities of most league clubs these days, it is also one which can be a real heartbreak unless the boy and, of course, his parents fully appreciate that time, patience and understanding must be brought to bear. Not every player who gets to the top of his 'class' in schools' football goes on to fulfil his promise in the hurly-burly of league football. Yet the failures are few and far between, because coaching has been developed almost to a fine art these days. The setbacks which occur in the early stages of a youngster's career are accepted as part and parcel of his apprenticeship.

Let me explain that point: In the first few months of a boy joining a league club straight from school, it is the task of the professional coaching staff to try and smooth out the rough edges, both from the point of view of playing and temperament. One has to remember that the youngster has entered a completely new football world from that which he was accustomed in the school sphere and it may take six months or so before he really understands the set-up and routine.

Whereas previously the budding schoolboy player turned out each week for his school side and was judged on the form he showed, the changeover to the league sphere involves him in a continuous training routine such as lapping, sprinting, roadwork, and, as a diversion, P.T. and games, before he gets down to the most important of all – ball practice. Again, in the early part of

A MAN AHEAD OF HIS TIME

his apprenticeship to professional football, he will find himself playing with and against boys who are a little older.

That's when the first setback often occurs, because it is in these junior matches that he finds the game much harder than he knew it as a schoolboy. I have come across many boys who, even in the first few months with a senior club, have got the impression they would not make the grade because they haven't been as successful in the 'breaking-in' games as they were at school. That's where the time element comes into the reckoning.

It's the job of his instructors to press home the fact that provided he continues to take in his lessons and understand what they are meant to achieve, the young footballer is on the right path towards advancement, even if the results are not immediately evident. In other words, there must be no attempt to run before the art of walking has been mastered. In my coaching experience I have found that once a youngster puts his schoolboy successes in the background and begins to understand the aims of his coaches, he starts to make progress. It is then, having acclimatised himself and got the 'hang' of things, he settles down. So much so that before long his play improves and he is knocking hard at the door for promotion.

But how often do we find that, even after making the senior limelight and perhaps being talked of as an international footballer of the near future, our young footballer hits another phase which results in a sudden loss of form and an enforced spell in the reserves?

I have seen this happen so often in the past and I am never surprised when I hear of this or that club deciding to rest a promising boy. My advice to these players who have the temperament and the ability to make good is never to allow these temporary setbacks to undermine your confidence. True, plenty of patience is required on all sides, but if a young player is imbued with enthusiasm and determination to learn he will soon find himself back in the reckoning.

I often wonder how many of our present-day stars ever cast their minds back to when they were soccer apprentices. Fortunately, at Old Trafford, our experienced professionals are still young enough to remember their 'schooling' period. They are always ready to help the club's juniors through their 'teething' troubles. That spirit can play a tremendous part in giving the embryo footballer the confidence which is such an essential part of his training.

School football

As a professional soccer coach I am, of course, always interested to hear of boys being given every encouragement and help in playing association football during their schooldays. But I also hope I am broad-minded enough in my belief that sport of any type, provided it caters for the desires of the pupil, is an important part of our educational system. It is for this reason alone – and not because I am concerned with the development and grooming of budding football talent – that I am alarmed to hear, on my travels up and down the country, of the seemingly growing number of headmasters and teachers who have set their faces against soccer and insist on rugby being played in their schools.

This restriction is enforced in many grammar schools, particularly in South Wales, but it does not stop there. You will find it applies in schools in England, Northern Ireland, and Scotland with equal force. Where boys should have freedom of choice in their recreational activities, now they must play the rugby union game no matter whether they have an aptitude or a liking for this particular sport. I am not suggesting that rugby, to the exclusion of soccer, is the general rule at grammar-school level. Thank goodness that is not the case. But the tendency for the association game to be pushed in the background is much more prevalent, I believe, than at any other time since the war. Again, I do not suggest for one moment that the majority of grammar school boys would rather play soccer. But at least the choice should be theirs to make for themselves. Those who prefer to play with the round ball are surely entitled to the same facilities, encouragement, and coaching given to those taking up the rugby code as their recreational pursuit.

Not so very long ago, I met a headmaster who quite seriously suggested rugby was the better game for developing a boy's character and that, in any case, once a lad left junior school for grammar school he soon forgot soccer. This is utter nonsense. The whole thing, in my opinion, smacks of snobbery and is against all the unwritten laws of tolerance, which is an essential factor in teaching a boy to be a sportsman.

My advice to the headmaster was to visit any of the big league club grounds on a Saturday afternoon and to discover for himself the number of secondary and grammar-school badges to be seen among the thousands of youngsters going through the turnstiles. It's the playing of games which should be the most important consideration, having full regard to the interest shown in either or both codes by the pupils. If a boy wants to play rugby union at school no obstacle should be put in his way. Alternatively, if soccer has more appeal, then by all means provide equal facilities. For who would dare suggest that rugby has a greater educational value, or vice-versa, in moulding our citizens of the future?

I've mentioned South Wales as a kind of 'black spot' in putting the bar on soccer. Figures prove my point. In South Wales, for instance, there are 240 schools affiliated to the Schools FA, as against 470 in membership of the Welsh Schools RU And in the same area, 99 grammar schools play rugby and only nine play soccer!

To my mind, as a Welshman, these are staggering statistics, which prove what an uphill fight those who are trying to put Welsh football back on the map have on their hands. In fact, I have heard it suggested that if John Charles had not been encouraged as a boy in developing his soccer prowess by a sympathetic schoolteacher he would have been lost to the game and perhaps blossomed forth as an outstanding rugby union three-quarter. But soccer was big John's first love – and at school he was allowed to make his own choice.

In Southern Ireland, at school level, Gaelic football is the order of the day. Some junior clubs have been known to put a 'life' ban on any playing member going over to association football! That, I believe, happened to Johnny Carey when he was a junior in Dublin. But here, of course, it turned out to be a blessing in disguise – one from which Manchester United and Eire, who received such great playing service from Johnny, profited to the full.

The Perfect Footballer

Who are the most complete footballers you have seen since the war? That's the question which was fired at me in a recent sports quiz, and I must admit that while the names of Tom Finney, John Charles and Alfred Di Stefano came quickly to my mind, I would be very rash indeed to claim they possess all the soccer talents.

Though club managers, coaches, trainers and scouts probably

A MAN AHEAD OF HIS TIME

dream of unearthing the player who has them all, the perfect footballer is as yet unborn. While great names have floated across the post-war soccer scene, a close study of their make-up would undoubtedly reveal they were lacking in one or other of the major essentials required to bring them into the category of the ideal footballer.

Perhaps that's what prompted several members of the audience to query my choice of the three players whom I consider have sufficient talent to put them in a class apart. Everybody agreed that Charles is a great player, but the argument waged fast and furious on whether he makes the most of his powerfully-muscled frame by really getting 'dug-in' when it comes to tackling an opponent. And the doubts raised against my selection of Finney and Di Stefano, two brilliant ball-players, were that for players of such undoubted skill in an attacking sense, they have their limitations when their teams are fighting a defensive battle.

To my way of thinking these arguments do not stand up. It's true that for such a fine physical specimen, Charles remains one of the gentlest players and never throws his weight about as one might expect from such a giant. But it is equally true to say that 'Big John' doesn't need to adopt tactics of that sort because he plays football with his head as well as his feet. He is a 'brainy' type who, in one swift stroke, can completely change the run of the game. You can ask many of the world's top goalkeepers whether or not he makes full use of his physical powers when it comes to shooting. I'm sure they will agree with me that there is no-one else in the world who can hit a dead ball with such deadly force.

And Finney and Di Stefano? Well, they come into my idea of footballers who are not far short of the ideal standard by virtue of their brilliant positional play and the skill they have developed in ball-control.

Both have match-winning qualities, the ability to collect a loose ball in their own half of the field and outwit the opposition before laying on a goal pass for one of their forward colleagues. Finney and Di Stefano are also goal-getters on their own account, and that's another reason why I rate them as having more all-round ability than many other stars who, perhaps, remain great footballers in a particular position.

Charles, Finney and Di Stefano are men of many parts in football as attacking players and their efficiency and ball-skill remains unimpaired no matter what position they occupy. If the question had turned on the best players I have seen in any one position since the war, then, of course, many other names would have come into the reckoning.

Ferenc Puskas, the 'galloping major' of Hungary fame, would be an automatic selection at inside-forward, not only for his defence-splitting passes, but for his power-shooting with either foot. And, of course, one could not omit the 'Maestro' himself, Stan Matthews, as outside-right. His special brand of ball-juggling has thrown so many players into utter confusion.

Again, one can conjure up many more names in thinking of players who couldn't be bettered in their normal club positions – players such as Len Shackleton, the 'Clown Prince' of inside forwards; Stan Cullis, who as Wolves' and England centre-half, combined a powerful defensive style with forcefulness in supporting his colleagues in attack; and Ireland's present captain, Danny Blanchflower of Spurs, an outstanding wing-half. Danny ranks as one of the world's best ball-players, but the factor that causes me to hesitate in including him in my list of 'complete' footballers is that I feel his skill is much more pronounced in attack than in defence.

And the perfect footballer?

A MAN AHEAD OF HIS TIME

Well, we are still awaiting perfection in this great game and, who knows, one day the player will be found who combines most of these attributes – perhaps a mixture of Finney, Di Stefano, Stan Matthews as ball-players, the stamina of John Charles, and the sheer determination and drive of Duncan Edwards.

It takes all these mixtures to make a great team, and you may have noticed that the most successful clubs do strive to arrange their forces so that they have a ball-player at full-back, wing-half and inside forward playing alongside individuals who provide strength in the tackle and shooting power. Yes, brains and brawn can be mixed to good effect. Yet even those players well-endowed physically must have the skill to go with it.

Ability alone is not enough.

Reach Sport
www.reachsport.com